ALSO BY ROB NETO

Beyond the Grate
Into the Darkness Beyond
Beyond Hope

Sidemount Diving The Almost *Comprehensive Guide 2nd edition*
Available in English, Dutch, German, and Spanish

BENEATH THE JUNGLE OF COZUMEL

Connecting the Crowns

Book 1

ROB NETO

Published by Chipola Publishing, LLC,
Greenwood, Florida 32443, U.S.A.
www.chipolapublishing.com

Cover design by Rob Neto

Author photography by Jen Neto

Printed in the United States of America

PUBLISHER'S NOTE

This book is a memoir. The accounts in it reflect the author's recollection of experiences over time. Be aware that the author's recollection is not always the best. All persons within this work are actual individuals. There are no composite characters. Some names have been abbreviated and no surnames were used to protect the privacy of those individuals. Some events have been compressed, and some dialogue has been recreated.

ISBN: 9781961612129

DEDICATION

This book is dedicated to the memory of Brendan Napier.

TABLE OF CONTENTS

ACKNOWLEDGMENTS

I'd like to thank the readers of my first three novels, *Beyond the Grate, Into the Darkness Beyond,* and *Beyond Hope.* Those novels have been a success because of you. It means a lot that my books are being read by so many. After the first novel, you kept coming back for more. You wait, sometimes not so patiently, for the next release. This is truly humbling.

I especially thank those that have left reviews. I read every review and use the comments to improve my writing. I sincerely believe *Into the Darkness Beyond* is a better book than *Beyond the Grate,* and *Beyond Hope* is better than both. Each subsequent book continues to improve. That's because of the reviews I've received on my earlier books. Even though this book isn't a novel, I've used the lessons learned from the reviews of my novels in this book as well.

I would also like to thank all of the other authors I have been reading over the past year. Your words and writing styles have certainly had an influence on my own writing. I no longer read simply for entertainment. I now read as a way of research so I can incorporate styles that I like into my own writing. That doesn't mean I don't enjoy the books I read. I certainly do.

One such author that influenced me is Patrick Taylor. Pat

wrote and published his Lost & Found series which detail the solo hiking and mountain man adventures he experienced over the years. I had the pleasure of receiving an advanced reader copy (ARC) of his most recent book, *Lost & Found: Navigating New Lives & Love*, and this book inspired me to begin writing my own series about my exploration projects in the water-filled caves of Cozumel and Florida. This book, *Beneath the Jungle of Cozumel: Connecting the Crowns,* is the first of that series. I had a lot of fun writing it and reliving those adventures. You can be assured there will be many more adventure books to follow.

I would also like to acknowledge the dive buddies and friends that joined me on these adventures over the years. I changed most of the names to protect privacy, not to withhold credit. Your assistance and companionship on these trips and during these dives have been an inspiration. I wouldn't have had as much fun exploring the caves of Cozumel without you. If you've been included in the book, even with a name change, it is because I thought you deserved mention.

Finally, I would like to thank my wife for supporting me throughout the writing of all of my books, particularly this first adventure book. She was right there alongside me for the adventures in this book, particularly the one horrible experience we had. It wasn't easy for either of us to relive through the words in these pages. She's also been an invaluable source to me. I embarked on this writing journey many years ago but only recently began to devote more time to it. This is my fourth book to be published over the course of a year and a half. She has not only been a sounding board for ideas I've had but also my first and last editor for each book that I've written. That means she's read each book at least twice. Her suggestions and advice have been invaluable to me.

ROB NETO

FOREWORD

The idea for the *Beneath the Jungle of Cozumel* and *The Hidden Rivers of Florida* series came to me after reading a book titled *Lost & Found: Navigating New Lives & Love* by Patrick Taylor. I "met" Pat on Facebook. I don't recall exactly how our paths crossed, whether one of his posts came up on my feed or I saw a comment he made on someone else's post. It doesn't matter. What matters is that we made an instant connection, and we've interacted with each other frequently since.

I've learned a lot from Pat about marketing my books and getting them into the hands of more readers. Most of Pat's books have been on an Amazon bestseller list at one time or another. Some of them even live there. I've joked with Pat that this book is going to knock his book out of the top spot at some point. I can only dream that it will, even if just for an hour. What makes this even more fun is that as I was working on this book, Pat began writing his first fiction book. We both crossed over into new genres. I've really enjoyed reading Pat's adventure books and am looking forward to seeing how he does in the world of fiction.

When I started writing this book, I had no idea it would turn into a series. I thought I would be able to cover all of my adventures in one book and be done with it. That couldn't be further from the truth. I currently have two more books in the Cozumel series planned with the potential for a fourth and fifth book. The Florida series will have at least three books, as well. And who knows? My adventures in Cozumel and Florida may lead to many more. There's still a lot to be done in both locales!

The accounts in this book were written from memory. While I did use my old dive logs to get the order of the dives and the timeline correct, I didn't keep very detailed narratives or a journal. If you were a part of these adventures at any time, you might notice some discrepancies. I do believe what's written here is mostly accurate, and the overall story does describe how the exploration progressed. The minor discrepancies that may or may not exist don't detract from the end outcome one way or another.

Anyone who has read my novels might also notice some incidents in this book that are also in those books. As authors we write what we are familiar with. In the novels I write about cave diving, I use the experiences I've had during many of my dives to make the stories seem more plausible. You might have thought some of that stuff was pure fiction. While the stories themselves are, many of the predicaments Joey and Lindsey have found themselves in are similar to ones I've found myself in. So now you know those scenes aren't as far-fetched as you might have thought. What you may notice is that my writing style is slightly different in this book than in my fictional thrillers. I approached the writing in this book as if we are just sitting around a campfire telling stories. The tone is more conversational, less formal. I used the same approach in the *Sidemount Diving* book.

In no way is this book or any of the scenes included in it

intended to disparage the reputation of any living or dead person. The account is written as I remembered the events and the events are written from my own perspective. My interpretations of the things I observed involving other parties on these trips might not be correct. They are simply my opinions and not meant to be presented as factual information.

Finally, while I do explain some of the techniques and skills we incorporate when we cave dive, this is in no way meant to substitute for actual instruction and training in cave diving. If you are interested in learning how to cave dive, please find a qualified cave diving instructor and learn how to do it properly. Your life will depend on it.

There are places that no one else has been to since the dawn of time. We can't see what's there. We can see what's on the dark side of the moon or what's on Mars, but you can't see what's in the back of a cave unless you go there. There's a special feeling when you know no one else has been there before.

Sheck Exley (4/1/1949 – 4/6/1994)

PROLOGUE

I slowly moved through the low room for the third time in as many days. What was I missing? I overlaid my maps of Cueva Quebrada and Dos Coronas cave systems on Google Earth, and they indicated that the caves should connect in this area. The problem, besides being unable to find the connection, was that where I was in Cueva Quebrada was only twenty-eight feet deep. The area in Dos Coronas was thirty-four feet deep. I could very well be swimming above Dos Coronas with only a foot-thick layer of rock separating us. If that was the case, it might as well have been ten feet. There was no way to get through it, even if I did subscribe to the camp that thought destroying caves for exploration was acceptable, which I don't. Having two layers so close to each other wasn't normal for water-filled caves. There should be a connection. And it should be right in front of me.

The room widened a bit, and I looked to the right. About forty feet away, I noticed a drop in the floor. It looked to be about the size of a manhole, like you might see on the street only without the cover. I was too far away to tell if it was an actual opening to a layer below or if it was no more than an indentation in the rock, a bowl in the floor. I decided I would take a closer look on my way back. I pulled a line marker from the pigtail holder clipped to my harness and placed it on the guideline below me - line I had placed in this tunnel about six months earlier on a previous visit to Cozumel.

I wanted to check the remaining eighty feet of tunnel before looking at other leads. The overlays were telling me the closest the two caves came to each other was near the end of this tunnel. I had already been to the end of the guideline five times and not found anything. Something was bothering me about it, though. Something kept telling me I was missing the connection.

I continued following my line to the end of the tunnel, hoping to find whatever it was that was gnawing away at me. Hoping to find something I had missed during previous visits to this area. It was easy to miss leads. The first time going through a new tunnel, you tended to be focused on the big stuff. You looked for the larger openings. You looked for what you thought would be going cave. Going cave is the phrase we use for cave passages that continue on, hopefully indefinitely.

Sometimes you missed the real lead because you followed what looked like the obvious path. That path didn't always continue. Sometimes it just led you to a large room with no outlet. A dead-end. You backtracked and found a small hole that looked like nothing more than a nook but led to a much bigger tunnel than you were in. I remembered one such tunnel I explored. I initially followed the big passage, only to come to its termination a couple of hundred feet later in a large, round room. I backtracked and saw a small window in the wall near the ceiling, the tannic layer of water bisecting it about midway, camouflaging it. I swam over to take a look. I slowly moved through the hole and found myself in a much larger room. The passage opened up and I ended up swimming several thousand more feet before turning around.

It made no sense, but that was just how the earth cracked. The weak points gave way and created tunnels. The earth shifted and created fissures. The water flow carved out small rooms that went nowhere. I've encountered this on several occasions. That's why I never stop looking.

The connection to Dos Coronas had to be in the tunnel to which my maps kept bringing me back. I checked other tunnels in the area multiple times as well, but none of them went in the right direction. They all ended up curving away from Dos Coronas. I was visiting this tunnel for the third time during the same trip. I was certain the connection was in that location. I kept coming back despite it not being an easy area to get to.

It wasn't far from the nearest cenote, only about eleven hundred feet. To non-divers that might seem like quite some distance. Even to divers, considering that this was eleven hundred feet in a water-filled cave. To an experienced diver with thousands of cave dives, eleven hundred feet was a walk in the park. The path to get there wasn't so easy.

* * *

Why would I be doing this? What was driving me to dive deep into a water-filled cave, far from any possibility of ascending to the surface simply to find a connection to another cave? What could I possibly get in return for making this connection?

One could ask the same question of countless explorers from history. Why would Jacques Cousteau dive repeatedly into the deep oceans of this earth using what today we consider archaic and dangerous equipment? Why would Edmund Hillary attempt to reach the summit of Mount Everest after so many others had failed to reach it, many even dying in the process? Why would Neil Armstrong travel to the moon just so he could walk on it?

I can't answer for those men, and I'm certainly not putting myself into the same class of explorer. All I can say is that I'm just a regular guy who likes to explore caves. I explore caves because they are there, and I appreciate their beauty and enjoy the process of exploration. I enjoy studying the maps I've made and trying to determine where the best area to continue exploration would be. I enjoy finding passages that have never been seen by another set of eyes. I enjoy the solitude of being in a location *in* this earth where no one else has ever been and likely will never go. Growing up I used to love watching the original Star Trek. I loved the exploration of the galaxy and finding strange new worlds. Cave diving has allowed me to slip into that sci-fi fantasy and explore my own strange new worlds.

Going into those tunnels provides me with an exhilaration I can't describe. There simply are no words that come close to describing the feeling of finding a place where no one has gone before and being the only person on this earth that's ever been in that location. There are many places both in Cozumel and Florida where I can lay that claim. Sure, I've had plenty of friends accompany me on my dives. I've also done a lot of solo exploration.

Those of you that scuba dive might be thinking I'm crazy. We were taught in our very first training course to always dive with a buddy. It's safer to dive with someone else. That holds true in open water where you can ascend directly to the surface. However, in a cave with small restrictions and silt that can obliterate the visibility, sometimes diving solo is safer.

I don't see my claim to being the only person to have visited certain passages as a bragging right. I don't go around and tell everyone about these ventures. Very few people know about them. There's one particular cave in Florida that I've explored that only a handful of people know about. I've taken even less people to that cave and brought them to some of the passages I've found. No one else has been in more than half of the mile plus length of tunnels that I've lined in that cave. It isn't likely anyone else will ever go there. It isn't an easy cave to get to and it isn't an easy cave to dive.

I don't tell others about these places because I don't want to reveal where they are. I don't want others to know where these places are because I've dedicated so much time and effort to accomplish what I have, and I'm not ready to let someone go in and scoop my leads. This is another common phrase in cave diving to describe when someone jumps in on someone else's exploration project without collaborating with them. They find the end of the line that was placed in the cave and continue to push the passage even farther in. The worst part is when they never tell the person who is still exploring the cave. I've had that happen to me.

I also don't want someone going there and damaging the cave. Not that every cave diver damages the caves they dive. Most are respectful of the environment and leave behind nothing but bubbles. But one only needs to look at the more popular underwater caves in Florida, Mexico, and France to see the impact divers with poor buoyancy control or no respect for the environment have left. So I keep a lot of information to myself to protect the caves and the passages that I've found.

Now you may be wondering why I've written and published this book if that's the way I feel. Writing this book doesn't mean I feel any differently. I am still very protective of the places I have been. I don't reveal specific locations in the pages that follow. I don't provide any maps in their entirety of the caves I've explored. There's very little chance, if any at all, that anyone will ever be able to find the passages I've found and explored without devoting significant time and effort. I've been exploring the caves of Cozumel since 2011 and have spent hundreds of hours exploring, surveying, and mapping them. I know the caves intimately. It takes a lot of time, effort, and devotion to get to the point of familiarity that I've attained. Most people are looking for instant gratification. That rarely happens for very long in cave exploration.

The reason for this book is because there are people who like to read about adventures like this that will never be able to do something even remotely similar. It takes a lot of training, dedication, and sacrifice to dive at this level. I moved across the country so I could live ten minutes from some of the best cave diving in the United States. My career as a nurse made such a move possible. Not everyone has the time or resources for such endeavors. Not everyone has such a flexible career in terms of location. They might still enjoy reading about these adventures, though.

I mentioned Pat Taylor in the foreword. He writes books about solo hiking and camping in remote wilderness. He spent several years camping in the Frank Church Wilderness of Idaho during the winter months, sleeping in a tent in sub-freezing temperatures, and becoming one with nature. As much as I'd like to do something similar, I know that a lifestyle like that isn't possible for me at this stage of my life. So I live vicariously through Pat's books. I get to experience a little of what he did through the words he wrote. I only hope that there are readers who will live vicariously through the *Beneath the Jungle of Cozumel* and *The Hidden Rivers of Florida* series.

1

Continuous guidelines

Eleven hundred feet was a walk in the park for a seasoned cave diver. The distance wasn't the issue. It took about twenty-five minutes to swim through the maze of water-filled tunnels to the area I was interested in. That took into account having to stop and bridge the gaps between permanent guidelines with the spooled-up lines we carried. Running a line from just below the surface of the tannic stained cenote to the beginning of the guideline that was only ten feet inside of the cave entrance took me less than a minute.

Once the lifeline to the surface was secured to the permanent guideline in the cave, I swam three hundred feet through the middle of a halocline, breaking out of the blurriness and encountering the first gap in the line. A gap was a space between two guidelines, and it was usually more than ten feet long. This one was about fifteen feet long. I grabbed another spool of line and closed the gap between the two guidelines by securing one end of the line on my spool to one guideline and letting out enough line to secure the other end to the other guideline. If I just swam across the gap without connecting the two ends, I would not have a continuous guideline to the surface. This wasn't a big deal. I already knew the cave well enough to make my way through the maze of tunnels…as long as I had good visibility. If the visibility was disturbed, then it would be a very big deal. I could find my way around as long as I could see the walls and the floor and ceiling.

Without being able to see anything, that guideline was my only way of finding the opening to the surface. It was literally my lifeline.

We don't just go into these underwater caves blindly. That would be crazy. Some of you may be thinking that cave diving is crazy in and of itself. It might be, but cave diving without a continuous guideline is even crazier. It's suicidal. So many things can happen that make it unsafe to do that.

The guidelines we set in the cave are not there to get us into the cave. They help with that, but that's not their primary purpose. The very first person that ventures into an underwater cave runs a guideline from the opening through the tunnel that's being explored. Just like Hansel left a trail of breadcrumbs when he and Gretel made their way into the woods, we leave a line when we make our way into a cave. The difference is that our lines won't get eaten by fish or dissolved by the water, at least not right away. Most of the lines remain in the cave tunnels permanently.

These lines do what Hansel intended to do with his trail of breadcrumbs. They let us know how to retrace our path back out to the surface. Without them, well, it could be a bad thing. Why do we use guidelines? Why don't we just place our line markers on the floor of the cave and retrieve them as we exit? We place markers shaped like arrows and cookies on the lines to help us navigate. Dry cavers will sometimes mark walls with chalk to mark their way out. Why don't underwater cave divers do something similar? Why not forgo the lines?

If we didn't run lines through the passages, we would have to carry hundreds of line markers so we could place them close enough to each other to be able to see them. A typical two-hour long cave dive can mean seeing more than a mile of cave passages in an underwater cave. If we placed a marker every fifty feet, that would require more than one hundred markers! Second, if we placed the line markers on the floor of the cave, they would only help us get out if we continued to have good visibility in the cave. Those markers wouldn't do us any good if the visibility in the cave was suddenly diminished or completely gone. A dry caver only has to be concerned with having enough lights to get in and out of the cave. A cave diver needs lights, but also needs to not disturb the sediment typically covering the floor of the cave. Sediment, that if disturbed, will decrease, or even eliminate, the visibility in a water-filled cave.

I remember the first time I ran a guideline into a previously unlined cave passage. It wasn't a huge passage. Actually, it was rather small. I knew the visibility would likely be diminished just because of my movement through it. I knew that line would be my only indication of which way would lead me out of the passage and back into the main passage of the cave.

The risk of silting out an underwater cave is almost always present. Silting out means the sediment on the floor gets disturbed and rises into the water. Think of it as driving along a country road in heavy fog. Or for those of you in the colder regions, think of driving through a snowstorm. Only sometimes that fog or snowfall is so heavy you can't see an inch in front of your headlights. You might not be able to see an inch in front of your windshield! If you've ever encountered such conditions, you've probably pulled over rather than risk driving into another car or a deer, or even a moose. That isn't an option in an underwater cave. You only have so much air in your tanks.

While there are some caves with high enough current that any sediment that may have been in them is pushed off of the floor and out of the cave, those are rare. Even high flow caves, the caves with strong, fast current, have areas with sediment covered floors farther inside that are shielded from the current. No cave is immune to a silt-out. A fast current in a cave will not help clear out the silt more quickly. It can actually have the opposite effect. There's a cave in Florida not far from where I live where the visibility gets worse when the flow is higher. This is because the faster current stirs the sediment on the floor and pushes it up into the water column. This drops the visibility in the cave to well below ten feet. The visibility in that cave is better when the current isn't so strong.

There are three types of sediment in caves – sand, mud, and clay. Clay is the worst of the three. When clay is disturbed, cave divers will find themselves in the heaviest fog imaginable. They not only can't see that car driving toward them in the other lane, but they also can't see the front of their own car. They might not even be able to see the hood! It's time to pull off the road to a safe place where they won't be hit by that crazy driver who hasn't pulled over.

I remember my first time in a silt-out so bad that I couldn't see my dive light. I couldn't even see the glow from my dive light. The clay particles engulfed the beam and absorbed it. My only reference to my location was the thin white line I held in my hand. Without that line, I would have been left to wander aimlessly in the cave, running into walls, while trying to find visibility again.

In a clay silt-out, the visibility will be diminished, and possibly even completely gone, for several hours. Clay can cause true zero visibility conditions. I've been in clay silt-outs in Cozumel and Florida in which I couldn't see the light from my eight-thousand-lumen primary light. I don't mean the light beam. I mean the illumination from the light with it pointed at my face from just inches away. Not even a glow! For those of you that aren't familiar with how bright an eight-thousand-lumen light is, it's blindingly bright. Far brighter than the high beams on cars. In a clay silt-out, the environment becomes pitch-black. Close your eyes for a few seconds. That's what it looks like in a clay silt-out, and it lasts for hours. Good luck finding those markers on the floor in that!

I've also been in partial silt-outs. Those are almost worse than complete loss of visibility. The glow of the light can be disorienting. I've spent many hours moving through cave passages in both Cozumel and Florida with my eyes closed. With my eyes open, my brain insists that I should see something. With them closed, it gets what it expects.

Mud is almost as bad as clay except the dive light might still be visible. The glow will be there, just not as bright or defined. Mud particles also won't hang in the water column for quite as long as clay particles. Rather than several hours, they will only remain in the water for a few hours. That's more time than we allot in our scuba tanks for emergency situations. Mud will still be in the water column long after the air in the scuba tanks has been depleted. A cave diver in that situation will have to use the guideline to get out of the cave. Not all is good just because there's enough visibility to see a few feet in a mud silt-out. It's not. You won't be able to see those markers on the floor until you're just inches above them. That would be a slow and painful process from a mile inside of a cave, even from only a thousand feet inside of a cave!

At this point you're probably thinking back to my comment about being crazy. We, as cave divers, must be crazy to subject ourselves to these harsh environments where the visibility can be obliterated with the errant kick of a fin tip and leave us in complete blackness with the only reference to the exit being a thin piece of string that looks like it can break at any moment. When you put it that way… I've even had someone comment on one of the videos on my YouTube channel asking why we don't use something more substantial. The line we use may be small, but it's durable in most environments.

Besides clay and mud, there's sand, which is the most benign. The particles are large enough that they quickly fall back to the floor. Visibility is usually restored in a matter of seconds rather than minutes or hours. Even when the sand is in the water column, there's enough visibility to see some things, maybe even the cave wall a few feet away. The problem is that it's rare to encounter only sand on the floor of these caves. There will usually be some mud or clay mixed in. So while the larger sand particles settle down quickly, the other stuff, the mud and the clay, hangs in the water and destroys the visibility.

I know what you're thinking. Now we sound really crazy for doing what we do. We would be, except silt-outs are rare events. Most cave divers will never see diminished visibility inside of a cave. Diminished visibility is more likely to happen in the smaller tunnels and during exploration. Because of this, I have experienced a fair amount of diminished visibility. More than the average cave diver. I've exited many caves not being able to see a thing. I'm still here, and it's because of the guidelines. Don't get me wrong, there's a lot of training and experience that also goes into it, but no amount of training and experience will get you out of the cave without a reliable guideline.

The possibility of diminished visibility is one of the reasons we place guidelines in underwater caves. It's the main reason. The lines aren't there to show us where to go on the way in. It's easy to swim into a cave and follow the tunnels. The hard part is getting out. It's kind of like flying an airplane. Flying is easy. It's the landing that's hard. So the guidelines are there to lead us out of the cave should we lose visibility. They give us something we can feel and follow out. They allow us to have a smooth landing. They are literally our lifelines out of the cave.

One of the rules of cave diving is to always maintain a continuous guideline to the surface. We secure the beginning of the line below the surface where once we return to it, even if we still can't see anything, we know we can let go and ascend to the surface where we can finally breathe without our scuba tanks and regulators. Why, then, do we have gaps in the guidelines inside of the caves if we depend on having a continuous guideline? Shouldn't those gaps be eliminated? Shouldn't there always be a continuous guideline? As with anything, there are limits to actions that can be taken to make things safer. Sometimes not having a gap can make things a little riskier, so we intentionally place gaps in the lines to increase safety. Clear as mud?

Most caves are mazes of tunnels that go in all directions. Some tunnels continue for hundreds, or even thousands, of feet before abruptly ending. Other tunnels may eventually loop back and connect to the main tunnel or some other section of the cave. Take a look at the original line map of one of the caves in Cozumel below. You can ignore the dashed lines; they are roads on the surface. The solid lines are the cave tunnels that have been lined, surveyed, and mapped. You can see how confusing it can get, especially in the center of the cross-section. And this is just what had been found and explored in that cave at the time. There are more tunnels on my map of this cave that are not depicted in this cross-section from the original map.

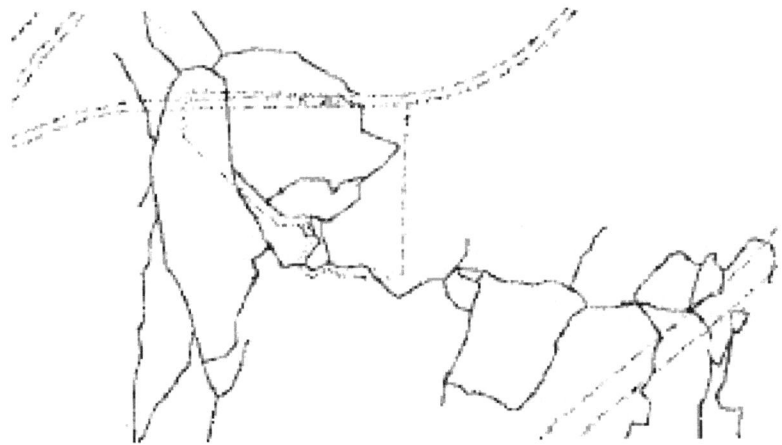

The guideline in what we call the main passage, the main tunnel that leads from the opening in which we access the cave, is typically a single line that continues for thousands of feet. There will usually be offshoot tunnels along the main tunnel. I say usually because that's not always the case. There are some caves that are linear and have no offshoot tunnels or don't have any offshoots for several hundred or thousands of feet. Most caves in Mexico, those in Cozumel included, have multitudes of tunnels. So many that they can't even be called offshoots.

We choose to not connect the guidelines from these offshoot tunnels to the guideline in the main tunnel because not everyone is going to leave the main tunnel. For one reason or another, the offshoot tunnels aren't that popular. It could be because they're just a short run that dead-ends or loops back into the main tunnel. It could be because they get small and beyond the comfort level of most divers. It could also be that it leads to another section of the cave that divers visit, just not that often.

Regardless of the reason for the gap, when divers go into these offshoots, they use a line from spools they carry with them to connect the main guideline and the offshoot tunnel guideline before heading into that section. These are referred to as jump spools because they are used to jump from one guideline to another. The jump spools establish a continuous guideline back to the surface. On the way out from that section, the jump spool lines are removed so the guidelines can be restored to their original state. When other divers go into the cave, they then don't have to deal with a line intersection if they intend to go beyond that area.

Line intersections occur when you have a line tied onto another permanently. In cave diving, we call them line Ts because many of them exist at ninety-degree angles or close to it. An intersection creates a fork in the tunnel and a decision must be made about which way to go. The decision is easier on the way in. It doesn't matter which line you follow unless you're trying to get somewhere in particular. However, on the way out, you typically only have one option to get yourself out of the cave. You might recognize which line to follow if you have good visibility. If you're in a silt-out, it becomes much more difficult.

You'll read about several line intersections that I had to swim past. Line Ts, such as the ones described in this book, won't typically be found in most underwater caves. They are more likely to be encountered farther back in the tourist caves or in non-tourist caves. Non-tourist caves are caves that aren't frequented by most cave divers. Line Ts are more likely to be found in caves being actively explored and surveyed because it makes it easier for the explorers. Most of the caves I've explored in Cozumel have a lot more line intersections than are typically found in a cave.

Many years ago, while diving a Florida cave, I came across several line intersections in close proximity to each other more than two thousand feet from the opening. They all had line arrows pointing back the way I had come. I decided I didn't need to place any additional arrows. The arrows already on the lines told me what I wanted to know. Until I arrived at an intersection which had the arrow pointing the way I was going. It was easy enough to deal with. I could place my own marker at the intersection. Except the intersection looked very familiar. I thought I might have looped back to where I had started. The disorientation to my exact location in the cave was unnerving enough that I quickly turned around and made my way back. I never went beyond a line intersection without marking it with my own marker after that.

We have methods we use to deal with line intersections when we are exiting a cave, so we don't have to rely on memory, something I did in that last example. Relying on memory may work in good visibility when you must only recall two or three intersections. However, if the visibility is diminished and the lines aren't visible, you'll need to know how to get out using tactile senses. Your memory may also be put to the test if you pass by several line intersections on a single dive. I think the most intersections I've gone past on a single cave dive was seventeen. And I did that dive many times. That was in

Cozumel after finding a section that had previously been unexplored. This was a section that had more tunnels in it than all of the tunnels shown on the original map of the cave. You'll get to read about it in the next book in the *Beneath the Jungle of Cozumel* series.

If we typically leave line intersections in place during exploration, why not leave them after exploration is completed? We minimize the number of line intersections in certain areas of the caves we dive because it makes it easier to follow the guideline out of the cave in zero visibility. It's faster to follow a single line out than to have to stop and determine which one of two lines will lead you out the way you came in. When we can't see the lines, we maintain contact with them and use them to make our way to the opening of the cave. We do this by forming a circle with our thumb and forefinger around the guideline without placing any tension on it. We then swim above or next to the guideline as it passes through the circle we've formed with our fingers. When we encounter a line intersection, we feel for those line arrows or line cookies that I mentioned previously. We place them on the lines to direct us out of the cave. We feel the lines, searching for the line markers we left there on the way in, so we know how to continue out of the cave even in diminished visibility. We must trust the markers, even when we can't see them. We must trust them even when our brains are trying to tell us to go a different way. That happens more often than you'd think.

There are many procedures we must learn that just involve the guidelines. It's no wonder cave diving training is broken up into two to five day classes and has three levels of proficiency. This training is typically done over the course of a couple of years. There are some zero-to-hero cave divers out there, the ones that do the course in eight to ten consecutive days. New graduates of those courses will still be learning years after completion. They can't learn everything involved and become proficient in such a short time without some practice to reinforce the procedures learned. Hopefully they don't immediately rush to the back of the cave shortly after they complete their training and find themselves in a situation that leads to their demise. The ones that take their time and spread it out over several months or years and build their experience by diving the caves at the various levels of training are better cave divers. They give themselves time to absorb all of the information that gets fed to them in class and during training dives. They allow themselves time to develop the skills they learned.

The procedure for following a line out of a cave in zero visibility involves always maintaining contact with the line using one of your hands. If you arrive at a line intersection or a line wrap, you maintain contact with the line you were following while you determine which line you will continue to follow with your other hand. If you arrive at a point where the line is wrapped around a formation, one hand remains in contact with the line you've been following. You use your other hand to trace the line around the formation until you find where the line takes off again, making sure there is only one other line branching off from the wrap. Only when you have correctly determined you are on the line leading to the cave opening do you let go of the line you had been following. Familiarity with a cave helps to make this process more efficient. Unfamiliarity increases the risk.

I taught cave diving for many years. I always tried to put my students into situations in which they were forced to encounter a confusing line wrap because they exist in the real world. In fact, I used a real-world line wrap to conduct the training exercise! I had more than one student do that procedure incorrectly and end up going back into the cave, away from the opening, rather than continue out of the cave. Their mistake was releasing contact with the guideline, so they ended up back on the line they were following, only heading in the opposite direction. That can be a fatal mistake when an instructor isn't there to correct it.

All of this sounds like a lot of information to absorb, particularly for newer divers, which is why we tend to not have intersections in the section of the cave that's near the opening. We minimize the number of line intersections to simplify navigation and make things safer for newer, inexperienced cave divers who haven't been trained to deal with navigational decisions. We all have to start somewhere.

* * *

I arrived at that first gap, or jump, in the line about three hundred feet from where I began the dive. As I mentioned, cave divers carry jump spools, small spools made of Delrin or stainless steel, with anywhere from fifty feet to a hundred feet of line wrapped around them. We use the line to connect the two ends of the guidelines at either end of a jump. The free end of the jump spool line is wrapped around the end of the guideline nearest you, and the line is let out as you swim toward the end of the line opposite from you. Once there, the line from the jump spool is wrapped around the permanent guideline and clipped to the spool using the double ender bolt snap carried for that purpose.

The last thing that's done is a personalized line marker is placed on the line coming from the spool. This is that round cookie shaped marker I mentioned. We call it a non-directional marker, or simply a cookie. This lets anyone passing through know that the jump spool was placed there, and the diver is still in the cave so it shouldn't be removed. It's part of the continuous guideline to the surface that will get the diver out. Once the jump spool line is in place, continuing into the cave, following the permanent guideline, can be done knowing that if the visibility deteriorates, there's a continuous guideline to the opening.

After bridging the gap, I had another several hundred feet until I arrived at an area of the cave that I recognized from my many previous visits. There were formations in the area that alerted me that I had arrived. When I first found the passage, I didn't mark the guideline in any way because I had a feeling that the connection to Dos Coronas was nearby. I didn't want to leave any clues as to my exploration efforts. I didn't want anyone to scoop my lead so I kept it hidden.

There weren't many cave divers diving Cueva Quebrada. It wasn't an easy cave to access. The cenote entrance was deep in the jungle along a narrow, indistinct path. All that cave diving equipment that must be brought into the cave had to be carried through the jungle to the cenote. This included scuba tanks. That was well over two-hundred-and-fifty pounds of gear to carry on multiple trips through those four hundred plus feet of jungle while trying to keep from tripping over rocks and uneven ground. Most cave divers prefer to be able to back their trucks up to a picnic table and walk a few feet to the water. That doesn't happen in Cozumel.

Once I found my landmarks in the tunnel, I placed a line arrow on the guideline, pointing toward the direction I came from, back along my continuous line to the surface. I grabbed another jump spool and secured the line over the arrow. If the visibility happened to be diminished when I returned, I'd still know which way to go on the line by feeling the lines and finding my arrow. I knew the cave well enough that I would remember which way I needed to turn, but just in case, it was always better to have a reminder in place. This was especially true after passing through seventeen intersections. Thankfully, that wasn't the case for this dive.

With the end of the line secured around my marker, I swam away from the guideline in the direction of where I had placed line in the cave six months earlier. That line was out of the way, tucked behind a wall, and hidden from the main tunnel. I found my line and wrapped the jump spool line onto it, secured it back onto itself, and placed another marker on the jump spool line, a non-directional cookie this time. I glanced back at my dive buddy, David. I signaled him with my light, and he returned the signal. Why the pause? Because we were about to go through a section of cave I had named The Grinder.

2

Exploration, survey, and new discoveries

When I first got the opportunity to go cave diving in Cozumel, I knew very little about the underwater cave systems on the island. I had heard they were not easy caves to dive, but I hadn't heard why. I had already been cave diving on the mainland of Mexico on a couple of occasions and wanted to return to do more dives. However, at the time, they were going through their cycle of increased crime in that region, so we postponed a third trip until the cycle was over. It was during that waiting period that the opportunity to go to Cozumel with someone who had been diving in the caves there presented itself, and I couldn't pass it up. I didn't know much about those caves. The only cave I was aware of was Aerolito, and I only knew what I had read in a few articles that had been published about it by Germán Yáñez, a cave diver that lived on the island. Interestingly enough, I didn't even dive Aerolito during my first trip.

The first cave I had the opportunity to dive on Cozumel was Dos Coronas. During my first few trips to Cozumel, I had no idea Dos Coronas might be part of a bigger, more extensive cave system. I didn't know anything about Cueva Quebrada during my first trip to the island. As I mentioned, the only cave I was aware of was Aerolito, and that was because of all of the marine life found inside of its passages. I wouldn't learn about Cueva Quebrada until a year and a half after my first trip. It was right before my fourth trip to Cozumel that I became aware of its existence.

I did my first two dives in Cueva Quebrada during that fourth trip. It wasn't until after my second dive in Cueva Quebrada that I realized Dos Coronas might be connected to it. When I came to the conclusion that there was a possible connection between the two caves, I had already done fourteen dives in Dos Coronas and added almost a mile of line in the passages of the cave. As I learned more about the Dos Coronas cave, I became more excited about exploring it. What had begun as a small sea cave that might end up with a few thousand feet of tunnels was turning into a decent sized cave. We were finding so many unexplored tunnels that during my third trip to Cozumel, I focused on Dos Coronas and didn't dive in any other caves. Every single dive in Dos Coronas resulted in more unexplored tunnels being found and more line going into the cave. There wasn't a dive in which we didn't find unexplored virgin cave passage. It was an amazing time.

During those first fourteen dives, we were only looking for unexplored, virgin passage and adding onto the map I had created from my survey data. My focus in the exploration was to find virgin passages and expand my map. During my second trip to Cozumel I spent a couple of dives surveying the guideline that was already in the cave. I wanted to know what we were starting with and in what direction the tunnels we knew about were going.

Many underwater cave explorers go into caves and swim along the lined tunnels looking for areas that they think might have unexplored passages. In a previously unexplored cave or cave section, that's perfectly acceptable. You have nothing else to go by, and almost every lead you check is likely to result in leaving line in the cave. I've had plenty of experience doing that kind of cave exploration. However, once you've put some line in the cave and begin creating a map, there's a better approach to exploration.

That other approach is the one I always use when exploring caves.

I create my cave maps and overlay them onto Google Earth so I can see where the tunnels of the cave are in relation to points of interest on the surface. In the case of Dos Coronas, I looked at where the shoreline was in relation to the tunnels we were diving. If there was a cenote nearby, I'd look at the cave passages in relation to its location. I used the overlay to find Cenote Catedral, one of the cenotes we found during our exploration of Cueva Quebrada (more on that in book 2).

I not only look at where the tunnels are heading in relation to what's above them, but also in relation to other lined tunnels in the cave. There was no point in pushing a lead that would only tie into another tunnel thirty feet away unless it provided me with a significant shortcut to get to another area of the cave. I use the information I gather from my maps to determine where I want to focus my exploration efforts during my future dives. That was exactly how I approached my exploration of Dos Coronas.

As I was surveying the lines in Dos Coronas and plotting out the data, I noticed that the previous exploration team kept exploring tunnels going to the left. This didn't make sense to me. On the overlay, going to the left meant going back toward the sea. Going back toward the sea meant coming out of another reef opening and exiting the cave. While that would be good to know, and having a shorter route into the main part of the cave would be nice, the objective of cave exploration is to find going cave that heads farther from the openings, not toward them. I couldn't understand why they kept exploring leads that went to the left.

Unlike most of the caves in Mexico, the main entrance to Dos Coronas is in the reef. It's not a cenote in the middle of the jungle. While there is a cenote in Dos Coronas about six hundred feet from the reef entrance, it's not one we've used to access the cave. It just wasn't convenient. I did surface in it a couple of times to assess it. The time and effort it would have taken to find it, clear a path through the jungle, and haul our tanks and equipment in and out of the jungle for each dive wasn't worth the trouble. It was easier to enter through the reef opening and swim six hundred feet with an additional scuba tank than to overcome the challenges of the jungle. Sometimes options have to be weighed and the least troublesome followed. Had we found a cenote that would have cut fifteen hundred feet from our swim, cutting a path through the jungle would have made the effort worthwhile. We've experienced that and cut an eight-hundred-foot-long trail through the jungle to eliminate an hour of swimming. That was definitely worth the effort. More on that in the second book in this series.

The lines we were finding that were placed in the cave by the other team were heading west, directly toward the sea. They all ended in dead ends, or the tunnels got too small for a person to pass through. None of these tunnels were large, going passages. What was even more confusing was that there were a lot of potential leads to the right. These leads were completely ignored. They were not only unexplored, but there weren't any markers on the lines left as reminders to check them out on subsequent dives. Marking leads is a common practice in cave exploration. I started marking those leads as I found them and eventually checking them out as time allowed. That decision proved to be very worthwhile.

There had only been twenty-four hundred and forty-four feet of line in Dos Coronas when I first surveyed it. This included eight hundred and fifty-one feet of line I had placed in the cave during my first two dives there. When I returned to the cave during my second trip to Cozumel, I arrived at the end of one of the lines that had been placed by the other team. This line was heading in a northeast direction away from the reef. It ended in the middle of a large tunnel, and the tunnel kept going. There wasn't a wall. There wasn't a restriction. It was a large tunnel that wanted to be explored. It was beckoning me to keep going. It was screaming at me to explore it. I couldn't believe my luck. I couldn't understand why the other team hadn't continued going into that passage. I couldn't understand why they hadn't asked me not to explore Dos Coronas knowing that was there.

I tied the end of the line from my explorer reel to the end of that line and headed farther into the tunnel. The exhilaration was almost too much to bear! I had been in unexplored cave tunnels before, but this was the largest and longest one. This also became the first time I deployed all of the line from my explorer reel, more than one thousand feet! I wondered if this was how the original cave diving explorers felt twenty to thirty years earlier. Were they just as excited? Was the exhilaration on the same level as what I was experiencing? Did the feeling eventually become old because there were so many unexplored caves back then? I couldn't fathom how it would ever become old for me.

I was overwhelmed as I let line off of my reel in that passage. I was excited. I was the happiest I had ever been during a dive. I could barely keep a seal on my regulator mouthpiece because of the smile on my face. The exhilaration I felt was bubbling out of me. I don't remember all that much from that dive other than I had just swam through more than a thousand feet of previously unexplored virgin cave. All of the emotions I was feeling at the time filled my memory and still do more than twelve years later.

About twenty-five minutes after I tied onto the end of the other line, I let out the last bit of line from my reel. I was disappointed that I had come to the end of my supply of line on that reel. I was also happy that it wasn't the end of the passage. There was still going cave in front of me. I secured my final tie-off, leaving a loop on the end of the line so I could tie onto it the next day. I turned around ready to survey the line I had just set. I did have more spools with me, but as much as I wanted to continue, I had to put that off until the next day.

I would be breaking my own rule if I grabbed another reel and continued farther into the cave.

That rule is to only lay as much line as I can survey on the way out. I do this because I use the map I create later in the evening to determine where I will be focusing my exploration efforts the next day. I can't do that without having the survey data and plotting it into a usable map. I could go back the next day to do the survey like many others do, but that would waste precious time. Time wasn't a commodity we had a lot of on these seven-to-ten-day long trips to Cozumel. I'd rather be laying line in virgin cave passages every day than alternating days because I had to survey the line I put in the cave the day before.

Over the next thirty minutes or so, I focused on surveying the line and gathering data. Once I returned to where I had begun setting out new line, I tucked the survey notes into my thigh pocket for safe keeping and turned to David. I was still experiencing a high from having just swam through more than one thousand feet of virgin tunnel. David and I had become the first people to ever be in that location *in* this earth. We exited the cave, ecstatic with what we had discovered and accomplished. I couldn't get out fast enough and back to the house to plot the data so I could see where the tunnel had taken us.

A couple of hours later, back at the house, I plotted the data and saw that the tunnel was indeed heading in a northeast direction. I also saw that I had added more than twelve hundred feet of line, not just one thousand feet like I had thought. This was the first time I had emptied an explorer reel, and I didn't know exactly how much line it held. The excitement that filled me was even stronger! The best part was that there were still many more tunnels to be explored and lined. I saw a lot of potential leads and even marked some of them with my line markers and noted them in my survey notes to reference on later dives. There were so many. I didn't have time to mark them all.

I looked over my newly created map. All of the lines going to the left, back toward the sea, made even less sense once I saw where the tunnel we were in was heading. The tunnels on the left were only one to two hundred feet long. Why waste time with those short tunnels when the motherload of unexplored tunnel lay right at the end of the line they had left? I wouldn't have the answer for another couple of trips.

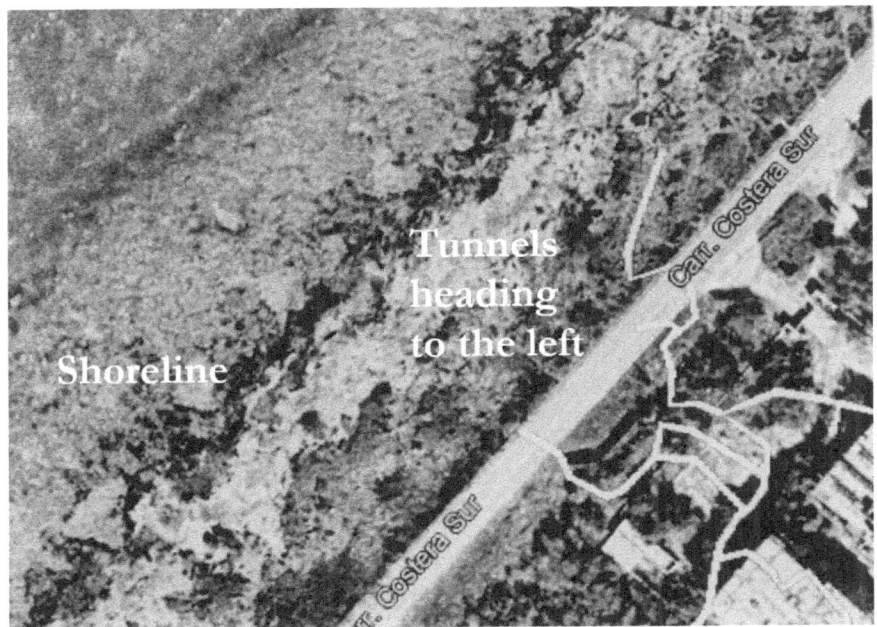

Tunnels heading to the left toward the sea.

* * *

I mentioned Germán Yáñez earlier. He was part of the original Cueva Quebrada exploration team in the nineties. I met Germán in 2009 when he came to Florida for a cave diving conference. I then met him again in 2011 during my first trip to Cozumel. From that point on, before each visit to Cozumel, I reached out to him and asked if there was anything I could bring him from the states. When I asked him before our fourth trip down, he requested that I bring some gold line to reline a couple of cave passages. Gold line is the type of guideline we use in the main tunnels of most tourist caves in Florida. It's thicker than the cave line we have on our personal spools and reels and has a sheath surrounding braided nylon line. Up until about 2010 or so, the line on our spools only came in white, so the color was also unique.

Gold line made its first appearance in underwater caves in 1989 after the death of Debra Reeves, a cave diver that had been diving with her boyfriend in Peacock Springs cave starting from the Orange Grove sinkhole. Peacock Springs cave is located in what is now called the Wes Skiles Peacock Springs State Park and is located in Luraville, Florida. If you've read my novels, you already know this story. Debra's story is a sad one, but it resulted in one of the most significant changes in cave diving – the use of gold line.

In 1988, Debra had entered the Orange Grove cave opening with her boyfriend. They were planning to swim along the main guideline until they reached turn pressure. In cave diving, this is typically one third of the starting air pressure in the scuba tanks. When they breathed one third, Debra and her boyfriend would turn around and begin their swim out of the cave. About thirty minutes into the dive, Debra had a primary light failure. Her boyfriend, who was leading the way in, noticed he no longer saw a light coming from behind him. He stopped and turned around to find Debra with a nonfunctioning primary light retrieving a backup light from her pocket. He faced Debra and provided light for her while she got situated. During this time, both divers inadvertently ascended to the ceiling of the cave.

Once Debra deployed her backup light, they signaled to each other that the dive was over. When there's an equipment failure, cave divers turn and exit. We have redundancy, but that's meant to help get us out of the cave after a failure, not to continue the dive. Debra and her boyfriend descended back to the guideline with Debra leading the way out. A few minutes later, Debra's boyfriend signaled her. She turned around and he communicated to her in hand signals that they were going in the wrong direction and should turn around. He didn't recognize the tunnel they were in and believed they had somehow gotten on the wrong guideline. Debra didn't believe him. After a couple of moments arguing using hand signals, Debra turned around and continued to swim the way she had been going. Her boyfriend, knowing that was not the right direction, turned and headed back from where they had come. That had to be one of the toughest decisions he ever made. I don't know if I could do the same thing as Debra's boyfriend under similar circumstances. That decision saved his life, though.

One thing that's drilled into the heads of cave diving students is that one fatality is better than two. You do what you can to save your dive buddy, but if things become critical, save yourself. It's a tough situation and one I've faced myself. Fortunately, in my case, it didn't result in a fatality for anyone. My dive buddy and good friend made it out of the cave unscathed. It was miscommunication and misunderstanding rather than confusion that led to him swimming off. It did result in being the inspiration for my thriller, *Beyond Hope*.

A couple of minutes after Debra's boyfriend turned to go the opposite direction, he came to the end of the guideline he was following. About fifteen feet away from it, against the wall on the opposite side of the tunnel he was in, was another guideline. He recognized this area as the location of Debra's light failure. He was at an intersection of tunnels. He swam across to the other line and followed it to the left and out of the cave. He removed his gear and raced up the street to the dive shop a couple of miles away to call for help. This was before mobile cell phones were commonly used. The shop wasn't far, though, and he held onto the hope that there was still time to save Debra. Unfortunately, there wasn't. Debra was found lifeless in the cave in the tunnel where they had argued about which way to go. Her scuba tanks were empty. She had drowned.

A couple of weeks later, members of the board of directors of two of the cave diving training organizations met to discuss Debra's death, analyze the details, and come up with a way to prevent a similar fatality from happening. Accident analysis was something that was still being done during that time. It was concluded that had the guideline in the main tunnel been distinguishable from the guideline in the offshoot tunnel, Debra would have known without a doubt that she was going the wrong way and wouldn't have gone down that tunnel. The board members had a cause and came up with a solution to prevent any further deaths from happening as a result of that cause. The decision was made to replace the guidelines in the main tunnels of all popular Florida caves with a thicker, different color line. Calls were made, and a supplier happened to have an overstock of gold-colored line that would withstand the harsh environment found in underwater caves. The supplier agreed to sell what he had at cost. Two weeks later, the guidelines in the main tunnels of Peacock Springs cave system, more than forty-five hundred feet, were replaced. It took another couple of months to replace the main guidelines in the other popular Florida caves. A plaque now sits at the opening in the Orange Grove sinkhole to commemorate Debra's memory and her unwitting sacrifice to cave diving.

* * *

I understood the need for gold line in the popular caves in North Florida and even in the popular caves on the mainland of Mexico.

Cozumel wasn't known for cave diving. It was known for its fantastic reef diving. Cave divers weren't flocking to the island to dive the caves beneath its jungle. I was diving the caves, but I was very familiar with them and very unlikely to make a mistake similar to the one Debra made. This led me to have one question for Germán - why place gold line in the Cozumel caves? Very few divers visit the caves of Cozumel. Besides Germán, I was the only one diving a few of the caves for many years.

Germán was diving them regularly at the time. He would occasionally bring other divers to them on guided dives. He wasn't diving them enough to monitor the conditions of the guidelines that were in those caves and the last few times he had gone into them with clients, several line repairs were necessary. He was also replacing the guidelines in those caves every two to three years due to their degradation. The harsh environment was causing the lines to deteriorate quickly. It was a safety hazard.

The water in the caves of Cozumel is very hard on the guidelines. The lines become so brittle they could not be depended on to get cave divers out safely in the event of a silt-out. Even now, whenever I'm diving in Cozumel, I test the guideline every dozen feet or so by tugging it to make sure it's not going to break. It would be bad if the visibility deteriorated, and I had to follow the line out only to have it disintegrate in my fingers. I've tugged at lines a few times only to have them break and drop to the floor in tiny pieces right in front of me. Germán explained that he wanted the gold line for its durability, not because these caves were becoming tourist attractions. He hoped gold line would last longer than the standard line that was used in the caves. It was a good idea on Germán's part. More than ten years later, the gold line we placed is still there and intact.

With safety being a concern, I was able to get three thousand feet of gold line donated by one of the cave diving training organizations.

I brought the gold line to Cozumel on my next trip. David and I spent a day diving with Germán replacing the old, brittle line with the new, more durable gold line. We placed fifteen hundred feet leading from one cenote and another twelve hundred feet leading from a second cenote, with the additional three hundred feet placed in an offshoot of that tunnel. Germán led the way and laid the line while David and I moved the permanent markers from the old guideline to the new gold line and pulled the old line up. On the way out, I surveyed the line we had just placed. Fortunately, David and I had spent the previous couple of evenings tying knots every ten feet onto the gold line. These knots were used to facilitate the survey process. Instead of bringing a tape measure into the cave, I counted knots to get the distance between survey stations.

During the previous three trips to Cozumel and laying thousands of feet of line in the caves, I had become very fast and proficient at surveying knotted line. I was able to keep up with Germán and David as we exited. I brought up the rear of our team while they cleaned up the old guideline. After the dives, I got coordinates to the two cenotes we accessed. Later that evening I plotted my data and overlaid the map onto Google Earth using the coordinates. That's when I figured out why all the lines were going to the left. The other exploration team had been trying to connect Dos Coronas to Cueva Quebrada. They had known the two cave openings were close to each other. The opening to Dos Coronas was south of the main sea opening to Cueva Quebrada so they kept pushing to the left, thinking they were pushing toward Cueva Quebrada.

The problem was they weren't surveying and overlaying. They weren't paying attention to the direction the tunnels were going where they were laying line. They knew they had started out going east in the cave and they knew Cueva Quebrada was to the north of the passages in Dos Coronas. They assumed if they kept pushing to the left, the direction they believed was north, they would eventually run into Cueva Quebrada. They went too far to the left. This had them doubling back in tunnels that ran almost parallel to the main tunnel.

In underwater caves, we follow the tunnels and see where they go. We don't use compasses to determine direction except when doing survey. Most cave divers don't even carry a compass with them when cave diving. Compasses don't provide very useful information unless they are being used for survey. The opening to the cave may be to the north, but heading south is necessary to get to a tunnel that heads toward the opening. The tunnels constantly turn one way or the other and intersect with others. They are literally mazes! A compass doesn't do any good to get a diver out of the cave because of this. This is one of the reasons why we use lines in the caves. Without having any type of reference in underwater caves, we might think we're going in one direction, when we're actually going the opposite way. Because the tunnels twist and turn, we might think we're heading north, but we could have made several turns and ended up heading south instead. It's possible to try to keep track of it in our heads, but that's not a reliable method. The more turns we make, the more difficult it is to keep it all sorted.

Apparently, the other team hadn't checked their compass headings or overlaid the map. They may not have even created a map during their trip. The maps I made and overlaid showed me that all of those tunnels going to the left, toward the sea, were also going away from Cueva Quebrada. The big tunnel at the end of their line that I added more than twelve hundred feet of line to was actually going toward Cueva Quebrada. It was heading to the northeast, right where Cueva Quebrada was located. The maps I created gave me a new focus for my exploration. It was no longer just about finding unexplored tunnels in Dos Coronas. It was about finding the connection to Cueva Quebrada!

3

A bumpy beginning in a strange new place

At the time of my first trip to Cozumel, I had been cave diving for about six years. Four of those years I lived in Florida only ten minutes from some of the best cave diving in the state. I had done some exploration and found unexplored tunnels in those caves. I hadn't done a lot of it, though. The opportunity simply wasn't there like it might be in Cozumel.

Florida is considered to be one of the world's cave diving meccas. There are a lot of caves in the northern part of the state and a lot of people visit Florida to dive those caves. If you want to learn how to cave dive, you go to Florida to do it. There is Mexico, but the international travel aspect deters some Americans. I had done hundreds of dives in the Florida caves. I started working on becoming a cave diving instructor about a year after moving to the state and had been teaching cave diving for three years by that first trip to Cozumel in 2011. With several hundred cave dives, many of them in the caves located only ten minutes from where we lived, I had come to know them very well. It was like driving around in my neighborhood. I knew the passages. I had the maps of the caves imprinted in my mind. Like I said, I had even surveyed and mapped some tunnels I had discovered. I wanted more, though. I wanted to find more unexplored tunnels and put line in them. I wanted to survey them and create maps. I needed to do more than just visit the caves. I wanted to explore them much like the early cave diving pioneers had explored them. The opportunity for that type of exploration was harder to come by in Florida. The caves had been scoured by the early explorers in the 1980s and 1990s. The only potential for exploration was far back inside the caves, thousands of feet from the entrances. That wasn't the case in Cozumel.

My cave diving adventures in Cozumel started with a post on an internet board dedicated to cave diving. That post was an open invitation for anyone interested in joining a trip to dive the caves of Cozumel. The potential to do real cave exploration and find previously unexplored passages was mentioned. I had read articles about the caves in Cozumel. One particular cave that was often written about due to the diversity of marine life located within its walls was Aerolito. It was the Cozumel cave most people were familiar with and the one most cave divers that ventured onto the island would dive.

Cozumel caves had the reputation for being advanced caves requiring special skills to dive them. This left me with the impression that they would be a bit too advanced and the logistics too difficult to overcome. I didn't know exactly why. Unlike the caves on the Mexican mainland in Playa del Carmen to Tulum, Cozumel caves weren't a popular destination. Renting tanks on the island was nearly impossible unless you were doing guided dives with a dive shop. That meant you had to have a guide with you when diving in the caves there. I had done guided dives in the mainland Mexico caves, but that was so I could learn the logistics of getting to the caves and who to pay for land access. The right guide will also show you some cool places that you might not otherwise find in only a dive or two in the cave. They can be worth the expense for short visits, but they were unnecessary for repeat visitors. And guided dives weren't going to lead to virgin passages.

Cozumel has never had many cave divers living there. Over the several years I've been visiting Cozumel, I've only known of three cave divers offering guided dives and only two at any given point in time. Scheduling guided dives there isn't easy. Finding the people who offer guided dives is even more difficult when you consider there are hundreds of dive operators on the island. There are a lot more recreational divers so that's where the focus remains.

The last exploration in the Cozumel caves occurred in the early 1990s. Not much exploration had occurred there again until the late 2000s. While the trip announcement mentioned the potential for cave exploration, I didn't think there could be much more exploration to do, although I was hopeful that I was wrong. It was common knowledge that there were more opportunities for underwater cave exploration in Mexico than in Florida. I was hoping that was also the case in Cozumel. I did ask myself that if there was potential for cave exploration there, why hadn't anyone been exploring the caves throughout the 1990s and 2000s?

When I saw the invitation, I couldn't pass up the rare opportunity. It wasn't so much about exploration opportunities as it was just to be able to dive in caves where not many others had been. Even to this day, probably less than one hundred people have been in the caves of Cozumel. There was also the challenge of diving in caves that had the reputation for being complex and difficult caves. I wanted to expand my experience as a cave diver. Yes, I was hopeful I would encounter a virgin passage or two. I wouldn't be overly disappointed if I didn't.

I discussed the trip with my wife, Jen, and we decided to go and be a part of this for a few days. Jen was already scheduled at work and couldn't get the entire time off, so I went down a few days before her. It was a good thing that it worked out that way. We couldn't find direct flights into Cozumel, so we had to fly into Cancun. That meant taking a bus to Playa del Carmen, doing the bag drag to the ferry, then taking the ferry across to Cozumel, at least for me. Because Jen was coming down three days later, she would fly Maya Air from Cancun to

Cozumel. That left me with checking an extra piece of luggage and bringing down all of our dive equipment because Maya Air had a strict weight limit on luggage. They flew smaller, prop planes and didn't have room for the standard fifty-pound checked bag per passenger that the major airlines had. You could only bring what you could carry on with you.

My arrival in Cozumel on that first trip happened with minimal information on the location of the rental house where the group was staying for two weeks. All we were told was that it was on the corner of two streets. When the ferry arrived in Cozumel, I disembarked, collected my luggage, and hailed a taxi. I directed the driver to the cross streets in my broken Spanish as best as I could. I knew enough Spanish to get by, but most of my background was speaking medical Spanish while working in various emergency rooms in southern Arizona. I could determine if you had *dolor de panza* or *cabeza* (stomach- or headache) and tell you *no empuje hasta que lleguemos al parto* (don't push until we get to labor and delivery). Directions were an entirely different thing.

Addresses in Cozumel are a bit different than in the United States. Street numbers are not commonly used. Many addresses are listed by using cross streets rather than numbers. The name, typically a number, of the street is followed by the word *entre*, Spanish for between, and the other two streets between which the house is located. That left you with several houses on both sides of the street to choose from. It was helpful that the house where we were staying was on the corner of two major streets and there was a sculpture of a giant conch shell in the small roundabout circle in the middle of the intersection. What wasn't helpful was that two of the four corners had houses situated on the lots. At least I had a fifty-fifty chance of locating the correct house. Another problem was that both houses at that intersection were surrounded by ten-foot-tall walls. The listing I was sent showed a photo of the house. The problem was that I couldn't see the house from the street!

After driving through the conch shell intersection three times, I asked the taxi driver to drop me off on the side of the road, not sure if I was at the correct location. I had wasted enough of his time. Taxi drivers in Cozumel are paid flat rates, so there was no meter running. I gave him a nice tip to make up for the time we spent driving aimlessly through that intersection. He left me on the side of the road with two large suitcases, a carry-on roller, and a backpack. I was on an island I had never been to before, having no clue where to go. It was hot and humid, and I broke out in a sweat almost instantly. I dragged my bags behind me toward the first ten-foot-wall hoping the house where we were staying was behind it. I checked the large gate, but it was locked. I walked around the corner to the other wall and found a second gate. It was also locked.

I returned to the intersection and waited for the light to change. When the light was favorable for me, I made my way across the street, bags in tow, to the other potential house. There were no gates on one side, so I dragged my luggage behind me along the other wall, my shirt completely soaked in sweat by now. There was a gate at the far end of the property from the corner and it happened to be open. I finally felt a glimmer of hope. I reached the gate and peeked inside. The buildings within the walls looked nothing like the house in the listing I had. At least that narrowed it down to the other house, as long as I was at the correct intersection.

I crossed the street and tried the gates again, like they might have magically unlocked themselves while I was wandering around across the street. They were still locked. I banged on the thick wood repeatedly to no avail. I could barely hear the knocking myself because of the sound of the traffic behind me. I found myself walking back and forth along the sidewalks of Cozumel trying to figure out whether I was at the correct location or if I had misunderstood the directions. I did this all while carrying a backpack and dragging behind me one hundred and fifty pounds divided among three suitcases full of dive equipment.

I finally gave in, connected to the internet, and got in touch with the group organizer. In 2011, international roaming wasn't included with most mobile plans. Every text cost fifty-five cents to send and ten cents to receive and data was charged by the megabyte. I shuddered as I thought of the expensive charges I was incurring while I watched the images slowly and painfully unveil themselves on my phone screen. I knew the longer it took to appear on my screen, the more I was being charged. Roaming fees be damned! I was tired of standing in the hot sun at a busy intersection in a foreign country with thousands of dollars of dive equipment. I was also hungry and thirsty. The beginning of the Pink Floyd song *Money* began playing in my head as the megabyte usage increased while my search results for the house downloaded and the messages I was sending to Ygor, the trip organizer, uploaded. Fortunately, Ygor responded almost immediately and told me someone was in the house. I sent another message and another fifty-five cents to let him know the gates were locked and I had no way of alerting those people that I needed to be let in. I had knocked loudly, but no one had responded.

About five minutes later, someone finally opened the front gate and greeted me. There had indeed been others inside the entire time. They had been there for several days already and took a day off from diving. The problem was that no one told them I was coming, and I had no way of letting them know I was there. The house was located about fifty feet from the gate I was knocking on, and I didn't know the people that were there, as I had never met them, so I had no way of contacting them. I began to wonder about how the logistics of the cave diving were being handled.

I'm not the most social person. I'm an introvert and prefer to be by myself or among close friends. Group trips were not something I typically sought out. Besides that first trip to Cozumel, I had only gone on two other group diving trips. The first one was my first diving trip a year after getting certified. Jen and I went to Ambergis Caye, Belize. That trip was mainly so Jen and I could learn the logistics of international dive trips. During the week in Belize, we decided we could have better experiences by booking our own trips. The second group trip was a liveaboard to the Bahamas a year later. A liveaboard is basically a small cruise for divers. We spent a week eating and sleeping and diving from the boat. There are liveaboards that can accommodate forty to fifty divers. The one we chose to do only had ten divers including us on the one-hundred-and-five-foot-long sailboat. It also had five crew members. That was more our style.

This trip to Cozumel was only the third group trip we had done and the purpose of that was to dive caves that I thought I would never have the opportunity to dive again. While I knew Ygor from online interactions, I hadn't met him in person before the trip. I only knew one other person there that week. He was a cave diver I had met in Florida, but he was diving the day I arrived. Here I was meeting new people for the first time, in Mexico, not knowing what the plan was and the three people in the house not having much more information themselves. I had at least been able to get off of the street and into an air-conditioned house.

The group that had arrived earlier in the week wasn't that large, so I was given an option of rooms to choose from. I claimed one of the empty rooms accessible through the courtyard that overlooked the pool. I immediately turned the air conditioner on high and settled in to unpack my dive equipment. I laid everything out on the bed to inventory and got it ready for the next day of diving. The excitement of what I was about to do the next day finally hit and almost became overwhelming. I couldn't wait to get into the caves of Cozumel!

After my arrival in Cozumel, I learned there had been ongoing exploration in some of the caves there in recent years by a group of divers led by Ygor. I believe they had started going there only two years prior in 2009. Ygor and his team had been exploring a cave named Sin Nombre, Spanish for No Name. Sin Nombre had two cenotes that were located in the middle of a construction project near the cruise terminal. If you're ever in Cozumel, you can see the cenote from the road in the Royal Village Shopping Center next to the Hard Rock Café. If I also happen to be there, you might see me pop my head up to say hi! There's a second cenote farther back in the shopping plaza. The cenotes would later become centerpieces of the shopping center.

During the construction project of the shopping center, part of one of the buildings the crew was working on collapsed. The column they had set in the ground was located above a cave tunnel and the ground failed to hold the weight of the concrete and rebar. The column collapsed into the cave tunnel. This occurred overnight so no one was injured. The managers of the project prohibited all diving from that point forward. Ygor's team had to find a new exploration project.

They started working on Cocodrilo, another cave on the island that had been previously explored and mapped. They were hoping to extend the length of that cave inland. There was nothing near the cenote entrance and they quickly abandoned that project. It became a place to allow new divers on the trips to dive while exploration was taking place at another cave.

That other cave was Dos Coronas. Ygor had learned of a hole in the reef not too far offshore that was popular with snorkeling tours. It was fairly easy to access from shore. He looked in the area and found the entrance to Dos Coronas. That became Ygor's new focus in Cozumel. That was the trip before my initial trip to Cozumel. He must have found it during his final day of diving because there was only a few hundred feet of line in it when I did my first dive there. During my trip with the group, they were focusing on finding the going cave passage in Dos Coronas. They may have already had the objective of trying to connect it to Cueva Quebrada at that point. It was never mentioned, so I don't know for certain.

Ygor was staying on the island for two weeks. He had opened the trip to interested cave divers and made a general announcement on the cave diving social media site. I think it might have been his first group trip to Cozumel. There wasn't much organization to the trip. There were groups of divers that would be arriving at varying times. Ygor didn't limit days of arrival or the head count. There was one main group during the first week and another group the second, but that was by chance. Some of the first group of divers stayed a few days into the second week and some of the second week divers arrived a few days early. And then there were some of us that overlapped the two weeks.

Jen and I were part of the overlap group. I arrived on a Wednesday and Jen arrived two days later on Friday because of her work obligation. We both stayed until the following Tuesday. It was a good thing Jen arrived after me because I'm not so sure she would have taken well to the bag drag around a strange city in another country looking for a house hidden by ten-foot walls. I was relieved she wasn't there for that. I definitely would have been incurring those roaming charges much sooner, and we might have never returned to Cozumel.

4

New openings, virgin tunnels, and getting stuck

I woke up my first morning in Cozumel and headed into the kitchen looking for a cup of coffee. I find it difficult to begin my day without a jolt of caffeine coursing through my veins. My brain has trouble functioning until after my second cup. If I could feed it to myself intravenously, I might consider it. Although, I do love the taste of a fresh cup of black coffee and would have to have a cup while receiving my caffeine drip. The kitchen was empty, but someone had already been in there and brewed a pot of coffee. I found a clean mug in one of the cabinets. As I poured myself a cup someone else walked into the kitchen.

"Ahh, coffee is ready! Do you know if it was made with bottled water?"

I stared back at him. I knew the water coming from the tap in Mexico was unsafe to drink. I didn't want to come down with a case of traveler's diarrhea my first day there and miss out on any diving. I looked around the kitchen. There was a five-gallon half full water bottle turned upside down on a countertop dispenser. Surely, the coffee had been made with that water. Why would anyone use water from the tap? Just then, another person walked into the kitchen.

"I can't remember if I made it with that or the water from the faucet. I'm down here so much I drink the tap water. It never does anything to me."

I turned to the sink and poured the possibly contaminated contents of my mug down the drain. I then grabbed the coffee pot and did the same.

"Sorry, I'm not taking chances with Montezuma's Revenge my first morning here. I'd like to get some dives in this week." I laughed to try to keep the mood light. I didn't know either of these guys.

I rinsed the coffee pot with water from the bottle, poured out the rinse water and filled it to the top, hoping that the water in the bottle hadn't come from the hose spigot outside. I discarded the used coffee grounds from the Mr. Coffee and rinsed the filter basket with bottled water as well. I carefully poured the potful of water into the Mr. Coffee, grabbed a fresh filter, which happened to be next to it on the counter, and shoved it into the basket. I popped open the coffee container and scooped a few heaping spoonfuls of ground coffee into the filter. With everything set up, I hit the brew button and stood next to the coffee maker as the wonderful, dark, bitter smell began to emanate from the machine. My mouth began to water waiting for the first taste of the piping hot liquid.

I'm a bit of a coffee snob. I like freshly ground beans, filtered water heated to the perfect temperature, and the two combined in a French Press, allowed to steep for a few minutes. This wasn't instant coffee, but it wasn't much better. I had no other options if I wanted my daily morning dose of caffeine. I hadn't seen any coffee shops during my ventures around the intersection the day before. I was going to have to explore the area whenever I had the opportunity. For the time being, Folgers would have to do.

We discussed dive plans as we caffeinated, and I ate some buttered toast. I would have to make a run to the supermarket after Jen arrived so we could get some food for ourselves. Ygor split the divers into three groups, and we were each assigned to different caves – Aerolito, Cocodrilo, and Dos Coronas. I was with the group going to Dos

Coronas, a cave I hadn't heard about until that morning. I was a little nervous about the idea of diving in a *wild*, untamed cave my first day on the island, but I was also excited. We headed to the dive site to set up our equipment. There were five of us in the group, which was a rather large group for cave diving, never mind for a small cave. We decided to split up and do our own dives. I went off to see what I could find by myself. The other four split up into two teams. It was fitting that Dos Coronas would be the first cave I ever saw in Cozumel because it led to so much more over the following years.

We had been told the general area of the opening but had no specific details. One of the divers had been there earlier in the week. He had followed another diver and had an idea of where the opening was located. We placed our tanks in the shallows just off of the rocky shore. It was a bit of a challenge. The constant surge against the rocks created an interesting surface both above and below the water. Walking on that craggy, uneven surface was a bit perilous at times. We braved the conditions and headed into the water after gearing up, careful not to step on any sea urchins hiding in the crevices of the rocky bottom. The surge wasn't horrible, but it didn't make things easy. We struggled to get our fins on and our tanks clipped in place as we were shoved back and forth by the movement of the water. Water is such a powerful force when in motion. It's certainly nothing to take lightly. Once geared up, we swam out to the reef about a hundred feet offshore

I arrived at the reef and swam toward the north, parallel to the shoreline, looking for the cave opening. About thirty feet back from where the reef sloped down, I found a depression in the sea floor. It was almost a perfect circle, reminding me of the meteor crater in northern Arizona that I once visited, only much smaller. There was a swim through on the side opposite from the shoreline that came out on the reef. After checking that out, I turned around and headed back through. That's when I saw it. On the side closest to the rocky shore was a small opening in the bowl. I headed across to investigate. I didn't see a line from outside the entrance, so I tied the end of the line from my explorer reel to a large rock outside of the opening and ventured in expecting to find another line somewhere in the cavern zone, the first area of the cave that was still illuminated by daylight. There was no line. I continued into the cave slowly letting line out from the reel sweeping my light beam back and forth expecting to find a line at any moment. There was no line to be found. Several minutes later, about one hundred feet in from the opening, I knew I hadn't found the main entrance that we had been told about. I couldn't believe my luck! My very first dive in Cozumel and I was in an unexplored, virgin cave.

The visibility was hazy due to the surge moving the water in and out of the opening. The sea floor was only about fifteen feet deep at this point and at that depth the surge was still significant. I was being knocked around a bit. I slowly followed the wall to my right around a bend. The floor and walls were covered in coral and sponges of various colors. They were mostly of the orange and yellow variety. Occasionally, I saw some red peeking out. The wall started to curve to the left to form a room about twenty feet wide and only fifteen feet long. At the bottom of the wall, on the far side from where I had entered, was a small restriction, barely large enough for me to fit through. It was so small I almost missed it. I swam to the opening and stuck my arm and my head inside of it, shining my dive light into the darkness beyond. The cave passage opened into a much larger room than the one I was in. The wall on the opposite side looked to be about thirty feet away. I tried to push myself into the restriction by finning. I barely moved. I tried to pull myself through. I was too big. I backed out into the small room and pulled one of my sidemount tanks off, swinging it around so it was in front of me. I held the tank in that position and swam forward into the small restriction again.

It was a tight squeeze. I struggled a bit and almost decided to stop and back out. Then I saw it. I saw a line covered with crusty coral about twenty-five feet in front of me. It was crossing from left to right about three feet from the far wall. The growth on it had caused it to blend in with the wall when I had looked through the small hole from the other room. With all forgotten except that line, I pulled harder and squeezed myself through the restriction until I finally popped into the next room. I stopped and looked back at the hole I had just come through. It wasn't there anymore. It hadn't caved in. It just wasn't visible. There was enough silt on the floor that I had stirred it up, and the hole had disappeared in the cloud that had formed. If it wasn't for the line from my explorer reel poking out from the silt, I wouldn't have had any idea where my exit was located. I was thankful for that guideline.

I turned away from the silt cloud, hoping it would settle down by the time I was ready to head back through the hole hiding inside of it. I saw the crusty line about twenty feet away and swam toward it. I found a large orange line marker on it. It was shaped like an arrow and pointed to my right. That was the way out toward another opening. I rubbed away the silt and coral that had started growing on the marker to read the writing on it. It had two crowns drawn on it with a permanent marker. I was in Dos Coronas. I felt a little defeated. I thought I had found a new cave. Then it occurred to me. I had found a second entrance to Dos Coronas. The excitement returned.

I tied my line onto this guideline, placed one of my own markers on it, pointing in the direction I had come from, and began following the line I had just tied into. I decided to go to the left, away from the other opening. I wanted to see what else was in this cave. I swam slowly, taking in my surroundings. Everything was covered in pastel colored coral and sponges. There wasn't a smooth surface to be found. I was diving inside of a reef. This was like no other cave I had seen before. It was amazing!

I reached a bend in the line. There was another line arrow on it belonging to someone from the exploration team during the previous trip. It had coral growth on it so it couldn't be from earlier in the week. It was pointing back behind me. I looked to the left, where the line continued. It was a low bedding plane and seemed to go for some distance. I decided this was a good place to turn around. I had already been on the dive for about thirty minutes and was nearing my turn pressure in my scuba tanks. I marked the location with a line cookie, turned around, and began surveying the line. I arrived back at the intersection I had created and took a compass heading for the line I had tied into. This was a heading going toward the other opening. I swam along the line I had placed in the cave, continuing to get survey data.

Half a minute later, I arrived at the restriction I had pulled myself through and assessed it. The silt had started to settle down already. It was hazy, but I could see the hole again. I had been stuck in there only twenty minutes earlier. I had to pull myself through with one of my tanks held in front of me. What if I couldn't get back through? I should have thought about that before going through it. I still had the other opening I could look for. However, I hadn't been to it and had no idea what it looked like, what the passage between where I was and that opening looked like, or how far it was from my location. I also didn't know if the guideline was continuous or if there were gaps along the way. What had I gotten myself into? The excitement of the exploration and seeing another line had taken over and put me in danger.

I pushed the thought of not being able to get back through the restriction out of my head. I got in so I'd get out. I unclipped the same tank, swung it around so it was in front of me, and pushed it through the haze into the small hole that would lead me back out of the cave and to the surface. The tank took up a good portion of the hole and I found myself wondering how I had fit. The better question was how was I going to get back through. I followed my tank into the restriction.

I struggled a little as I felt the borders of the hole squeezing in around my body. I pulled my way forward, struggling to get closer to the exit. And then I popped out. For some reason, it was much easier to pass through going out than it had been going in. I let out a sigh of relief. I was going to live to dive again.

I continued to survey the line I had placed in the tunnel forty-five minutes earlier. As I swam forward, I saw a pinpoint of light ahead. That light grew larger as I got closer until I could see fish casually swimming outside of the cave opening. I reached the end of the line where I had secured it and wrote down the last of the survey data. I did the math and quickly added the distances between all of the survey stations. I had only placed two hundred feet of line in the cave, but I had discovered another opening. I was happy.

The exit hadn't taken nearly as long as the entry into the cave. I still had plenty of air in my tanks, so I decided to look around the reef. Maybe I would find another entrance. I continued toward the north. A few minutes later I encountered another opening. This one was slightly larger than the first one. I grabbed my explorer reel and tied the end to the outside of the opening. I entered the cave and found myself in a taller room than what I had seen in the previous opening. It was a bit narrower. It was more of a tunnel than a room. I followed the tunnel around to the left. Then it started to curve to the right and became even smaller. At some point I had to turn sideways to fit in the tunnel. The walls were too close together for me to fit with scuba tanks mounted at my sides. I doubted I would have been able to fit with tanks on my back. I felt a strong current coming from inside of the cave trying to push me back out. This tunnel definitely led into a cave. I kept going, excited that I had found another entrance on my first dive in Cozumel.

I reached the end of the tunnel. The walls came together, and I found myself at a dead-end. That couldn't be right. I felt a current. The water had to be coming from somewhere. I swept my light around looking for the source of the current. I moved closer to the wall and felt a distinct change in the temperature of the water moving past me. It was much colder. The current was freshwater coming from somewhere inside the cave. This meant it was definitely coming from somewhere beneath the jungle. The water was a couple of degrees cooler than the saltwater I was in. I felt the cold water coming from the right. I moved forward and looked in that direction. There was a narrow slit in the wall just around the corner. It had looked like a dead-end, but the wall curved to the left then to the right only giving it an appearance of ending. I pointed my light into the slit and saw a small restriction near the floor. It was much too small for me to fit through, even with one tank off. I might have been able to fit with both tanks pushed in front of me, but I wanted to have more air in them if I was going to do that. If I got stuck on the other side, I would need time to figure things out. I didn't have much time with tanks that were just under half full.

I tied the line to the wall, cut it, and placed one of my line markers on it. I grabbed my notes and began to survey on the way out. The tunnel was only two hundred and thirty-two feet long before the no mount restriction, but I was certain it was another entrance to Dos Coronas. That brought the count to three. I still hadn't seen what was being called the main entrance.

I surfaced and met with the other divers on the shore and excitedly told them about my findings. They were happy for me and surprised. They were anxious to go look at the openings during the next dive. We had two dives planned for the day, so we stripped the hardware off of our tanks and swapped them out for the full tanks we had awaiting us in the van. Less than ninety minutes later we were back in the water.

This time I headed for the original entrance to the cave which was south of where I had been. The other divers would also go that way and then check out the openings I had found after the dive. They weren't too interested in penetrating them after I told them about the restriction I had to go through. I followed the other divers toward the original opening. They had been in that entrance while I was off finding the other two. There was already a line in place from the opening to the beginning of the permanent guideline that had been placed there by someone earlier in the week. It would stay there for the duration of the trip. This opening was about one hundred feet off of the shoreline in the first reef fifteen feet below the surface. It was slightly bigger than the opening I found during my first dive. There was also a lot of coral and sponge growth around the perimeter of the entrance. A brief glance at it might make it appear as nothing more than a duck under in the reef. It was so much more!

Going through the cave was a bit of a blur. There was so much to look at that I had sensory overload. The floor and walls leading from this entrance resembled what I had seen during my earlier dive, only there was a lot more color. It looked like someone had taken a giant pallet of pastel paints and swung it around the room splashing the color onto the surfaces. I recalled going through a restriction from the lower level to a level about seven feet shallower, but the specifics of the tunnel escaped me. It was so much to take in. I ended up in a large room that seemed to be covered in even more coral. Not the smooth, flat type of coral you find in brain or elkhorn coral, but coral like stony or tabulate varieties. It was uneven and sharp. This room looked similar to the one I had reached from the other entrance, only it was bigger. I followed the line until it took a sharp turn to the left. Directly in front of me was a dark void with no line in it.

The rest of the cave didn't matter at that point. There was more virgin tunnel to be explored. I placed a line arrow on the guideline and grabbed my explorer reel. I unlocked the spool, let out some line, and secured it to the permanent guideline. I then swam into the void. I slowly moved forward, sweeping my light beam from left to right, taking in as much as I could. The tunnel seemed to continue forward so I did as well. The ceiling began to slope down. I kept going. The craggy floor faded away and transformed into a muddy sediment. Before I knew it, I was squeezed between the ceiling and the floor. The passage continued, but I thought it best that I didn't. The clearance was low and the sediment on the floor had been disturbed by my movement through the passage. I knew I could fit if I kept going, but this was only the first day of diving. There would be more opportunities to come back and push it farther. I secured my line to a protrusion sticking up out of the sediment on the floor. I cut the line and placed one of my line markers on it. I had just been in my third unexplored, virgin passage of the trip. It was only the first day of diving.

I surveyed the new line. I had placed another three hundred and seventy-nine feet of line in the cave. That brought my total count to eight hundred and fifty-one feet on the first day. I was more than happy with the results of these dives. I would have been happier to place all of that line in one continuous tunnel, but it was still a good day of exploration. I continued to survey the line that was already in the cave out to the opening. I remained focused on the survey work and didn't look around at the cave. I could do that another day. I made it out of the cave faster than I expected. I still had lots of air in my scuba tanks so I decided to swim along the reef and see if I could find a fourth entrance. This time I went south.

Two minutes later I found another opening in the reef. I couldn't believe my luck! I positioned myself in front of it and felt a cool current coming from inside. More freshwater. It was time to see where this hole took me. Unfortunately, it didn't go very far. I entered the opening and went to the right, the only way I could go. I had to turn sideways. This wasn't like the tunnel I found during the previous dive where I had to turn sideways. The walls in this tunnel were so close together I would have had to turn sideways even if I didn't have any tanks on. My shoulders wouldn't fit between them. I was able to push in about twenty-five feet before the fissure crack got so small I couldn't go any farther. My chest was too deep. I already had to turn my head sideways to fit it between the walls. I looked around as best as I could to see if I had missed a larger opening. There wasn't one. The fissure continued forward, but it was too narrow. I couldn't even fit one of my arms into the crack in front of me.

I started to back out. The crack was too small to turn around. I moved back a few inches. Then I couldn't move anymore. I wiggled my hips and shoulders and tried to push myself backwards. I couldn't even move an inch. It felt like something was catching me on the left side, so I moved my left hand back to feel around. Fortunately, there was enough height in this crack that I could move my arms. I wiggled some more. It felt like my tanks were A framing. When I backed up the bottoms of the tanks got caught by the uneven rock around me and were jammed in, not allowing me to move back anymore. The straps on the tanks also got caught and I couldn't move forward either. I was stuck.

I wiggled back and forth. I tried to shake the tanks loose. I pushed and pulled. I wasn't making any progress. The thought of dying twenty-five feet inside a fissure crack in water that was only twenty feet deep entered my mind. How ironic. I had been more than five thousand feet inside multiple caves. I had been more than two hundred feet deep below the surface inside caves. And here I was, about to die twenty-five feet inside a cave only twenty feet deep. I looked at my pressure gauges. I still had plenty of air in my tanks. The depth was in my favor. I easily had a couple of hours of air to figure things out. I just had to remain calm. I took a moment to breathe and think. I had to do this on my own. No one else could fit in this fissure crack. No one would be able to help me get loose. If I died in the crack, they would have to cut me into little pieces to remove my body.

Once I was relaxed, I moved my hands back alongside my tanks. The bottoms were stuck and keeping me jammed in, so I needed to get them away from the floor and the ceiling between which they were trapped. I was still sideways. It seemed counterproductive, but I pushed myself farther into the crack as I put pressure on the lower half of the tanks. Sometimes you have to go farther in to be able to get out. I felt the tanks start to move. I pushed harder with my hands and my feet. The rock finally released my tanks. I kept my arms back to continue to push the bottoms of the tanks in. I stretched my legs out and felt for something to anchor myself on. It wasn't easy moving my feet around with fins that stretched out more than a foot from the tips of my toes. The walls of the crack kept grabbing the fin tips. My heels finally found some footing, and I bent my knees to pull myself back. I moved back about a foot before being stopped again. I wiggled my body as I continued to hold my tanks in and pulled back with my legs. I continued this process for about fifteen minutes.

Twenty minutes after I had entered that narrow slit in the reef, I finally emerged back into the clear blue waters of the Cozumel reef. I had never been so happy to be out of a cave. Well, it was more of a crack than a cave. I didn't leave line in that crack or survey anything. It wasn't worth it. I was happy to be alive back on the surface and out of the cave, but I was excited about the coming days of more cave diving in Cozumel.

While I wanted to go back and continue to poke around in Dos Coronas, I also wanted to see other caves on the island. Dos Coronas wasn't a very long cave at the time. I think after the eight hundred and fifty-one feet I had put in it that day, I was able to claim more than half of the line in the cave. I didn't think there would be much more potential in Dos Coronas. Was I ever wrong!

5

Cocodrilos, more virgin tunnels, and unknotted line

It was a beautiful day. The best kind of day to be out laying in the sun taking in the rays on a beautiful island in the Caribbean. That wasn't what we were about to do, though. We were about to descend into the chocolate milk brown, murky water into which we had seen a small crocodile escape the previous day. It wasn't a hatchling. It also wasn't adult size. The crocodile was what I'd call a toddler. I didn't know if that was more dangerous or less. We went into the water, anyway, knowing the potential risk. One time wasn't enough. We were back to do it again. None of us were thinking about the possibility of mama croc also lurking in the dark recesses of the cenote, at least not until a few hours later.

What could be below the surface of that water that would entice us to do such a thing? Why would we expose ourselves to this unknown danger? Beyond that muddy layer of water was the dark world of one of the underground river systems that meandered all along the west coast of the small island of Cozumel. Befittingly, this particular cave system had been named Cocodrilo, the Spanish word for crocodile.

Two days earlier, my first day in Cocodrilo, I swam through the large, dark tunnels reconciling what I encountered with the mental image of the maps I had studied. The main tunnel was large. I estimated it to be twenty to twenty-five feet from floor to ceiling and between fifteen to thirty-five feet wide in places. The formations were unusual. They didn't look like the formations I had seen during my previous trips to dive the caves on the mainland of Mexico. They were the same shape. They were the stalagmites and stalactites commonly found in caves that were once exposed to air. However, the formations and the walls were a dark brown. They were almost black. Many of the formations were leaning or fallen over. Some of them were broken. These weren't recent breaks. It looked like they had been in that condition for centuries.

I followed the main tunnel and noted the offshoot tunnels whenever I saw line intersections. The published maps seemed to be inaccurate. They provided a basic sense of the layout of the cave passages, but they were not exact. There seemed to be some discrepancies between the distances on the map versus the actual distances in the cave. The offshoot tunnels were farther from each other than the map indicated. It almost seemed as if someone had distorted the image of the map and squeezed the top and bottom of it closer together. It would be nice to resurvey the cave and produce a new map. It might even lead to finding new passages.

On the second full day on the island, I did my first dive in Cocodrilo, my third dive in Cozumel. I happened to find an unexplored, virgin tunnel on that dive. The trip was turning out better than expected. I had hoped to do some exploration in Cozumel, but I didn't expect to be laying line every day. The tunnel I found wasn't extensive, three hundred and fifty-nine feet of previously unseen and untouched cave that looped back to the main tunnel. But it was a virgin cave tunnel, and it was beautiful. It was also different in appearance from the main tunnel. It was much smaller, and the formations had more color. They weren't like the ones found in the dark cave of the main passage. They had splashes of white and yellow. The best part was that I had found it during my first dive in the cave. I was three for three and had placed new line in more than twelve hundred feet of virgin cave passage. This was going to be a great trip! Or so I thought.

I only did one dive in Cocodrilo that day. Jen was coming in on a midafternoon flight and I had to meet her at the house. I continued to incur roaming charges, and we sent text messages to each other throughout her travels. I wanted to make sure she didn't have any issues, especially after how she had started her day. Her arrival in Cancun was uneventful and she was able to get onto an earlier flight than we had booked for her on Maya Air. About $20 worth of roaming fees later, I met Jen at the house shortly after my dive, depriving her of having to do her own bag drag. I walked out of the gate just as her taxi was pulling up. I had already brought her dive equipment with me on my flight and prepared it so all she had to do that evening was relax. That was a good thing as her morning had been quite stressful. She had overslept, hitting the snooze button on her alarm repeatedly; something she still does. It's also something I've done which is why my alarm clock sits on the dresser in the opposite corner of the room from my side of the bed. By the time I get to it and shut it off, I'm awake. Jen's snooze antics caused her to almost miss her flight. We weren't sure she would make it to the airport on time to make the gate. She did get there and boarded the airplane, but she was not showered and a bit unkempt. She hadn't even had time to brush her teeth. The first thing she did after getting to the house was clean up.

For Jen's first dive the next day, we went back to Cocodrilo and surveyed the guideline in the main tunnel starting from the cenote opening. I had already surveyed the tunnel I found, as well as part of the guideline in the main tunnel the day before. However, the line along the first four hundred feet or so from the opening lacked knots. That made the survey work a little more involved and required two divers.

Underwater cave explorers typically tie knots every ten feet along the guidelines being used for exploration. This makes it easier to survey once it's deployed inside the cave. We spool out the line, securing it to formations in the cave each time we change the direction we're heading, and create stations. On the way out, we take compass headings, notate depth, and count knots to get the distance between the stations. When a survey station falls between knots, we estimate the distance. That's how underwater cave maps are created. It may not seem like a very accurate method, but it can be when done by a skilled surveyor.

Not all cave explorers bother to tie knots in their lines. Some use a tape measure to determine the distance between stations instead. This method is more accurate but can be very time-consuming. Tape survey also requires a second diver and several dives to survey the same area I was able to do alone in one dive using knotted line survey. There's also an electronic device now available that is placed on the line and slides along it, recording azimuth headings, depths, and distances. That wasn't available in 2011. I still don't own one of those. I enjoy the process of surveying caves. That device would take that away from me.

Occasionally, lines without knots will be found inside underwater caves. If the guideline in the cave needs to be replaced, the diver replacing it may choose to not use knotted line. That's what I suspect happened in that first four hundred feet of tunnel. The line had deteriorated and was replaced with unknotted line at some point. So we had to employ tape survey if I was going to be able to add the tunnel I had found to my map. I needed to do that because I needed to begin the map from the opening and the unknotted line began at the entrance to the cave.

I brought a one-hundred-foot-long cloth survey tape, the kind used in construction, on the chance that we would need to use it. Jen took the dumb end, the beginning of the measuring tape where the zero was, and I held onto the smart end, the reel and the end that would provide me with the length of the segment of guideline we were measuring. Jen swam until she reached a survey station, a point where the guideline was wrapped around a formation in the tunnel and changed direction. She held the dumb end at the bend, and we stretched the measuring tape along the guideline. I then read the number on my end. We did that for four hundred and forty-two feet before we made it to the section of line that had knots. While there were some longer segments, the longest one measuring eighty-eight feet, most of them fell into the range of two feet to twenty-one feet in length. There were very few runs longer than that. There were sixteen measurements we had to get. It was time-consuming, but it helped us become more familiar with the passage. In addition to providing me with data to create a map of the cave on paper, the process of surveying a cave also helps me paint a mental picture of the cave in my mind. It helps me learn the cave better. It also helps me decide where I want to focus my exploration efforts on subsequent dives. I mention the lack of knots and our efforts to survey because it becomes notable on the worst dive of my life on the fourth day of my first Cozumel trip.

* * *

The week two group arrived on the evening before my fourth day of diving. Some of the week one divers had flights back home scheduled the next day. Others, like Jen and I, weren't leaving for another two or three days. There was a bit of overlap among the various divers, and this put us over capacity with regard to the bed count and people count in the rental house. There were five bedrooms containing eight beds. Jen and I were one of two couples out of fifteen people that were there that Saturday night. That meant we were five beds short.

Jen and I had been in a bedroom with two beds. I gave up the second bed as my equipment staging area and we traded with one of the other divers, Amy, who was in a room with a single bed. Jen and

Amy were the only female cave divers on the trip. Amy's bedroom was inside the house and our bedroom was accessible from the courtyard surrounding the pool. We stripped the bed and moved our belongings inside. Amy moved into the courtyard bedroom along with Roger, one of the guys on the trip. Other bed assignments were made. The other couple had been there since the first day and were already set up in their room. A couple of guys shared one of the full-size beds sleeping head to foot. The four remaining divers had to sleep two on the couches and two on the floor in the living room. Logistics. At least we were all able to go diving.

I woke up early the next morning and quietly entered the kitchen to get a pot of coffee going. I had placed myself in charge of that duty after my near-miss experience with tap water that first morning. I'm typically not a morning person, but I'll wake up early to insure I get untainted coffee. As I walked down the hall, I got a glimpse into the living room and the four guys crashed out in it. The only one that looked comfortable was the guy on the full-length couch. The others didn't look like they had a restful night. I wondered how they would feel during their dives later.

After coffee and breakfast, Jen and I headed to Cocodrilo. We had three additional divers joining us – Greg, Jose, and Brendan. Greg had arrived the first day of the trip. Jose lived on Cozumel. Brendan arrived the evening before and had volunteered to sleep on one of the couches. He got the short end of the stick on that. Not only did he have to sleep on a couch but being the shortest of the four relegated to the living room, he got stuck on the love seat. When I saw him earlier that morning, he was folded up on the love seat mimicking a contortionist. I could tell Brendan was tired, and even though he was young, he was feeling the discomfort of the love seat in his back.

Brendan and I got to know each other a little as we set up our dive equipment next to each other in the parking lot of the beach resort where the Cocodrilo cenote was located. We also got plenty of strange looks from the loads of tourists that were arriving for a day on the beach enjoying the sun and drinks. Because Cozumel sees a lot of cruise ship traffic, there are lots of day resorts. They offer beach, pools, lunch, and drinks, but no overnight accommodations. It was a Sunday, but it was the beginning of high season so there were a couple of cruise ships in port. That meant the resorts had plenty of customers that day. The cruisers were probably wondering what five people were doing setting up dive equipment in the parking lot of a beach resort. Diving wasn't allowed from the beach. Little did they know that the reef surrounding the island was not our intended destination.

As Brendan and I were talking, I learned that he had been cave diving in Cozumel on previous trips and was familiar with the caves, particularly Cocodrilo. I also learned that Brendan and Ygor were very good friends. In fact, Brendan had saved Ygor's life on a previous cave dive. Ygor had an issue with his rebreather during one of their dives together. A rebreather is a device that is designed to scrub out the carbon dioxide we exhale. It uses absorbent to bind with the carbon dioxide so that the air that's left can be breathed again. Even though the air is recycled, rebreathers still require a scuba tank with diluent air and another scuba tank with one hundred percent oxygen. The diluent and oxygen replenish the air in the loop when necessary, allowing the oxygen content in the rebreather to be breathable. Apparently, the air in the closed-circuit loop Ygor was using wasn't being scrubbed of carbon dioxide properly and Ygor took a carbon dioxide hit. It incapacitated him to the point where he couldn't swim. He was barely able to maintain consciousness.

Normally, if such a thing happens, the diver switches from the rebreather to breathing directly from a scuba tank. The diver then ascends to the surface where there is an unlimited supply of air. The problem was that Ygor and Brendan were inside an underwater cave.

There was no surface. At least not for more than a thousand feet. Ygor had already gotten too much carbon dioxide in his system, and he couldn't slow down his breathing. A carbon dioxide hit takes time to recover from, more time than they had. With a malfunctioning rebreather, Ygor couldn't remain on the rebreather loop and had to breathe directly from his bailout scuba tank. Ygor had to get to the surface as quickly as possible if he was going to survive.

Brendan grabbed Ygor and pulled him out of the cave. He dragged him through hundreds of feet of cave passage until they were back in the opening and able to ascend to the surface. Ygor was barely conscious enough to keep a seal on his regulator mouthpiece and keep water out of his lungs. During the times he tried to assist Brendan by swimming, it became harder to breathe and he almost passed out. His carbon dioxide hit had been a bad one. If it hadn't been for Brendan, Ygor would have died that day. Brendan was more than just a competent diver. When he told me about that dive, he was very humble. He believed anyone could have and would have done the same. Brendan was just that kind of person. He wasn't egocentric.

That morning, Brendan was going to guide us to an air dome room that was located almost three thousand feet from the murky entrance of Cocodrilo. It was an unusual occurrence to find an air-filled room in Mexican underwater caves. This was a special treat for our first trip to Cozumel. The room was about a kilometer from the entrance, so it would take nearly an hour to swim to it. Once there, we planned to surface, enjoy some snacks and drinks that we had stuffed into the pockets of our exposure suits, get some photos and video, and head back after about thirty to forty minutes.

Brendan was diving a prototype rebreather. It was a semi-closed rebreather. This type of rebreather only required one scuba tank filled with an oxygen-enriched gas called Nitrox. This was what we referred to as the drive gas. The semi-closed rebreather allowed the Nitrox in the scuba tank to last three to eight times longer than it would if breathed through a standard regulator. It was much easier to get scuba tanks with Nitrox than with one hundred percent oxygen in Mexico, so a semi-closed rebreather was more practical.

Brendan's rebreather had been designed and built by Ygor. Brendan had been diving it for several months and was very familiar with it. We talked quite a bit about the rebreather and how it differed from other rebreathers. I had purchased one of Ygor's earlier rebreathers, one similar in design to the rebreather Brendan was about to use. Because I had experience on a similar rebreather, Brendan asked me if I wanted to take his that day, and he would use my scuba tanks. I declined. I didn't have a lot of experience with rebreathers at the time, and I didn't feel comfortable diving a rebreather that I didn't have any time on into a cave the first time I used it I would be very thankful for that decision about forty-five minutes later.

We finished setting up our equipment and carried the scuba tanks to the water's edge, tossing a few rocks into the water to scare away the small crocodile we had watched escape into its depths the day before, and the larger crocodile that might also be in there watching us. I was going to make sure the others were positioned between me and the deeper section of the cenote until we descended into the clear water just inside the cave about six feet below the surface. Well, everyone except Jen. I kept her on the other side of me.

We geared up and descended below the surface into the black water and rushed to find good visibility as we followed the guideline that Brendan had secured to a rock on the shoreline. He would be tying the other end onto the beginning of the permanent guideline inside of the cave, the unknotted line. The water suddenly became clear as we descended below the muck. I glanced around and saw the other divers. I didn't see a crocodile, small or large. That didn't mean one wasn't somewhere nearby, so my guard remained up. We made it through the small opening into the cave. At least I thought it was small. I couldn't see it through the mud. I merely followed a line. Once through it, I could see the cave passage we were in, and it was large. I hadn't realized just how large it was during the two prior dives. It wasn't that I hadn't looked at it, but rather that there had only been two of us each of those days. The first day in Cocodrilo, I was diving with a fellow by the name of Larry, and the second day Jen was with me.

On this third day, there were five of us. We could all see each other. Five powerful underwater lights transformed the cave into a different place than I had seen the two previous days. Two lights did a good job providing light in the immediate area, but five lights allowed one to see a lot more inside of a dark cave. The almost black walls of the cave were all illuminated. Very few shadows remained. The sight was breathtaking. I was happy to be taking the rear position on this dive. I was about to see the cave like I hadn't seen it on the previous two dives.

Brendan led the group. He had been to the room on two other occasions. Greg had been there once but wasn't certain as to the route to take to get there. It wasn't a straight shot. There were a few navigational decisions that had to be made on the way, including a few line Ts. Jose was a local cave diver who was along to assist with topside communications. We were in Cozumel, Mexico and having a local at some of these dive sites was helpful, especially at a cenote located on the grounds of a resort. Jen and I brought up the rear, along for the ride, and ready to really see the cave this time. It was her second dive in this cave and my third. It was our first time going to the dome room. We followed behind the others enjoying the additional lighting they provided. The cave was magnificent. The passage was large, and all of the lights helped us to get a real appreciation for its beauty. Having three powerful lights ahead of us brightened both the cave and our spirits. We could see so much more of the cave and get a true feel for the size of the passage.

Until we lost sight of the three divers we were following.

6

My worst dive

We were falling behind the other three divers. They had abruptly started swimming faster. Jen and I looked at each other, confused about the sudden change in pace. The five of us were not only experienced divers, we were experienced cave divers. Jen and I didn't know what was going on or what had caused the three ahead of us to suddenly pick up their pace. If we were closer to the opening, I might have thought the crocodile we had seen the day before was chasing us, but we were one thousand feet inside the cave. I looked around anyway, just in case.

The plan was to do a leisurely swim through the underwater cave passage. Our destination would take us an hour to reach, and we didn't want to overexert ourselves and breathe through the limited air in our scuba tanks before we got there. We also had to reserve enough air for the hour-long swim back. I shrugged my shoulders at Jen and indicated we should maintain our normal pace. The others would either slow down, allowing us to catch up, or we would lose them and alter our dive plan. I didn't feel like swimming that fast and tiring myself out on such a long dive.

The other three divers swam around a corner, and we lost sight of them for a few seconds. Jen and I had been in this cave the day before and knew we would see them again when we rounded that bend. The relatively narrow section of tunnel we were in transformed into a wide, long room at that point. We might not be any closer, but we would at least see their lights ahead once we turned the corner. We continued at our own pace, swimming about fifty feet per minute as the distance between us and the other divers increased. We rounded the corner and saw the other three divers. They hadn't gotten as far as we had expected. One was in a vertical position, ascending toward the ceiling. I couldn't tell which diver it was because of the darkness and the distance. It was strange though. Cave divers rarely went vertical. We didn't want to kick up the sediment on the floor of the cave and destroy the visibility in the passage. Ascents and descents were made in a horizontal position, much like an airplane taking off and landing. I wondered what was going on. Had he seen something near the ceiling? Was there an opening to a cenote that we had missed? I had been in this area on two previous occasions and hadn't seen anything of interest up there.

Then I saw it, and my heart began racing. I blinked my eyes rapidly, hoping they were playing tricks on me. Unfortunately, they weren't. A second stage regulator, the one that was placed in the mouth and supplied air to the lungs, dropped down along the vertical diver's body and came to a stop next to his feet, hanging from the hose it was attached to. My eyes quickly traced the line of his body up to his head. As I got to his head, I watched it drop forward. There was no regulator in his mouth. He had lost consciousness.

Jen and I sprinted forward to offer assistance. My mind was still grappling with what I had just witnessed. I was still having difficulty believing it was happening. We reached the unconscious diver at the same time as the other two divers. We swam that fast. To be fair, we hadn't been exerting ourselves prior to that, unlike Greg and Jose, who had tried to keep pace with Brendan. I was now close enough to recognize who it was that had lost consciousness. Even this close I was having trouble believing it. Brendan couldn't be unconscious. He couldn't be drowning right there in front of us. Why was this happening? I had just met him and already knew he was a really nice guy. No one deserves to die this way, but Brendan really didn't deserve it.

I thought Brendan might have experienced a carbon dioxide hit. He was breathing through a rebreather. Sometimes the scrubber fails and not enough of the carbon dioxide is removed. That had happened to Ygor. Sometimes a valve fails, and the same air remains near the mouthpiece. A carbon dioxide hit could also happen when a diver experiences overexertion, such as by swimming too fast. The question that remained was if his was a carbon dioxide hit, did the hit precede the sprint, or did the sprint precede the hit?

Greg had one of his regulators extended and tried to get it into Brendan's mouth. I grabbed Brendan's arm and began pulling him and Greg down toward the guideline that was secured to formations rising up from the floor of the cave. We were in a large section of the cave, and we needed the guideline to keep us on the right path out of the cave to the surface almost one thousand feet away. The room we were in was tall, maybe twenty feet from floor to ceiling. We had about a fifteen-foot descent. My objective was to get to the guideline so we would not lose orientation of our location in the cave. From there we could begin our exit toward the surface, toward unlimited air. I was finally beginning to accept the reality of the moment. We were in a race against time, and the odds were not on our side. It was difficult to control my breathing. Adrenaline was flowing. I was focused on saving Brendan, not on my respiratory rate. Had I been using a rebreather, I would have been overbreathing the circuit loop and risking my own carbon dioxide hit.

Bubbles were escaping my regulator exhaust valve almost continuously. We always planned to reserve one-third of the air in our scuba tanks for emergencies. I found myself wondering if it would be enough. I was breathing too fast. The only thing in our favor was that this was the beginning of the dive, and the cave was shallow. We still had lots of air in our scuba tanks, but we were in a large room with offshoot tunnels. It would be easy to drift off of the guideline and get lost. When we got close to the guideline, I grabbed the regulator that was dangling from Brendan and clipped the attached bolt snap to the line. The thought of leaving his body there to recover on a later dive flashed through my mind. I quickly shoved it aside. There might be a chance to save Brendan. I had to hold on to that hope. I also wanted to make certain we didn't lose contact with the guideline while we situated ourselves to begin our exit from the cave.

Once secured to the line, I looked away and toward the ceiling, hopeful that I'd see an air pocket large enough to get Brendan's head above the surface of the water. Unconscious, he couldn't seal his lips around the mouthpiece of the regulator to keep water out of his lungs. To keep *more* water out of his lungs. I was certain some water had already entered them. The only hope we had was an air pocket. And even that was not very promising.

I didn't see any air pockets.

We began preparing for our exit. Greg was on Brendan's left; I was on his right. Jose took position behind Brendan ready to trade places with one of us if we should tire. Jen got in front of us ready to lead the way out, keeping an eye on the guideline so we wouldn't have to. That allowed us to focus on trying to keep Brendan alive. All of this happened in a matter of seconds. None of it had to be communicated. We just fell into our respective positions and did what we had to do. We began our race toward the cave opening.

Deep down inside, I knew our efforts were futile. We were an eighteen-minute swim from the surface. Brendan had lost consciousness in the water-filled cave. The air in his lungs had already been replaced with water. The chance for survival was very low. But we couldn't just leave him there. We couldn't give up. We had to try. We had to do everything we could to save him. Hopefully our efforts wouldn't endanger any of us and result in another victim. We swam hard and fast, the one thousand feet of cave between us and the surface seemed like one thousand miles.

It took us a matter of seconds to get ourselves situated around Brendan and begin exiting. Greg and I took turns holding a regulator in Brendan's mouth as we pulled him along, hoping that it would get some air into his lungs. I knew it was unlikely, but we couldn't give up. We had to try everything we could to save Brendan. Like Brendan had done when he saved Ygor. We followed Jen as she watched the guideline and made sure we were going the right way. Cave divers should always verify their own navigational decisions, but this situation was different. We had to trust Jen to guide us out, to not get us lost. If we focused too much on looking for the thin, mud-stained line that led us out of the cave, we would slow our exit. If Brendan had any chance of living, we had to get out of the cave and back to the surface fast.

I glanced at the guideline every minute or so. I wasn't confirming our route. I didn't watch it long enough for that. That would have slowed us down. I only looked for a second or two. I was looking for knots. I was thankful for the survey Jen and I had done in the cave the previous day. While it wouldn't affect the outcome of the situation we were in, it provided me with information. It provided me with some hope. It provided me with a small distraction. Because of that survey, I knew when I saw a lack of knots that we only had about four hundred and forty-two feet remaining until we were in the cenote. That meant we were more than halfway back from where Brendan had lost consciousness. Normally, that distance would take about nine minutes to swim. We were swimming much faster. We were in an all-out sprint to the surface. I pumped my legs as fast as I could. I focused on tightening and loosening my muscles as my legs went through the motions necessary to get us out of the cave. I switched from doing a modified frog kick, the standard finning technique preferred by cave divers, to the flutter kick to see if that would move us faster. It made no difference so I reverted back to what I was used to and what I hoped would get us out faster. I could feel the strain in my muscles as they neared exhaustion. One thousand feet was a long way to swim at the pace of a sprint. It had to be done. It was the only way we might be able to save Brendan.

The smooth, knotless line came into view. We were more than halfway back to the cenote. I could stop glancing at the line. I could just follow Jen's light. I couldn't ease up on my legs. I had to keep pumping them. I had to move faster. I glanced over at Greg. I could tell he was getting tired. Greg was a large man. He stood about six feet five inches and enjoyed his food. He wasn't obese, but he also wasn't thin. He wasn't used to swimming this fast either. Somehow, he was keeping up. We were all pushing ourselves to our limits. What had taken us eighteen minutes to swim into the cave only took us eleven minutes to swim out. We had swum fast. We made it to the small opening. Jen moved aside and let us through. I got in front of Brendan so I could pull him. Greg pushed from behind. We got into the cenote and ascended the last six feet through the murky water. The thought of crocodiles lurking in the darkness flashed through my mind. Hopefully, the way we hurried into the cenote from the cave and up to the surface would keep them away rather than cause them to come for us. We didn't need any other complications.

As soon as we broke the surface, I saw Jen already there stripping off her tanks and harness. I wasn't sure how, but she had gotten around us. I flipped Brendan over so that he was floating face up. Jen grabbed him and struggled to get him out of the water and onto solid ground. Brendan wasn't a big guy, but his tanks and rebreather were still attached to his harness, adding another hundred pounds. I knelt on the ledge and quickly shed my own scuba tanks oblivious to anything else around us. Before I knew it, Jose was pushing on Brendan's chest repeatedly, performing some of the best chest compressions I've ever seen. Jose's eyes were wide, the fear and shock inside of him evident. Brendan's legs were still submerged in the brown water. After a couple of minutes, I relieved Jose and took over chest compressions. Greg pulled Brendan's mask off his face and was about to do rescue breathing when Jen stopped him. The standards had recently changed. There was a higher likelihood of survival for compressions only CPR. Jen and I were both ER nurses.

I heard Jen yell, "Go call 911!" I glanced up briefly and saw a woman, a tourist who had been taking photos of the cenote, pale and shocked at the scene that was unfolding in front of her. I was so focused on Brendan when I surfaced that I hadn't noticed her. But she noticed us - five *frogmen* emerging from the dark, murky swamp only a few feet in front of her. She probably had no idea there was a maze of cave tunnels below her feet. To her, it had to look like a scene from *Creature from the Black Lagoon* as we broke through the surface in our black wetsuits and hoods.

"CALL 911!!!" Jen yelled again. Was that even the right number in Mexico? I had no idea. I should have researched that before the trip. How could I know that vital piece of information might be needed? It didn't matter. I didn't have my phone on me. It was in the van half a football field away and I couldn't leave Brendan to get it. I had to keep pushing on his chest. I had to keep his blood pumping through his body. Hopefully the pale woman could find someone nearby that knew the correct number and would get an ambulance on the way.

The woman ran off in a panic. I hoped she was running for help and not just running away. I didn't know if she would get someone to call for help or if she would simply disappear, psychologically scarred by what she had just witnessed. Jen began cutting away Brendan's wetsuit with a pair of trauma shears she kept sheathed on her harness. We continued chest compressions, Jen and I taking turns to keep from overexerting ourselves. We repeatedly checked for a pulse. Nothing.

I didn't know how long we did chest compressions. I did know it wasn't going to bring positive results. I had worked enough cardiac codes in my career to know what death looked like. It was too late. Brendan had pink froth bubbling out of his nose and mouth every time we pushed on his chest. His lungs had been filled with water for much too long. His pupils were fixed and dilated, a sure sign of death if the dilation wasn't caused by life-saving medications. Only a miracle could save Brendan at this point. I wasn't one to believe in miracles. The local ambulance service, the Cruz Roja, finally arrived and took over, their efforts short-lived. Brendan was pronounced dead. We were devastated. I took Jen into my arms, and we held each other tightly. If I had accepted Brendan's invitation to take the rebreather on this dive, it would have been me lying dead with my feet still in the muddy water of the cenote.

7

What killed Brendan?

We dialed Ygor's number and listened to it ring. There was no answer. He was either still on his dive in Dos Coronas or hadn't retrieved his phone from the van yet. We contacted the group of divers that had gone to Aerolito. They had just exited the water. About thirty minutes later, after quickly loading their tanks and equipment into their van, they arrived to help us with our equipment and to be there for emotional support. We were all in disbelief at having lost a friend in such a tragic event.

The rest of the day was a blur. We were in shock at what had happened. Most of us had lost at least one friend to a cave diving fatality. I still vividly remembered receiving the news of the death of a friend in Jackson Blue cave in Marianna, Florida only two years earlier. He had also been diving a rebreather and it was surmised that carbon dioxide from overexertion had caused him to lose consciousness. He was diving with a friend who witnessed the death. That fatality occurred nineteen hundred feet from the cave opening in an area with exceptionally high current.

Brendan's death was the first time any of us on that trip to Cozumel had been in the water or on a cave diving trip and someone died during a dive. It was one thing to read about it online or get a call from a friend. It was another thing to experience firsthand. It felt like we had been punched in the gut.

Ygor felt a lot of guilt. It was his rebreather that Brendan was diving, and rebreathers had a reputation. Not the good kind. The saying goes that rebreathers are always trying to kill you, and you have to keep them from doing so. It's not a completely deserved reputation, but there's some truth to it. When diving a rebreather, you had to remain attentive. You had to constantly monitor it.

When we got back to the house, Ygor took the rebreather and dropped into the pool in the courtyard. He spent an hour underwater trying to find a reason for Brendan's death. He put that rebreather through every test he could think of. Ygor had built it, and he knew it intimately. Several of us watched, ready to pull him to the surface if he lost consciousness. It was a tense time. One fatality was enough. We didn't need a second one.

Ygor made it out of the pool alive. Everything checked out with the rebreather. It performed flawlessly. That left three other possibilities. Brendan had overbreathed the rebreather causing a carbon dioxide hit, he had a medical event, or the scuba tank he was using had contaminated air. Brendan was a young guy and physically fit so none of us thought he had a medical event. While a carbon dioxide hit was the most likely cause, none of us could believe someone as experienced as Brendan would let that happen. It was preventable.

The third option, contaminated air, was a possibility. We didn't have a way to test the air in the tank. Resources on the small island of Cozumel weren't plentiful. We couldn't drive to a local store and pick up a carbon monoxide analyzer, the one gas we thought could be the culprit. Several of us contacted divers we knew on the Mexican mainland to see if they could help. It was only an hour ferry ride across. Unfortunately, we came up empty. No one bothered to analyze their scuba tanks for carbon monoxide.

The next morning we got word of the autopsy results. The blood tests revealed a concentration of carbon monoxide in Brendan's blood equal to eight hundred parts per million (ppm). That eliminated the possibility of overbreathing the rebreather and taking a carbon dioxide hit. Our final suspicion of contaminated air had been confirmed.

The World Health Organization recommends carbon monoxide levels be below nine ppm for any eight-hour period and below twenty-five ppm for any one-hour period. Those recommendations are for a surface environment, not underwater. Divers Alert Network recommends less than ten ppm in a scuba tank. Period. There's no range of time associated with that recommendation.

Eight hundred parts per million.

Eight hundred ppm produces physical symptoms within twenty minutes and is fatal within one hour. Those numbers are for people standing in a room on land. Submerge yourself in water with increased ambient pressure and symptoms come much more quickly. At the depth we were diving, the carbon monoxide content was effectively doubled. Equivalent to sixteen hundred parts per million. Physical symptoms appear within five to ten minutes at those levels. The way a rebreather works meant the concentration was diluted. That explains why Brendan didn't begin his sprint sooner. It took the carbon monoxide twice as long to build up to deadly levels in his bloodstream. When he bailed out and took a breath directly from his scuba tank instead of filtering it through the rebreather, he got an undiluted megadose and immediately passed out.

The question we had was why hadn't anyone else experienced issues with carbon monoxide. Why was everyone else doing fine? We quickly figured it out. Brendan was using a scuba tank filled with a higher concentration of oxygen called Nitrox. The rest of us were using scuba tanks filled with air. The facility that filled the tanks used different compressors to fill the air tanks than it did for the Nitrox tanks. The intakes for those compressors were in different locations. It was possible for carbon monoxide to contaminate one set of tanks and not the other.

Then Greg mentioned he had issues the day before during his dive. At the time, he thought it was a rebreather issue. He thought he was experiencing channeling in his scrubber which would have meant getting a higher concentration of carbon dioxide. He did not think it was a breathing gas issue. That possibility never occurred to him. The incident happened the previous day, while Jen and I were surveying the first four hundred and forty-two feet of line in the passage. Greg had been in a small room off to the side of the opening of Cocodrilo conducting his own survey work. This room had been named the Artifact Room because of all the ancient Mayan artifacts and sea fossils found in it. Greg was obtaining video of the room for an art project he was working on. He started feeling disorientation on that dive and bailed out to his air-filled tank. The feeling passed and he switched back to breathing from his rebreather.

Switching back to the closed-circuit loop is common practice when diving rebreathers. If there's an issue, you stop breathing from the rebreather circuit, go through a troubleshooting checklist, and if everything checks out, you resume breathing from the rebreather. A few minutes after switching back to his rebreather, Greg felt disoriented again and bailed out a second time. He went through his checklist again, felt better by the time he completed it, and resumed breathing from the rebreather a third time. When the disorientation returned a couple of minutes later, Greg decided to stop tempting fate and, rather than breathe from the rebreather again, he continued to breathe from the air-filled tank and surfaced from the dive. He had implemented the three-strikes rule.

At the time, Greg thought one of the mushroom valves was folded over and he was feeling the effects of elevated carbon dioxide levels. This is one of the problems which could occur that was nearly impossible to troubleshoot in the water. He did the appropriate thing by ending the dive. Greg was also using Nitrox to supply his rebreather. It never occurred to him that the gas in the tank could be the issue. Bad gas was a very rare issue in scuba diving. It wasn't something many divers gave any thought to. Had Greg not bailed out when he did, he would have likely suffered a similar fate as Brendan. Only he would have been alone when it happened.

None of this information would bring Brendan back. However, it was a natural response by cave divers to analyze cave diving accidents and fatalities. Our group wanted to know the cause so we could take action to prevent future fatalities from happening for the same reason. Accident analysis was a significant part of cave diving training from which the safety guidelines for cave diving were derived. Everyone in our group was aware of carbon monoxide and its dangers. It was briefly mentioned during the initial open water scuba diver training course. *Briefly*. It was glossed over. There was a single line, maybe two, in the student manual of the largest training agency in the world. It was so uncommon that no one thought twice about it. Or was it?

We wrote a statement to post on the social media platforms. News of cave diving fatalities gets out quickly. We wanted to let everyone know what happened so we could avoid the usual speculation about the cause of death that typically followed a cave diving fatality. We also wanted to let everyone reading it know that they should be testing their breathing gas. After posting our statement we began learning about more incidents that had happened to other divers on the island. These were near misses rather than fatalities. They involved symptoms of illness early in the dive – nausea, headache, dizziness, disorientation, and confusion. Symptoms similar to what Greg experienced on his dive. Symptoms that might cause someone to suddenly increase his or her swimming pace. These people decided they were too unwell to continue their dives and surfaced, just like Greg had. They were in open water with a direct ascent to the surface. Greg had been no more than one hundred feet from the cenote. Had Brendan bailed out to a different tank, to one of his air-filled tanks, the outcome might have been different. Or maybe not. The carbon monoxide levels in his bloodstream could have already been too high at the time that he bailed out. He might have maintained consciousness another minute or two. We'll never know.

Carbon monoxide doesn't kill right away. Above the water it's a long process. It can take hours to deprive organs of life-sustaining oxygen and cause the heart to shut down. Underwater, it's the loss of consciousness, followed by the regulator falling out of your mouth, and your next breath bringing water instead of air to your lungs that kills you right away. You drown. If you're exposed to carbon monoxide long enough it can kill you as well, even without the water. It suffocates you. The molecules bind with hemoglobin, not allowing oxygen molecules to bind. Hemoglobin's affinity for carbon monoxide is two hundred and forty times more than its affinity for oxygen. When your hemoglobin is deprived of oxygen, it creates disorientation and eventually unconsciousness. The only treatment for it is to breathe one hundred percent oxygen for at least twelve hours. This was a treatment I administered a few times during my time as an emergency room nurse. Severe cases were put inside of a hyperbaric chamber while breathing one hundred percent oxygen. Neither option was available to us one thousand feet inside of a water-filled cave.

Once learning the cause of Brendan's death, everyone in the group ordered carbon monoxide analyzers to add to our dive kits. We weren't going to let something like this happen to us or anyone we went diving with again. Since Brendan's death in 2011 I haven't been on a single dive without first testing my scuba tanks for carbon monoxide. For several months after that dive with Brendan, I held my breath every time I was diving with someone who stopped moving for more than a couple of seconds. A few times I started to reach out, thinking something had happened, fearful that the person I was diving with had just lost consciousness. The fear that lived within me had me on guard for many years. The post-traumatic stress was significant. During that time I was doing two hundred and fifty to three hundred dives each year. I was teaching a lot and diving a lot on my days off. I began to dive solo quite a bit. It was less stressful and more enjoyable. Whenever I was diving with someone else, I saw Brendan rising toward the ceiling with no regulator in his mouth. It was something I never wanted to experience again.

It wouldn't be carbon monoxide that would take a student or another dive buddy, though. In addition to testing my own scuba tanks, I also tested the scuba tanks of everyone diving with me. Some teased about the testing, but they hadn't witnessed what I had. They didn't know what I had gone through. It's difficult to unsee the death of someone you know. I had witnessed many deaths in the ER and ICU, having worked in healthcare for almost fifteen years before Brendan died. But those deaths were all in hospitals where death was common and often expected. This was my first witnessed death in a recreational environment. It was my first witnessed death of someone I knew outside of a professional relationship. Hopefully, it will be the only one.

8

Why I returned to Cozumel

After the experience of watching a friend die right in front of me on a dive, you might be asking why I would go back to Cozumel. Why would I want the reminder of what happened that day? Wasn't I fearful that it could happen to me as well? Those were all valid concerns. Those were questions I asked myself.

We knew the cause of Brendan's death. We had an idea of how the carbon monoxide had gotten into his tank. The filling station had implemented measures to never allow that to happen again. They installed inline carbon monoxide analyzers and relocated the air intake for the nitrox compressor. But most importantly, we had our own carbon monoxide analyzer, and we were never breathing from a scuba tank again without analyzing the air in it. Cozumel wasn't to blame. Cozumel wasn't the cause of Brendan's death. Carbon monoxide infiltration of the air going into scuba tanks wasn't an issue unique to the island.

There had been a cave diving near-fatality a few years earlier in Florida. The diver was also using a rebreather. He started behaving strangely during the dive and almost lost consciousness. He was fortunate to make it out of the cave, but he suffered long-term effects that kept him from diving again. It sounded all too familiar. The victim's friend, who had been diving with him, had kept the rebreather and scuba tanks used during that dive. He hadn't added more air to the tanks. The only thing he did was replace the absorbent used to scrub the carbon dioxide from the exhaled air. He went diving and used the rebreather almost a year later. He wanted to see if he could figure out what the issue was. Several minutes into the dive he began having his own issues. He quickly bailed out to his emergency scuba tank and aborted the dive. Fortunately, he also survived. Unfortunately, he ended up spending more than a month in an intensive care unit recovering from severe lung damage. Several years later, he still had significant aftereffects and was also never able to scuba dive again.

After he was discharged from the hospital, he decided to have the gas in the scuba tank used with the rebreather analyzed. The results were shocking. The gas was not only bad; it was toxic. In addition to carbon monoxide, the results revealed several other contaminants, including oil. This tank had been filled at a local Florida dive shop. The air compressor at this dive shop was located adjacent to the parking lot and divers regularly backed their vehicles up to the compressor to get their tanks filled. On one occasion, I witnessed a UPS truck parked and running next to the building because the parking lot was full. The truck's exhaust was going directly toward the compressor intake.

Carbon monoxide contamination can occur at any scuba tank filling station. These events resulted in the reevaluation of my own scuba fill station and placing the air intake far from any possible exhaust fumes or other contaminants. Even with those precautions, I still analyze every single tank that gets filled from my scuba tank fill station.

* * *

A couple of months after we returned home from Cozumel, Greg, the diver that had a near miss with carbon monoxide, called me and proposed a return trip. I told him I was in and to let me know the details. I waited and waited but heard nothing back. A couple of weeks later, I asked Greg if he had started making arrangements. He hadn't but promised he would. He was anxious to get back and try to regain access to Cocodrilo so he could continue his project. Another couple of weeks passed, and I asked again. He still hadn't looked for a rental house or settled on dates. Other things had kept him distracted.

I decided to take matters into my own hands. I did some research and found a few houses large enough for a small group that were available during the month we had planned for the trip. I gave Greg the details and asked him if it was okay to reserve one of the houses. We had put the invitation out to other members of the previous trip, including Ygor. Only one other person, Roger, expressed an interest in going. So I asked Greg if he was agreeable to me inviting one of my former students to join us. He was. I invited David, a former student and a fellow nurse. That was David's first trip to Cozumel. David became a regular dive buddy and explorer on these trips.

With our small group confirmed, we agreed on dates for a week-long trip. I reserved the smallest house that could accommodate one couple and three singles. I then found a direct flight into Cozumel and made our flight reservations. I wasn't interested in doing the bag drag again.

We later found out that Ygor and a few of his close friends had returned to Cozumel about six months after my first trip. They were there to explore their new find in Dos Coronas. On the last day of the previous trip, they had found going cave that led to a deeper section. During their return trip they placed just under nine hundred feet of line in the cave. They were looking for the connection to Cueva Quebrada. They didn't find it during that trip. Every lead they pushed to the left ended in a dead-end or got too small to continue. They never returned to dive Dos Coronas again. They had given up exploring the cave. They probably thought there was no connection big enough for a diver to pass through.

My second trip to Cozumel happened four months after their trip, almost ten months after my first one. I organized the entire thing, from the rental house to the rental van and the scuba tanks. I had gotten the mobile number of the guy that rented the group the two vans we used on the first trip, and I called him to reserve the large van.

During my first trip in 2011, I had volunteered to go to the scuba tank filling station the first day. I wanted to see it and how it operated. It was quite impressive. It was the biggest tank filling operation I had seen. I have yet to see a bigger one. There were no banks of compressed air like were often seen in the US. They filled their scuba tanks directly from the compressors. The large air compressors were in a line about twenty feet long in the back of the warehouse and filled more than one hundred scuba tanks at a time. They had hundreds of tanks in the small warehouse in groups of filled and unfilled tanks. The compressors operated non-stop during high season. The men there worked hard.

There were employees constantly moving tanks around. They had several groups of tanks all throughout the open space. There were two large groups of filled tanks on each side and smaller groups of unfilled tanks in the center ready to get hooked up to fill whips and get filled. A couple of guys closed the valves, removed the whips from the filled tanks, and moved them out from the filling aisles. A couple of other guys brought over empties to fill the vacant slots next to the freed-up whips and grabbed the filled tanks and moved them in line with the other filled tanks. There was constant movement in the building. This was not a job for a lazy person.

I watched the process for picking up the tanks we were renting. Ygor didn't speak much Spanish, so communication was not the easiest, but somehow, he had managed. I did speak a bit of Spanish and stepped in. This simplified the process. I continued to go to the fill station each morning to pick up filled tanks and each afternoon to drop off used tanks. I had no intention of returning to Cozumel on my own at the time. I was simply being helpful. But doing so helped. When I arrived at the fill station the first day of the second trip, the manager recognized me. I told him our plans for the week and what our tank needs would be. He agreed to rent me tanks with certain provisions in place.

This was one of the hurdles I had managed to overcome to be able to do these types of dives in Cozumel. You can't just go to a dive shop and rent tanks. None of the shops will rent tanks unless they are taking you on dives. I don't know if it's a liability thing or if they think you're going to take the tanks and never return them. You couldn't even rent weights from a dive shop on Cozumel unless you were diving with the shop. Weights are necessary to counteract the positive buoyancy of the neoprene wetsuits and the air in our lungs. With no weights available, we had to bring our own to Cozumel every trip. Fortunately, carryon bags weren't weighed. I eventually solved that issue and started storing weights in Cozumel along with a set of cave diving equipment.

My primary focus for this return trip to Cozumel was Dos Coronas. I also got to see Aerolito de Paraiso for the first time. In fact, Aerolito was our first dive during this trip. It was fairly easy access, so we used it for a shakedown dive to get our tanks and equipment sorted. It also ended up becoming another exploration project of mine. One which I'll write about in the third planned book in this series, *Beneath the Jungle of Cozumel: Shooting Stars*.

After our shakedown dive, we headed to the resort where Cocodrilo was located for a late lunch. The owner had banned diving after Brendan's death. It had been ten months since his death, and we were hoping he might have had a change of heart. Greg was especially hopeful because he wanted to get back to Cocodrilo to work on the art project he had started. We arrived at the resort and were seated at a table in the restaurant. We ordered drinks while we looked over the menu. Some of us ordered soda, which came by the bottle because fountain drinks aren't commonly found in Cozumel. Greg ordered iced tea, which came by the glass. Once we decided on our meals, we asked if the manager was available to speak to us. Greg ordered an iced tea refill.

The server got the manager and brought him to our table along with a new glass of iced tea for Greg. We introduced ourselves to the manager and told him who we were. Everyone but David had been on the previous trip. Greg, Jen, and I were on the dive with Brendan, and Roger had been with the group that had been diving in Aerolito and showed up half an hour after we had surfaced. We asked the manager if he thought there was a chance the owner would someday allow us to access the cave again hoping he might give us access that week. One of the things we wanted to do was place a memorial at the location where Brendan died. Greg also wanted to continue to work on his project, but we didn't mention that part.

Unfortunately, the owner was not on the island and wouldn't be returning for at least a month. The manager told us he would ask him about it, but he didn't think the owner would be open to allowing diving there anytime soon. The event was still too fresh in everyone's minds. The owner was also not local to the island and had gotten some pressure from the other resort owners about it. He felt a bit alienated and was trying to reestablish a good rapport with them. We understood and thanked the manager for his time. Maybe it was the truth or maybe it was a kind way to refuse access. Either way, the result was the same. We wouldn't be diving Cocodrilo during our stay. Shortly after the manager walked away, the server brought our appetizers and Greg asked for another iced tea refill. A few of us ordered a second soda.

We were not optimistic about getting access, at least none of us besides Greg were. It was worth a shot to politely ask, though. Greg was the most upset about not getting access. He was an artist by trade.

He spent many years working on set design in the theater and also did paintings and sculptures on his own time. He had started a new art project during the previous trip and was getting more images for it when he had his issue and had to abort the dive. Greg was gathering video of the main cave tunnel and the Artifact Room in Cocodrilo. He slowly swept his video camera back and forth as he swam through the tunnels. He then spent countless hours stitching the frames together to produce a three-dimensional image of the cave passage. This image included the formations and walls as well as the shape of the tunnel as it snaked its way through the earth. Greg had already amassed thousands of video frames and dedicated hundreds of hours to the project. Without access to Cocodrilo, the project was dead. We would try to gain access again in the future, but I wasn't very hopeful we would get it.

Our meals were served, and Greg asked for another refill. By that time, Greg was on his fifth or sixth iced tea. We ate our food and talked about our dive plans for the rest of the trip. The rest of us were disappointed about not being able to dive Cocodrilo, but it wasn't the end of the world. We still had Dos Coronas and Aerolito to dive, both beautiful caves. We decided to alternate our days between the two caves. Dos Coronas only had about twenty-five hundred feet of lined passage at the time, but Aerolito had twenty thousand feet of lined passage. It would take a while to learn that cave.

We finished our meals and requested *la cuenta*, the bill. We told the server a combined bill was fine. We would figure out what each person owed. Unbeknownst to Greg, iced tea did not come with free refills. Each new glass that was brought out was a new drink charge. Cozumel not only doesn't have soda fountains, it also doesn't have free refills on anything but coffee with breakfast. Even the coffee is usually limited to one refill. Greg had been ordering more and more iced teas, not realizing each order was adding another $2.50 USD to his bill. I think his iced tea intake for that meal cost him $20. That was more than my entire portion of the bill!

Greg remained a bit grumpy the remainder of the trip. It wasn't the iced tea bill, although that became the joke of the trip at each meal and probably contributed to his foul mood. It was losing access to Cocodrilo that had him on edge. This was understandable with such a large project being cut short. He had even brought a printout of what he had done in Cocodrilo during the previous trip. That printout took up an entire wall in the rental house! He had devoted a lot of time to it. A couple of days into the trip, after a particularly bad dive for him, we returned to the house and he tore the printout off the wall, tearing it into pieces. The loss of access was getting to him.

I was disappointed that we wouldn't be able to get back into Cocodrilo. I felt I needed to do that dive to help me come to terms with what had happened to Brendan. For the previous ten months since losing Brendan, I still had flashbacks while on other dives. As I stated, there were times my students or dive buddies would stop moving momentarily and I almost reached out to make sure they were still alive. These flashbacks would go on happening for more than a couple of years. Even now, more than a decade later, I occasionally think about that dive, and I can still clearly see Brendan rising to the ceiling. It's not quite as bad as it used to be, but it's there.

Even with the disappointment of not having access to Cocodrilo, we were in Cozumel, and we had caves we could dive. Dos Coronas became my new passion.

9

Lobsters, corals, and cowries! Oh my!

Having done our shakedown dive at Aerolito, we were ready to hit the rocky beach and head to Dos Coronas. We were eager to see the new area that had been found by the others at the end of the previous trip. David and I teamed up while Greg and Roger formed a second team. Jen has never been fond of small cave tunnels, so she happily spent the day on the beach relaxing in the sun and occasionally taking a dip in the water to cool off.

I quickly found the main entrance to Dos Coronas. During my two days diving there on the previous trip, I had made some notes of some features on land that made it easy to triangulate the opening in the reef. I didn't swim directly to the opening like I do now. That first time back, I ended up finding the crack of death before finding the main opening of Dos Coronas. I instantly recognized the Crack and knew I was too far south. The Crack also appeared even smaller than it had when I first found it. I headed north toward the main opening. A few minutes later I encountered the small hole in the reef surrounded by coral, sponges, and a couple of dinnerplate-sized angel fish patrolling the perimeter as they fed on the coral around it. This opening looked a lot more inviting than the Coronas Crack of Death.

This was my third time entering the cave through this opening, which was named Dos Coronas I because it was the first opening to be discovered and lined. I hadn't paid much attention the previous two times I had entered it. There had been too much going on. This time would be different. I entered the cave and began to take in my surroundings. There was a lot going on in the first twenty feet. I took my time and moved slowly so I could appreciate the beauty around me. The spool that had been in the opening during the previous trip was gone. It had been removed so non-cave divers wouldn't be tempted to follow the line into the cave. I grabbed one of my jump spools and prepared to run a line to the permanent guideline. I tied the end of the line from the spool to a large rock just outside of the opening and began my way into the cave. There was a school of small fish swimming just inside. They took up the entire opening left to right and top to bottom. The beam of my dive light hit the fish and made them shimmer and resemble a curtain of shiny beads. I felt like I was about to enter Greg Brady's room during his hippie period on the Brady Bunch. The fish parted for me as I approached them, making a hole large enough to pass through.

Just on the other side of the curtain of fish to my left was a pod of lobsters hanging out. Most of them were upside down and clinging to the ceiling of the cave. I stopped for a moment to observe them. I counted at least ten lobsters before their movements made it too difficult to keep straight. They were jammed in close together and the introduction of my bright light got them stirring. A couple of the lobsters even dropped from the ceiling down to the floor two feet below. There were a lot more than ten lobsters and they were all a decent size.

A few feet later I came to a concrete filled five-gallon bucket that was almost entirely engulfed by a large white sea sponge. The bucket was lying on its side against the wall to the right. There was a two-inch diameter pipe that rose out of the center about two feet. The pipe probably once held a sign warning untrained divers to stay out of the cave. The sign was no longer there. It likely broke off and was carried out to sea during a storm surge.

I looked around the small room I was in. The cave was full of color. There were yellows and oranges and reds. Almost every surface was covered by sponges and coral. I was already about thirty feet inside the cave. If I didn't know any better, I would have thought I was in a coral swim through not a sea cave. I followed the wall to the right, taking in the scenery. I had looked at it during the previous trip, but the excitement of being in a new cave kept me from really appreciating everything. This time I took my time and enjoyed the moment. This was what cave diving was all about.

The permanent guideline was tied to a protrusion coming out of the floor a short distance after the bucket. I secured the line from my spool to it and continued farther into the cave. By this time, I could no longer see the daylight streaming in from the opening. The only light behind me came from the dive lights being held by David, Greg, and Roger. A few feet after tying my line to the permanent guideline, I came to a sharp turn in the passage that went vertical. I looked up into the small circular multicolored tunnel that was shaped as if a giant corkscrew had been twisted in and out of it, leaving the void I was staring into. I studied this odd shaped tunnel and thought about how I was going to approach it so I could fit through the restriction with minimal contact with the cave. I had gone through with no issue during my previous dives into this opening, but I just pushed through in the excitement and was lucky that I didn't get stuck. This time I was taking it slowly and learning the cave. I wasn't going to leave it to luck, especially after my experience in the crack during the previous trip. I rotated my body and began my ascent into the corkscrew, twisting as I progressed through the borehole into the level above.

When I was about seven feet shallower, I popped out into a wide room. This was the room where I had extended the line into the low bedding plane on my second dive in Dos Coronas. I moved forward to give room for David and the others to follow. As I waited for them, I took in my surroundings. The variation of colors continued. It seemed that every surface of the room was covered by coral and sea sponges. It amazed me that I was more than one hundred feet inside of the cave, on a different level than the opening, and there was still so much sea life. Coral had even started to grow on the guideline that had been placed there a couple of years earlier. I didn't realize coral grew that quickly. Apparently, it can grow anywhere from one to four inches per year. I was witnessing the miracle of a coral reef developing inside of a cave.

I thought about the disadvantage of the coral being on the guideline. If we lost visibility and had to rely on the line to get us out, it would be interesting. I touched the end of a piece of coral that was growing on the line. It was sharp and pointy. It wouldn't feel good against our bare hands if we had to exit in diminished visibility. I could almost feel the papercut-like abrasions that would cover my palm if that happened. I swam forward, pinched the line along one of the few bare spots left on it, and tugged to make sure it was still intact and durable. It would be a bad thing if it became our lifeline to the exit and snapped in two. Fortunately, it didn't break or disintegrate. I arrived at the line intersection where I had started to run my line into the low bedding plane ten months earlier and chose a spot on the guideline that had the least amount of growth on it. I marked the exit line with a line marker and followed the line going to the left.

About twenty-five feet away from the line intersection was the second restriction. The corkscrew was the first. This one wasn't quite as long or small. It was a straight pass through without the need to manipulate our bodies to get to the other side. I moved through it, careful to keep from touching the walls with my tanks. It was close. As I was getting to the other side of the restriction I saw movement below me on a shelf to my left. I shined my light in that direction and saw a small shell with a nickel-sized area that was colorful and glossy while the rest of it had a dull, uneven coating. The coating looked like a growth, possibly coral. Closer inspection revealed the shell to be a cowry, and it was slowly moving along the floor of the cave. At this point, I was about one hundred and fifty feet from the opening out to the reef. I couldn't believe I had found marine life this far inside of the cave.

I moved past the cowry and about twenty feet later came to another restriction. This one was about half the size of the previous one, and I had to remove my stage tank and push it in front of me if I was going to fit. I stopped and unclipped the bottom bolt snap, pulling the bottom of the tank around so it was straight out in front of me, and carefully moved through the opening. I could feel my tanks gently scraping against the walls on either side as I slid through the hole. Next time I would have to tilt to one side so that wouldn't happen. When I emerged from the restriction I looked back and saw that I had not damaged the walls. There was no sign of me having been through there other than a light spatter of dust from the percolation of my bubbles on the ceiling. I signaled to David, who was pulling his stage tank and a sidemount tank off to push ahead of him. I also saw the lights of Greg and Roger behind him.

The tunnel was bigger on the other side of the restriction. It seemed the guideline also had more growth on it than the guideline we had already passed. The walls and floor were still covered in coral and sponges. If I hadn't seen it with my own eyes, I wouldn't have believed that almost three hundred feet inside of this cave, it still resembled the reef on the outside. Actually, it had more growth on it than the reef we had come from. I reflected on how amazing nature was.

I arrived at another line intersection. This was the intersection I had created during my very first dive in Cozumel when I found Dos Coronas II, the second opening to the cave. To the left, the line went through the small restriction that had required me to remove a sidemount tank. I looked at the restriction and thought about when I first found it. It was indeed small. I considered using that entrance for our next dive in Dos Coronas. I turned back to the line intersection and placed a marker on the line leading out the way I had come and continued following the line to the right. This was a fairly long straight tunnel for the next three hundred feet or so. I had gone down this tunnel during the first dive of my previous trip, but I turned around when the line made a sharp left into another bedding plane. I wished I hadn't turned so soon because this was the path to the new section that was found after I had returned home. I had no idea what was on the other side of that bedding plane, but I was anxious to find out.

I followed the line as the ceiling began to slope down and close the distance between it and the floor. I arrived at the location where the line made a sharp left, and I shined my light toward the bedding plane. It was maybe fifteen inches from floor to ceiling, less in some spots. It was low enough that I would have to remove my stage tank from where it was mounted above my left sidemount tank and push it in front of me. I repositioned my stage tank and slowly followed the line to the left, trying to be careful not to disturb the visibility for David, Greg, and Roger. The bedding plane was wide, so I was able to position myself about five feet to the right of it, allowing the divers behind me to stay closer to the guideline.

About fifty feet later, I saw one of the saddest things I had ever seen inside of a cave. To the left of the guideline was the skull of a large turtle surrounded by pieces of its shell. The skull measured almost a foot long. It was nothing but bone. The skeletal remains had been there a long time and picked cleaned by the other living organisms in the cave. The turtle must have gotten itself lost and died in this spot, about four hundred feet from the Dos Coronas II entrance. I circled my light beam around it to alert the others, not that they could miss it.

I continued past it. The ceiling finally began to rise, giving us more room.

The cave's appearance transitioned at this point. The rough coral covered floor continued to the right. I also noticed another low bedding plane about fifty feet away. I believed that to be where I had tied off the end of the line I had placed during my first dive into the Dos Coronas I entrance. I couldn't see my line. It was too far away, but I knew it was there. If I had gone a little farther, I would have found this tunnel. Everything seemed to be connected.

In front of me were fewer coral and sponges. The floor became a smooth tan colored rock. It appeared we were finally getting far enough from the opening that reef life could no longer survive in the darkness. There wasn't enough to sustain it. I was about five hundred and twenty-five feet inside of the cave. As I continued farther into the cave, the floor fell away into fissure cracks. There were cracks to my right and left, with the occasional crack crossing the middle of the tunnel. I shined my light beam into them and could see another floor about eight to ten feet below. The cracks were too small to get through, but that must have been the deeper section that the other team had found.

I also noticed small restrictions on both walls. They were circular holes about a foot and a half to two feet in diameter. I considered looking into them, but the restrictions were small enough I didn't think I would be able to fit through any of them, at least not without removing my tanks and pushing them in front of me. I made a note of them for possible future exploration. I continued following the guideline. About seventy-five feet later I arrived at a much larger fissure crack than the ones I had encountered so far. It cut across the floor of the tunnel. The guideline stretched out above the crack and ended a few feet farther on top of a smooth curved shelf. Beyond that was a dark, almost black, sediment that continued as far as I could see.

I thought that was strange. I hadn't seen anything similar from the entrance to this point. I didn't expect the cave to transform again so soon after the coral line. I was only about six hundred feet from the Dos Coronas I opening.

A couple of feet from the end of the line, another line was tied into the guideline I had been following. It went down and to my left into the large crack. This crack was big enough for me to fit without having to remove any tanks. I checked the pressure gauge on my stage tank. I had breathed the air down close enough to where I would be switching to one of my sidemount tanks in the next minute or two. The shelf on the other side of the fissure crack looked like a convenient place to leave a stage tank, so I began breathing from one of my sidemount tanks and removed my stage tank. I closed the valve and tucked the hose into the hose retainers. I then clipped the tank to the line and set it on a bare spot on the shelf. With my tank secured, I dropped down into the fissure crack. When I saw the size of the crack from below, I was glad I had left my stage tank behind.

10

Passage to Hades

With my stage tank safely secured to the guideline, I went headfirst into the fissure crack. This had to be the way to the new section of the cave. We were told it was in a deeper section through a fissure and a restriction. As I descended into the fissure, it got smaller and I had to turn sideways to fit. At the bottom of the fissure, there was a white sea sponge on the ceiling just above and to the right. I was quite surprised by it. I hadn't seen any sea life in the past seventy-five feet. I didn't expect to see anymore. The sea sponge was large. It was about the size of a basketball. It didn't help that the fissure we were in was small. There wasn't much room left to get around it.

I did my best to carefully move past the sponge, trying not to disturb it. A couple of feet beyond the white growth was an even smaller restriction in the wall to the right. The guideline disappeared into it. I had already removed my other stage tank and was holding it in front of me to get through the fissure crack. I pushed the stage tank into the small hole and pulled my body in behind it. I had to bend at the waist to maneuver my way through the restriction. Once my finned feet were through the hole I saw the guideline curve to the left. I followed the line and found myself in a small room with a dark, sediment-covered floor. It resembled the floor on the shelf ten feet above me where I had left my first stage tank. I had arrived in Hades.

I turned around to watch for David. He had to remove a sidemount tank in addition to his stage tank and hold both in front of him to get through. The visibility was also reduced for him. I took credit for that. I had barely touched the cave. There wasn't a layer of sediment on the floor between the beginning of the fissure crack and the beginning of Hades. In fact, it was solid rock all the way through. However, the water flow had deposited a thin layer of dust on the walls and the floor, and even the ceiling. When we moved through the small space, it disturbed the dust and this in turn made the visibility "foggy". This meant David was not only pushing two tanks in front of him, but he was also going through in limited visibility.

In hindsight, I should have let David go first. Not only to give him better visibility going through, but also because if he happened to get stuck in the restriction, he would be stuck between me and my only way of getting out of the cave. If he got stuck, I would also be stuck! These are the kinds of things one thinks about in these situations. The bigger diver should always lead the way in and follow out. I was once following another diver in a cave in Florida, and he got caught up in the water current and lost control of his body. The current pushed him into the cave opening, which was a rather small restriction. Only he wasn't pushed into it head or feet first. He was pushed into it tail end first, plugging up our only exit. I had to anchor myself against the wall and floor of the cave and pull him back against the current so he could straighten out his body and make his escape. To this day, we still joke about that dive and how he almost killed us both by imitating a cork.

To give you an idea of just how small the opening he corked was, I broke the battery canister for my dive light going through it on a subsequent dive. I was using a two-piece cabled dive light at the time, and the battery canister was mounted at the small of my back. When I tried to squeeze through, the canister was squeezed in between the ceiling of the opening and my back, and something happened to it. I found myself in complete darkness. I pulled myself into the cave until

I could reach back and flip the power switch. The light never came on again. The dive was over before it had begun, and I was left with a very expensive paperweight.

Fortunately, David didn't get stuck in the restriction leading to Hades. We would both make it back out to the surface. I would have the pleasure of exiting through this area in diminished visibility behind him, though. I thought maybe I should implement the bigger diver first in last out rule and lead the way out. Just in case. I watched the illumination from David's light fighting to make its way out of the cloud of dust I had left behind me as he slowly came toward me. The bottoms of his stage and sidemount tanks poked out of the cloud into the clear water between us followed by David's head. He stopped to readjust himself and get his sidemount tank clipped back on. We didn't know it yet, but he'd have to leave his stage tank unclipped to go through the next part. David didn't bother clipping his stage tank back onto his harness. He must have had a feeling about the passage ahead.

I wondered how Greg and Roger would fit through the restriction. Greg and Roger were big guys. They were bigger than David, but they had managed to get through smaller restrictions than I thought possible. I wasn't sure if they had been able to fit in the low bedding section before the turtle skull or if they had just decided to go see a different part of the cave. David indicated he hadn't seen them in some time, but the last time he saw them they were fine and had signaled for him to continue.

Typically, when diving in a group of three or more, each diver is responsible for keeping in contact with the diver directly in front and the diver directly behind. As the one first in, I only had to keep track of David. David kept track of Greg, and Greg kept track of Roger. The last communication David had with Greg, all was fine. Greg and Roger were big boys. No pun intended there. I wasn't worried about them being in the cave alone.

David and I continued around another corner and soon saw leaves, branches, and old bottles and cans scattered about the dark sediment on the floor. I knew instantly that there was a cenote somewhere above us. There was no other way that this debris could find its way more than six hundred feet inside of the cave from an opening in the reef. A cenote would also explain the dark sediment covering the floor. The sediment was from disintegrated leaves and branches. I made a mental note to look for the cenote on the way out.

This trash room area was right before the Devil's Throat (not to be confused with the open water dive site on the south side of the island). This was the next tunnel we were about to go through. We hadn't named it yet. That didn't happen until after the dive. The Devil's Throat is a series of baffles about fifty feet long connecting Hades to Winter Wonderland, the next section of the cave. This is not to be confused with Wonderland in Aerolito. We had to maneuver our bodies through the baffles to get through the tunnel. It reminded me of a pinball making its way through a series of random bumpers before it was spit out onto the open playing field in front of the flippers. Thankfully there were no flippers waiting on the other end trying to smack us back into the Throat. The second diver had to get through with very little visibility due to the silt that one couldn't avoid stirring up. David wasn't getting to see a whole lot on this dive.

There was not only a thin layer of dust on the walls and baffles, but the floor was covered in a thick tan layer of mud. Unfortunately, the small size of the Devil's Throat meant our movement through it would disturb that layer of mud. I moved slowly to minimize the disturbance and avoided touching the floor, but David was still left with very little visibility. It didn't help that no one had been through that tunnel in four months. I would have my turn at the number two position on the way out and have to exit in diminished visibility. That was always extra fun when moving through a restriction. When we surfaced from that dive a couple of hours later, David mentioned he felt like he was going through the Devil's Throat. That was how the passage got its name.

What we found on the other side of the Devil's Throat made it all worth the hell we went through to get there. That pun was intended. This was an area I named Winter Wonderland. The topography of the cave transformed from the rough, craggy sea cave with lobsters and sponges and corals seen throughout the first six hundred feet of tunnels into layered mounds of mesas with a white sandpaper rough surface and dark edges outlining the perimeter of each layer. It reminded me of the plateaus found in the Grand Canyon after they received a light dusting of snow. It was absolutely awe-inspiring. David and I hovered there a few feet above one of the mounds in that first room shining our lights around it and visually taking everything in. It was an amazing sight.

The transformation the cave made going from the sea cave we had entered, to the smooth surfaced walls and floor, through the Devil's Throat, and into one of the most beautiful rooms I've ever seen in a cave was shocking. It felt like we were in a different place altogether. It was difficult to believe that we were still in the same cave we had entered back on the reef. David and I continued following the line that had been placed by Ygor's team of divers during their trip four months earlier. They had hit it hard, or so I thought. I'd end up not thinking what they did was such a great feat a couple of years later once I'd surveyed the line they had placed in the tunnels. You might recall that I mentioned it was twenty-four hundred and forty-four feet. That included the eight hundred and fifty-one feet of line I had placed during both dives that first day of my first trip. It also included seven hundred and ninety-six feet of line that had been placed in the shallower first section of the cave. There were only an additional eight hundred and ninety-eight feet in the deeper section of Winter Wonderland.

David and I continued through Winter Wonderland and took in the beauty of the cave. We were in awe. It looked like nothing else I had seen in any other cave, both in Florida and in Mexico. It didn't resemble Cocodrilo or Aerolito. It didn't look like it should be inside of a cave. It truly looked like a winter scene on the plateaus of Colorado or Utah. It was unique. We made it to the end of the guideline. We were about thirteen hundred feet from the opening. This was where the other team had stopped. This was where I began to truly explore Dos Coronas. I tied the line from my explorer reel to the end of the line and began my way into virgin cave territory. The cave kept going and going and going. I let out hundreds of feet of line as I swam faster and faster, listening to the gentle hum of my reel quickly spinning as I let line off the spool. I stopped occasionally to secure the line around a formation whenever the tunnel changed direction. Other than that, I just kept going farther into the cave.

The formations were everywhere, and they were breathtaking. The stepped hills continued on both sides. We also saw what appeared to be floating shelves of formations sticking out from the walls. The shelves stuck out three or four feet, secured to the walls behind them. Nothing held them up from below. These suspended shelves held several stalagmites standing at attention. Some of them resembled people standing in groups, a preacher standing among followers. Along the center of the tunnel was a path of coarse white sand. The low spots had gatherings of darker sand. This wasn't the same as the sediment I had seen back in the Trash Room. This was dark and coarse piles among the light-colored path. I wondered what had caused these strange bowls of darkness.

I zigzagged my way along, often having to choose a tunnel from the multiple options in front of me. I couldn't believe the other team that had been there four months earlier had left all of this unexplored. They had spent several days in this cave trying to push to the left. They hadn't even added nine hundred feet of line to the cave. I had no idea at the time what their objective was. My only objective was to find unexplored virgin cave, put line in it, and survey it.

The cave went through another transformation shortly after I had started running my own line. I began to see dark, reddish brown ponds of water on the ceiling. They looked like dark, foreboding clouds over our heads. The ceiling was uneven and offered pockets of deeper areas in each room we moved through. These areas were filled with reddish-brown tannic water. I ascended to one of the pockets and poked my head up into it. The water temperature dropped a couple of degrees, and the visibility became blurry. It took on the appearance of gasoline in water. The tannic water was brackish. The water we had been swimming in was saltwater. These tannic ponds continued for several hundred feet. I named this part of the cave the Swamp Land.

One of the most surprising things I saw in the Swamp Land area of Dos Coronas was a spiny lobster. I recalled the pod at the opening of the cave and thought to myself, this little guy is lost. Only it wasn't so little. This was one of the larger spiny lobsters I had seen. Its body was about nine or ten inches long and it looked healthy as can be. I was swimming through the center of the tunnel the very first time, laying line, almost two thousand feet from the cave opening, and a spiny lobster came crawling out from under a shelf into the middle of the tunnel as if to question my presence in its abode. I stopped what I was doing and hovered over it, amazed, my exploration momentarily forgotten. This lobster had somehow made it all that way into the cave, through Hades and the Devil's Throat. And it was getting enough food to keep itself alive.

I thought the lobster's cave residency must have happened recently. There was no way it could survive in a dark cave, completely devoid of light except for the lights we brought in with us, and with no food other than maybe some plankton in the water. There certainly wasn't its regular diet of snails, crabs, and clams this far inside the cave. Several years later, the spiny lobster was still there and thriving. I look for it every time I swim through that area. There are times I don't see it, but most of the time, it's there and comes out to greet us.

I eventually came to the end. Not the end of the tunnel, but to the end of my line. I had deployed every inch of line that was on my explorer reel. I had nothing left for that dive. It was just as well. I still had to survey the line I had just placed in the cave, in addition to the line the guys had placed a month earlier so I could tie it back into the survey I had done on my first trip. At the time I didn't know exactly how much line was in the cave. I clipped my empty reel back onto its D-ring on the back of my harness, thankful I had brought additional spools of line with me so I could continue exploring the next day.

I reached into my thigh pocket and pulled my wetnotes out. It was time for the real work to begin. There's a saying in healthcare. If you didn't document it, you didn't do it. I'm sure that can be applied to many professions. It can also be applied to cave exploration. If you don't document what you find, you might as well not have put line in the cave. Lining the passages is only one part of exploration. Producing a map is the other part. In my opinion, producing the map of your findings is the more important of the two.

I use my maps to plan my next day of exploration. I don't go blindly into a cave and look for openings that I think might end up going somewhere. I like to look at the map and visualize the cave and decide where to focus my efforts during the next dive. I don't want to look on the left side of the tunnel I'm in if that side will only have me running into another known tunnel that runs parallel to it or if that side will only bring me back to the reef from where I entered. Eventually, I'll look at those tunnels as well so I can produce a complete map, but my primary focus has always been to find the tunnel that goes on forever. Or at least a very long distance.

Maps also provide documentation that you found something. There has been a rumor for many years that was started by a small group of cave divers. They claimed they found an unexplored section of cave passages in Aerolito. They also claimed they added forty thousand feet of line in that section, bringing the total length of Aerolito to sixty thousand feet. They never produced a map, and no one has ever found this fabled section that is supposedly twice the length of the cave that has been documented. And believe me, I've looked!

I began gathering survey data in Dos Coronas. Fortunately, I had encountered quite a few straight lengths of tunnel that allowed me to not have to secure the line to any formations for some distance. I was able to run the line close to a hundred feet in length a couple of times, and once I even had more than a hundred feet of straight line. This made the task of surveying easier. As I mentioned previously, the survey data we gather involves getting depth, compass heading, and distance. Each time we stop to get the depth and compass heading at a survey station, a location where the line changes direction, it takes a few seconds. We have to stop, set the compass next to the line while hovering midwater, and read the tiny numbers on the face of the compass. We don't have the luxury of stabilizing ourselves by kneeling on the floor of the cave. That would disturb the sediment and leave evidence that we were there. It would also disturb the visibility and make it difficult to read the compass. Those numbers are difficult enough to read in clear water! There's a saying in scuba diving - leave only bubbles, take only pictures. We have the same saying in cave diving. With exploration you can add *leave only line and bubbles to it*. The line is a necessary evil, both for safety and for documentation purposes.

A little less than half an hour later, I arrived back at where I had started laying out line. I marked this in my notes so I would know where to differentiate the line I had placed in the cave from the line that had already been there. I had asked Ygor for the data they had gotten from their exploration before our trip so I could tie any line I placed in the cave into what had already been lined and surveyed. I never received it. They wanted me to just send them my data. In one dive I had already put more line in that cave than they had during their previous trip. During all four of my dives in Dos Coronas, I had claim to more than half of the line in the cave. I would share with them if they shared with me, but it had to be a two-way street.

Cave explorers can be a bit possessive with their data. I'm not complaining about it. I'm the same way. We are possessive because we put a lot of work into our projects and don't want someone else to come in and take credit for it. Another reason is that we may still be working on the exploration project. If we share our data, that gives someone else the ability to get into the cave and do what we call *scoop our leads*. They can head to the ends of our lines and continue pushing the passages farther in. I wasn't scooping Ygor's leads. He knew we were in Cozumel. He knew we were diving Dos Coronas and adding more line to it. I had been clear with him that we were doing that. I had asked him for his survey data to tie my survey data into. He never asked us not to explore the cave. If he had, we would have respected that and stayed out of Dos Coronas. He had even asked me to send him whatever survey data I compiled. So he was aware of our intentions. I extended an invitation prior to my next trip, and they declined. I even discussed my exploration project with him a couple of years later at the Dive Equipment and Marketing Association (DEMA) convention and showed him the map I had created. As it was, Ygor and his team never returned to Cozumel to do any additional exploration in Dos Coronas. They seemed to have forgotten the project after that last trip four months before my second trip.

I still have a few ongoing exploration projects in Cozumel. I've never been worried about anyone scooping any of my leads. They would have to be extremely lucky to do that. I've been asked to share my data before. There's always the premise that it's for some scientific purpose. I'll gladly assist with any scientific projects, but I don't share my data freely. I've worked hard on those projects. Others are more than welcome to dive the caves there if they can get access to them. I only ask that the lines be left as they find them. I need them to not be changed so I can tie in new survey data without having to resurvey an entire section of cave.

I also ask that they respect my exploration projects. I've been exploring those caves since 2011, and I've put a lot of time and effort into them. If anything is found, I ask that the survey data be shared with me so I can add it to my maps and give the explorers credit for their finds. It's a matter of courtesy. That being said, it would take years for someone to become familiar enough with the caves to be able to figure out where to focus exploration efforts. It has taken me several years to become as familiar and knowledgeable with them as I am. Sure, someone can get lucky and find a passage I haven't come across yet. There are miles upon miles of passages there and I'm only one person. Someday I'll pass the data I've accumulated along to someone else. That won't be for a long time.

11

Dos Coronas joins the mile-long club

During the second trip to Cozumel, we put more than three thousand feet of line in Dos Coronas. Three days of diving meant an average of one thousand feet of newly lined and surveyed cave passage each day. The first couple of days we averaged more than one thousand feet each day. As we got farther into the cave from the opening, that number went down. We spent close to an hour during that last dive just swimming back to the section we wanted to explore. Such was the nature of underwater cave exploration. It was great when hundreds, even thousands, of feet of unexplored passage was so close to the entrance. Once that was lined, you had to have perseverance to keep exploring. You had to have the patience to swim an hour or longer just to get to the place you wanted to explore. You also had to make sure you had enough air to breathe. This is something that keeps a lot of divers from pushing cave passages much farther than a couple thousand feet. They want instant gratification, and they don't get that if they have to swim an hour before they begin to find any unexplored tunnels.

We had perseverance and patience. The main issue was how much air we could carry with us into the cave. We could only carry so many scuba tanks with us. The restrictions only allowed us to squeeze so much through them. The limit was five scuba tanks. Any more than five and swimming became difficult. The massive drag of such a large object moving through the water, against the flow, slowed the pace. The additional effort required to move such a mass increased respiratory rate. Adding a sixth tank resulted in no longer of a dive than using only five tanks. The sixth tank wouldn't get us any farther into the cave. It slowed us down and increased our muscles' demand for oxygen.

We looked for another access point. We hoped to find a cenote somewhere in the tannic pools above our heads that would give us access to the cave from the jungle. That never happened. The freshwater from the rain was seeping through the ground, through the rock, and into the cave to hang above our heads like dark clouds on a stormy day. None of them provided us with a way to reach the jungle floor above our heads. We didn't even have to poke our heads up into every pool. There would have been other signs. There would have been debris from branches and leaves. There might have even been some old trash discarded by locals visiting any such cenotes. The sediment on the floor would have been dark like it was in Hades. We didn't find any of those things. So we just kept swimming like Dory from Finding Nemo.

By the end of the week, the length of explored and surveyed tunnels in Dos Coronas totaled more than a mile. The cave was starting to take form. It had taken on its own traits and personality. It was a cave by its own merits. Not that it wouldn't have been if it contained any less but breaking that mile mark in length was a respectable accomplishment.

On the way back from that first dive, I stopped to check out the cenote I was certain was above Hades. Before getting my stage tank from the shelf where I had left it, I pulled out one of my larger jump spools that contained about one hundred and fifty feet of line and ventured past my stage tank farther beyond the shelf. The floor transformed from the bare, light-colored rock beneath my stage tank to a fine, dark sediment with lots of leaves mixed in, similar to Hades and the Trash Room. I swam over this leafy sediment for about a hundred feet until the floor started to slope up into dark tannic water above me. I ascended into the black water and continued rising slowly. I could barely make out the beam coming from my dive light. It penetrated about a foot before getting lost in the darkness. I continued my ascent hopeful that I wouldn't encounter a crocodile hanging out in this unwelcoming environment. It was brackish water and slightly cooler than the saltwater I had just left. Hopefully, crocodiles wouldn't find that environment appealing. Fortunately, there were no such creatures. At least none that I saw. That's not to say one wasn't there. There just weren't any that were curious enough to come out and greet me.

I eventually saw light trying to penetrate through the murkiness. At first, it was just a faint dark red glow coming from above. As I continued to ascend, the glow got bigger and brighter. Eventually, I broke through the surface and popped my head above the water into the jungle above. I quickly spun my head around to check the surroundings for any potential danger. It was a small cenote, maybe about five feet in diameter. It wasn't a perfect circle. It was more of an oval shape. After the initial scan of the surroundings, I slowly rotated my body in the middle of the cenote, taking in more detail. This time I was looking at the jungle rather than looking for danger. There was some trash around the perimeter consisting of old beer bottles and cans. It wasn't a lot, and none of it looked like it had been deposited there in recent weeks or even months. I searched for evidence of a trail but saw none. Whoever had visited this cenote to drink beer hadn't been to it in years. Whatever trail had been made had been swallowed by the jungle and no longer existed.

I thought about creating a new trail. I thought about the possibility of accessing the cenote to cut off the six hundred feet of swimming from the entrance in the reef. Trying to get to this cenote would involve cutting our own trail through the jungle. We would have to find machetes on the island or bring our own with us from the US. I smiled as I pictured TSA seeing the shape of a large machete in the x-ray of my checked luggage and then opening it to confirm the long, sharp blade. Would they allow it to remain there? Even if I could get a machete to Cozumel, we might not find the cenote. The jungle was thick and the waterhole small. It would be difficult to locate. I wasn't sure it was worth the effort to try. The swim from the reef opening was only about twenty minutes and used one stage tank. That seemed like a much better option than hiking through the jungle with four or five tanks each in addition to our dive equipment. I dismissed the idea.

I descended a couple of feet below the surface and found a protrusion from the wall to which I could tie my line. I cut the line and secured it to the outcropping. I placed a directional marker with my initials on it near the end of the line. The arrow pointed up to the surface. I named the cenote after the Devil's Throat which lay below it. It became Cenote Diablo. After the dive, I did try to venture into the jungle from the road to see if I could find it, but the jungle was much too thick, and I didn't have the proper clothing or equipment to get through the brush. I abandoned that idea only a few feet into the thick growth.

David and I exited Dos Coronas content with what we had accomplished during that first dive back. We found Winter Wonderland, the most beautiful area of Dos Coronas. I had emptied my explorer reel, which held more than one thousand feet of line. I had found a cenote and, even though it would be too difficult to access through the jungle, it was still important information to have. It was somewhere we could surface in an emergency. Having an emergency exit was always a good thing.

12

Aerolito and Gotta Gotta Got Faith

We took a break from Dos Coronas to dive Aerolito the next day. Greg and Roger hadn't gotten very far into Dos Coronas and weren't thrilled with the cave. They wanted to dive Aerolito again. David was having a blast diving caves outside of Florida and didn't care where we went diving. I didn't mind learning more about Aerolito. I had only done one dive in the cave. I could put exploration aside for a day and be a tourist cave diver again.

During that first dive two days earlier, David and I had difficulty finding the main guideline in Aerolito. Greg and Roger, who had both been to Aerolito before, were moving a little slower setting up their equipment than David and me, so we began our dive without them. We entered the cavern and saw an opening to the right. We headed that way and passed through the hole. The hard, stone floor below us gave way to a mud-covered floor about five feet deeper. We dropped down to it and I found a line leading back the way we had come from, but in a deeper section. The line led to a large circular room located beneath the main opening to the cave. The tunnel leading to the room was fifty-six feet long. At the end of the tunnel, we arrived at a line intersection. The options available to us were to go right or left. The left side looked a little bigger, so I chose to head that way. I placed a line marker on the guideline leading back out toward the opening and continued into the cave. The passage circled around to the right. It

112

looked like the center of the room was an old collapse of the ceiling, but there was no opening in the ceiling. It appeared that part of the rock up there decided to give way. We swam around the hundred-and-eighty-eight-foot-long perimeter of the room. At one time this had been a large oval-shaped room before the ceiling collapsed and made it a roundabout of sorts.

We came back to the line intersection where we had left our non-directional markers. Just as we were approaching the intersection, I saw another light to the left, from where we had entered the roundabout. A moment later Greg appeared. Apparently, he and Roger followed our line from the entrance rather than running their own line to the main guideline. I waved to them and let them head off to the left. We exited the roundabout to go back toward the opening. I left my primary reel in place for Greg and Roger to use for their exit. David and I headed back to where we had tied off the reel so we could use David's primary reel to look for the main guideline again. We searched the cavern, the daylit portion of the cave, and found another line on the far-left wall.

This line was thicker than the white line we had found and looked to be yellow or brown. It was stained and difficult to tell the actual color. Thinking we had found the main guideline, we proceeded to follow it. The stained line brought us into a low, hazy tunnel. It was nothing like I had expected. I wondered if this was how most of the tunnels in Aerolito looked. If so, I finally understood why the caves of Cozumel had a reputation for being advanced caves. They were small and had hazy visibility. Even with those thoughts, I had a difficult time believing we were following the main guideline. Despite my doubts, we continued to follow the guideline I had found. A couple of hundred feet later, the tunnel became bigger, and the visibility got better. We could see as far as our dive lights would allow. Maybe this wouldn't be so bad, I thought. We no longer had to swim slowly and carefully so as not to disturb the visibility any more than it had been. We had plenty of room to move around and plenty of clearance to keep a respectable distance from the sediment covered floor.

The passage transformed from a low wide tunnel into a tall, narrow fissure crack through the rock. We left the muddy floor behind in exchange for smooth, bare stone. The tunnel was wider in the middle with the walls getting closer to each other as they approached the narrow floor and ceiling. It appeared to curve around to the right. We swam through the fissure for several hundred feet, passing some potential leads on both sides. We weren't in exploration mode, though. We were just getting a feel for the cave and what it had to offer. We were learning the cave.

We saw some sea life in this fissure crack. It didn't have the coral and sea sponges we had become accustomed to seeing in Dos Coronas. Instead we were presented with brittle sea stars, also known as serpent stars. These were small creatures with a body about the size of three dimes stacked on each other with five arms that stretched out five or six inches from their small cores. Whenever we came close to them, they pulled their arms in and tried to make themselves as tiny as possible. The creatures that had settled in the pockets of sediment had even dug small holes and disappeared into those bunkers, hiding from us as we intruded into their habitat. It wasn't the light that spooked them. They didn't react until we were almost directly above them. It had to be the movement of the water caused by our movement that alerted them to the presence of a possible predator.

The farther in we got, the less sea stars we saw. There wasn't much life in the cave at this point. The floors were smooth and clear and the guideline was free of growth. The line finally came to an end about twenty minutes after we had started following it. That put it at close to one thousand feet, maybe a little less because we had been taking our time moving through the tunnel. About ten feet from the end of the line, another line ran perpendicular to it. That line was even thicker than the yellow line we had just followed and it was orange. We closed the gap between the two lines with a jump spool and headed to the right into this new tunnel. A few minutes later we saw lights ahead of us and encountered Greg and Roger again. They were swimming toward us. Apparently, we hadn't tied into the main guideline that came from the cavern. David and I had found two lines, but still hadn't found the main one. Aerolito was proving to be a challenge. The four of us waved as we passed each other and continued in our respective directions.

Curious, David and I followed the orange guideline in the direction Greg and Roger had come from. The tunnel we found ourselves in was tall and wide, much wider than the one we had come from. I could see the wall to our left and nothing but darkness to the right. The ceiling got lower to the right, but the room continued beyond the penetration of our dive lights. The floor in this tunnel was flat and had a layer of mud covering it. It would be easy to silt the passage out and obliterate the visibility. Fortunately, there was plenty of room allowing us to swim several feet above the layer of sediment. We followed the line. As I mentioned, it was orange, but there were sections of it that had turned white. Closer inspection revealed the white was the growth of sea sponges on the line. They weren't as prevalent as what we encountered in Dos Coronas. There were some baseball and softball sized sponges growing on the line, but mostly it had just formed a layer around the line that continued on for several inches, sometimes feet. I imagined that in years to come, these might grow even bigger and longer.

We also saw more brittle sea stars. They were much bigger in this tunnel than the ones we saw in the fissure tunnel. There were a lot more of them as well. Most of them appeared to be hanging out next to their bunkers waiting to retreat for cover at the first sign of a threat.

115

Because we were maintaining more distance from the floor in this tunnel, our movement didn't disturb as many of them. We were able to swim by and watch them in their natural state.

A couple of minutes after we had turned into this new passage, we came to a large boulder in the middle of the tunnel. We ascended to swim over it and found ourselves in a halocline. This was my first halocline experience on Cozumel. I had experienced haloclines in the caves on the mainland of Mexico during the trips I made in the mid-2000s, but because I hadn't encountered one yet in Cozumel, I didn't expect it at that moment. I stayed close to the line and moved carefully over the sediment covered floor. I knew the visibility was going to be distorted for David behind me because I was disturbing the halocline. I didn't want to disturb the mud as well. The floor dropped away, allowing us to descend out of the halocline and get back into clear water. We swam between the house-sized boulder to our right and a wall to our left with the halocline just above our heads. This didn't last long. The guideline seemed to be routed right through the middle of the halocline. We continued on with distorted visibility, hoping to come to the beginning of the line and the reel belonging to Roger or Greg. We dropped below the halocline again momentarily. About twenty feet ahead, I thought I saw a reel secured to the line. It was difficult to see. It seemed to be located in the heart of the halocline as well. The reel belonged to Roger. His initials were on the side of the reel in large white letters written with a paint pen.

This was our first dive in Aerolito, and I was already amazed at the complexity of its tunnels. In about thirty minutes, we had swum a large loop around the cave, passing several offshoot tunnels. We briefly stopped and placed our markers near Roger's reel so he would not remove it if he and Greg returned before we did, and we followed the line from the reel out to the cavern. We wanted to see the route they had taken so we would know how to get to this line the next time. We swam and swam. We followed the line. It seemed never-ending. I expected to see daylight streaming in at any moment, but after three minutes we were still in the dark, both literally and figuratively. It was unheard of to have a primary guideline begin so far away from the opening of the cave. But in Aerolito, that's exactly what happened. We continued to follow the line. Right before we entered the cavern zone and finally saw some daylight, we went through the halocline again. We could also feel the current of freshwater moving through the borehole we passed through to get into the cavern. It took five minutes to get back to the cavern from Roger's reel. That meant the beginning of the line was about two hundred and fifty feet from the opening of the cave. I wondered how many dives it would have taken me to find that line on my own.

David and I took in the view of the opening from the far end of the cavern. It was an amazing sight. Rays of sunlight penetrated through the green hued water making it look like the heavens had opened up to us and were inviting us to ascend to them. The opening was wide with two peaks, the one on the left slightly higher than the one on the right. It looked like we were looking at the photographic negative of a mountain range with the light in the middle portraying the mountains and the dark stone surrounding it portraying the sky. After a couple of moments enjoying the view, we turned around and headed back into the cave, wanting to retrace our path, and possibly see more passages. The shallow depth of the cave meant we still had plenty of air in our tanks. We got back to Roger's primary reel and removed our line markers. Greg and Roger were still somewhere inside the cave. As we made our way back to our jump spool, we passed them heading back out. We waved again and continued on our way, retrieved our jump spool, and headed back along the fissure tunnel. We poked our heads into some holes we had seen on the way in but didn't see any lines. They had potential. I made a mental note of these areas and looked forward to returning to the house later that day to study the maps and try to figure out exactly where we had been.

My first dive in Aerolito had given me a lot of information, almost too much. I needed time to process everything we had found. As much fun as laying line in Dos Coronas was, I had really enjoyed Aerolito and was looking forward to doing more dives there.

* * *

When we began our second dive in Aerolito on our third day of the trip, David and I wanted to take the proper path into the cave. We wanted to find the passage to the main guideline that started two hundred and fifty feet from the opening. We entered the cavern and retraced the path we had taken two days earlier when we followed Roger's line. We found the borehole that took us through the first halocline in the cave and dropped below into the warmer saltwater with clear visibility. We followed the wall to our left. We swam for a few minutes, and I questioned whether I had gone the right way or stumbled onto another passage. Even though the swim had taken five minutes two days earlier, it always took a little longer when running line from a reel, and the information overload from that first dive had kept me from being completely aware of my surroundings.

I finally saw the stop sign often found near cave entrances shortly after doubts started to creep into my mind. I vaguely remembered seeing the sign while returning from the cavern two days earlier. I had been too busy looking at the cave to bother noticing a manmade object. Seeing the sign gave me confirmation that I was on the right path. A minute later I found the beginning of the main guideline in Aerolito. I was still amazed at how far back it began.

David and I enjoyed another nice two-hour long dive. We followed the orange guideline, passing the line we had come from two days earlier. It was much closer to the beginning of the guideline than I remembered. After about twenty minutes, the orange line transformed into a thinner, purple line and dropped into a large fissure. We followed it down and found ourselves about fifty-feet deep hovering over a hard floor covered with course gravel and sand. We wondered if this could possibly be connected to one of the leads we had found on our previous dive. As we continued along the line, we came across a line intersection with another line leading up into the ceiling to the left. We marked the intersection and continued straight along the line we had been following. A few hundred feet later, we arrived at the end of that line. The line stopped at the end of the tunnel and turned up, going through an opening in the ceiling to our left. The line ended a few feet below a yellow line in a fissure crack tunnel. It wasn't the same tunnel we had been in two days earlier, though. However, it appeared to be heading in the same direction. Instead of becoming more familiar with the cave, we were even more confused at the complexity. This was going to be a fun cave to learn.

* * *

The trip was going well. We were doing some fantastic dives in the caves. At this point, I had been diving in three different caves on the island of Cozumel, and one of them was quickly developing into a worthy project. But it wasn't just the caves of Cozumel that grabbed hold of my heart; the island was very special in its own way. In addition to the caves, I enjoyed the people, the food, the sites, and the atmosphere. It was a laid-back place with no sense of urgency. Island time was not only accepted, it was embraced. People didn't rush around to get places. They didn't stare at us like we were intruders. They were happy to have us on the island.

Cozumel depends heavily on tourism dollars. After Jacques

Cousteau did a documentary on the island in the 1960s, tourism flourished there. Today, there are more than one hundred dive centers taking divers out to the many dive sites that begin near the cruise ship terminal on the northern part of the island and stretch all the way down to the southern tip. Cozumel is also one of the most popular cruise ship destinations in the Caribbean, possibly in the world. During the high season, the cruise port is only closed once every other Sunday. On its busiest days, you can see up to eight cruise ships stopping in to let their multitudes of passengers get a quick glimpse at this part of paradise. More than two and a half million people visit Cozumel from cruise ships every year. Add to that nearly a million of us who visit by plane and stay overnight. The Cozumeleños know this and appreciate it.

When I first learned to scuba dive, I found out there were divers who visited certain destinations over and over. I thought to myself that will never happen to me. I want to see the world. I want to dive the world. Cozumel quickly changed that attitude. While I have been to many other destinations in the Caribbean and Europe, I keep returning to Cozumel. Part of it is the caves. I've been exploring those caves for years and there's so much more to do there. It's also the people and the atmosphere. I've made some wonderful friends in Cozumel and I always feel instantly relaxed when I step foot outside of the doors at the airport. I feel like I'm home.

During our visits, we make it a point to visit as many restaurants as possible and to support the local people as much as we can. We eat at the local taquerias quite a bit, but on occasion, we also like to check in at the turista locales for a change of pace. During this second trip, one such place we visited was Wet Wendy's restaurant, a touristy place just off El Centro. Wet Wendy's was the sister restaurant to the Thirsty Cougar, so it wasn't surprising that we enjoyed the food there. Wet Wendy's played good rock 'n roll music, but also had cover bands come in at night to perform for the patrons. We've seen some great talent there as well as some very entertaining acts.

One of the first couple of nights on this trip, we headed to Wet Wendy's for dinner. We were seated and ordered our drinks. Greg, being wise about the refill situation on the island, had a bit more self-restraint with his drink orders. We looked over the menu and Jen and I decided to share an appetizer. Greg and Roger were eyeing the same selection and agreed to share one as well. We placed our orders and started to talk about our experiences in the caves. We sat there discussing the dives and how much fun we were having and laughing at the difficulty David and I had finding the main guideline in Aerolito. David and I told Greg and Roger about Winter Wonderland and how beautiful it was, encouraging them to follow us to that section the next day. As we were talking, our appetizers were served. Greg and Roger looked down at their appetizer plate and then up at each other with expressions of dismay. David, Jen, and I watched them, wondering what was wrong with their food. Then Greg said, "What were we thinking when we agreed to share an appetizer?" Laughter broke out around the table and Roger quickly signaled the server and two more appetizers were ordered. Greg and Roger would each have one and a half appetizers. Diving does make you hungry.

The appetizers were quickly consumed, the plates cleared, and our entrees served. As we were working on the entrees, the band started getting ready for their set. The lead singer of the band was vaguely reminiscent of Richard Ramirez, the serial killer who murdered fourteen people during a killing spree in California during the mid-1980s. It wasn't him, though. At least, we didn't think it was. The band began their first set, and they were decent. They wouldn't be signing a recording contract anytime soon, but Richard's voice was in tune and the musicians were talented. As they played through the songs, it became apparent to us that Richard didn't have a strong grasp of the

English language. He was singing and most of the words were correct, but there was something off about them. Then the band began a cover of George Michael's *Faith*. It was kind of fitting with the exploration we were doing in the caves. We had travelled all this way in hopes of finding unexplored tunnels in these caves. We were heading beneath the jungle of Cozumel each day having faith that we would find something, or at least that we would have a great time looking. There was just one thing wrong with the band's rendition of the song. Richard's lack of command of the English language was really standing out with this one.

While Richard had done a good job mimicking the lyrics of the songs we had heard thus far, something happened when he had attempted to learn this song. The sounds hadn't transferred from the speakers to his mouth. Instead of belting out the chorus *'Cause I gotta' have faith; I gotta have faith; Because I gotta have faith faith; I got to have faith faith faith*, Richard sang *Gotta gotta got faith; Gotta gotta got faith; Gotta gotta got faith, faith, faith; Gotta gotta got faith faith faith*. We all burst out in laughter again. We continued to laugh throughout this entire song, especially during the chorus which was repeated at least twice more. It was the most entertaining song of the band's set. It was so entertaining that we returned to Wet Wendy's later in the week just so we could hear Richard's rendition of *Gotta gotta got faith*!

122

13

David pops his cherry; Greg blows his top

David and I had been able to convince Greg and Roger to head back to Dos Coronas with our descriptions of Winter Wonderland. David was happy no matter where we went. I was ecstatic to be going back to a cave full of unexplored, virgin passages. On our fourth day of diving, we went back to Dos Coronas. Jose, the local diver that was on the dive with us the day Brendan died, joined us for the day. We had reached out to him before the trip to let him know we were returning. He would have joined us sooner, but he had to work. This was his day off and he decided to spend it with us. David and I were looking forward to continuing our exploration in the cave after what we had found two days earlier. Jose was going to tag along with us, but he only had one stage tank and would be turning to exit before we did. Greg and Roger were going to try to get back to Winter Wonderland. They still hadn't been beyond the turtle grave. That day was also David's turn to take the lead in the next unexplored passage we found. Only he didn't know it. I was looking forward to seeing the look on his face when I let him know it was his turn to run the line into virgin passage.

We unloaded the tanks and equipment and moved the van up the road to a clear spot on the shoulder. We set up the tanks and suited up for the dive. I walked back to the van to hide our gear bags, clothing, and cell phones under the seats while the others continued to set up. Jen was spending the day at one of the beach resorts. I still had a small pouch with some tools in the possibility that they would be needed. Jose's dive light ended up not turning on, but fortunately, Greg had an extra one that he gave to Jose. We had gotten into the practice of hiding some smaller items under one of the short, bushy trees growing in between the rocks on the beach. Greg still had one of his gear bags that we used to keep the items together. My tool pouch, Roger's eyeglasses, Greg's shoes, and David's favorite ballcap went into that bag. Jose tucked his nonfunctioning dive light under a smaller bush next to it. With everything tucked away, we headed into the water.

We decided to enter the Dos Coronas II entrance. It looked like it would be a little less distance to get from there to Winter Wonderland. Greg and Roger were going to follow us and try to get to Hades and the Devil's Throat this time. I found the bowl marking the second entrance and headed into the cave. I arrived at the restriction and wondered if it had been such a smart idea to use this entrance. It was small and I was certain to ruin the visibility going through it. It was impossible not to. That was the plan and we were there, so I went for it. I unclipped my stage tanks and pushed them in front of me. I wiggled and pulled and finally popped out into the small room on the other side, a cloud of sediment following me through. I swam to the line intersection, placed my marker on the exit line, and waited for David. The hole was obscured by the silt cloud I had created. I wondered if Greg and Roger would be able to fit. I found myself once again questioning my decision to choose this opening.

David made it through, and I turned to continue into the cave. The room we were in wasn't that big and I wanted to give Greg and Roger space. The next four hundred feet went smoothly. I arrived at the shelf and placed my stage tank on top of it. David came in behind me holding his stage tanks out in front of him and quickly clipped one of them to the line. We dropped down the crack, arrived at the Devil's Throat, and made our way through the baffles, finally arriving in

Winter Wonderland. We were still in awe of the landscape. I hovered there for a moment thinking it would never get old to come through the Devil's Throat into such a beautiful, amazing room of formations. More than twelve years later, I still get that feeling.

We waited a few minutes for Jose, Greg, and Roger, but they never arrived. Maybe they hadn't gotten through the restriction. Maybe Jose had decided to stay with Greg and Roger. We were diving in two teams, so we decided to continue our dive. We would meet up with them later. David and I swam through Winter Wonderland and reached a point in the cave where I had seen a potential lead to more unexplored cave. Every lead to the right was unexplored because Ygor's team had only searched to the left. I stopped in front of this lead, swam off the line about twenty feet to investigate further, and confirmed that it did indeed keep going around the corner. I swam back to David, who was waiting at the line, and motioned my arms much like Vanna White when she was showing off one of the prizes on Wheel of Fortune. David stared at me. I made the motion of reeling a line with my hands and pointed at the dark opening to his right. Then I pointed at him and made the Vanna White motion back at the dark opening. He finally understood. I could see his eyes get wide and the smile appear in them. This was his first time leading into unexplored, virgin cave passage. Sure, he had followed me two days earlier when I emptied my explorer reel. It wasn't the same. At least it wasn't the same when you were first starting out in underwater cave exploration.

I'll never forget the excitement I felt when I placed line in a cave passage the very first time. I hadn't been cave diving for very long, maybe four years. Three of those years I was diving as what I referred to as a tourist cave diver. This wasn't meant to be derogatory. Tourist cave divers are people who don't live near any underwater caves and only cave dive when they take a long weekend or vacation to travel to the caves. I was a tourist cave diver for three years before moving to

Florida where I could be ten minutes from several underwater caves.

After a year of living in Florida, I began to understand the difference between being able to cave dive three or four times a year versus three or four times a week, sometimes more. It was the difference between visiting the caves and becoming a part of them. When you became a part of them, you learned to read them; you saw them in a different way. They became as familiar to you as your own town. As a tourist cave diver, you still needed maps and relied on the lines to navigate. As a local cave diver, you got to know the caves as well as you knew your own neighborhood. You didn't need GPS to navigate to the grocery store because you just knew the way. You knew what the streets looked like. The same thing happened in a cave that you went diving in frequently.

During my second year of living in Florida, I became more familiar with the caves. I started finding tunnels that no one else had found. These were typically tunnels that had low clearance and lots of sediment. The ceiling was too low to be entered with tanks mounted on the back of the diver, and disturbed visibility was certain to be encountered on the return. A sidemount configuration was best used to get into these passages but contact with the floors and ceilings was still likely.

Most underwater caves were originally explored before there was a form of diving referred to as sidemount diving. In sidemount diving, tanks are mounted on the sides instead of on the back. The original cave explorers were all diving in backmount configuration. This limited where they could go. There were some that would pull off their harness and tanks and push them ahead into low restrictions. But that wasn't the safest of practices. With the advent of the sidemount configuration, previously unexplored areas became available for exploration in a much safer manner. These were the types of unlined passages I was finding. They weren't extensive. I wasn't laying a thousand feet of line in a tunnel so low I could feel the floor below me and the ceiling above me. They were more in the two-to-three-hundred-foot length range. Some of them connected one tunnel to another. But they were previously unexplored, and I was the first, and only, person to ever be in those tunnels. I found several such tunnels in Florida before my first trip to Cozumel, but nothing that was ever very long.

My first extensive, regular size tunnel to explore and line was in Cocodrilo during my first trip to Cozumel. That was three hundred and fifty-nine feet long. The day before that, I put about eight hundred and fifty-one feet of line into Dos Coronas. However, that was three different areas over two dives. I had definitely been bitten by the exploration bug. The first passage I lined in Dos Coronas during the first dive of our second trip was my longest find. That was the one where I emptied all twelve hundred plus feet of line from my explorer reel. I was overflowing with excitement about that discovery, and I wanted to share the feeling with David. I wanted to have someone to talk to about the feeling of running line into a newly found passage. I wanted someone to share the joy with. Besides, it was still exciting to follow behind David as he laid line in this new tunnel.

David didn't have an explorer reel. He had a large primary reel that held four hundred feet of line. We had tied knots every ten feet into the line on the first evening of the trip to get it ready to deploy in virgin passage. David grabbed his reel, looped it around the main guideline, and started into the tunnel I had found. He slowly made his way forward, stopping to wrap the line around formations every time the tunnel changed direction. He was doing well. The line placement was safe yet would still be easy to survey. David had been studying the lines in the caves and he had watched me running line two days earlier. He had picked up on it quickly. The couple of times he missed securing the line during a direction change, I grabbed it and wrapped it around a formation behind him. This happens, even to me. You try to anticipate the need for a tie-off, but you don't always see it. This meant the second diver was tasked with correcting these omissions. This was line we would both have to follow out if the visibility became diminished. I didn't want to have any line traps.

A line trap occurs when the guideline slips into an area of the tunnel that's too small for a diver to go through. If the tunnel curved to the left and the line wasn't secured onto a formation on the right side, the line would be pulled in against the wall to the left. In some locations the ceiling dropped down enough to prevent a diver from being able to fit. Having a line in such a location could cause problems. If the visibility was negatively affected and required us to maintain contact with the guideline to exit, we would be trapped on the other side of the restriction of such an area. Or we would have to release contact with the guideline to get around it in the larger area. The problem with the second option is that we might not be able to find the line on the other side of the restriction in diminished visibility. Because of this we never want to lose contact with the guideline. That's why this situation is called a line trap. You were trapped on one side because the guideline was routed through an area you couldn't pass.

About twelve minutes after David started into his first virgin tunnel, his reel was empty. There was more tunnel ahead, though, and we still had plenty of air in our tanks. I unclipped my explorer reel, which I had placed new knotted line onto the evening before, and handed it to David. His eyes got wide. He hadn't expected that either. He tied the two ends together and continued running line farther into the tunnel. A couple of times he stopped, unsure of where the tunnel continued. I pointed my light beam at the continuation and made a slight circle with it. I had a lot more experience cave diving than David. Remember, I had been his cave diving instructor. I also had the vantage point from behind and could get a bigger picture of the passage rather than focusing on one particular point.

We finally arrived at a dead end. Or at least, there were no leads big enough for us to pass through. David tied the line to a formation and cut it. He started to turn back when I stopped him. I pointed at his line arrows and then pointed at the line. This was his line. He deserved the honor of marking it with his line arrow. He grabbed an arrow and placed it near the end of the line. He had just claimed his first exploration push.

David didn't know how to survey at this time. We had discussed it, but he had never done any cave survey. I pulled out my wetnotes and started to survey on the way out. I had done quite a bit of survey in Florida, even surveying existing lines just for practice, so I was fast at it. We soon made it back to the intersection where we had begun this exploration adventure. David had claimed just over eight hundred feet of virgin tunnel. Dos Coronas was two thousand feet longer than it had been three days earlier.

It was a great dive. We found more virgin cave passage and laid more line. We almost doubled the known length of Dos Coronas. We made it back out of the cave and to the reef. We ascended and popped our heads above the surface. Jose, Greg, and Roger were already on shore disassembling their equipment. David and I made our way to shore, unclipped our tanks, and walked out over the rocky surface. Greg immediately began yelling at us. He was angry that we had silted out the cave on the way in. Apparently, he had tried to follow us in through the small restriction at Dos Coronas II and couldn't fit. He blamed it on the silt we had caused. I explained to him that it was a small restriction and there was no way to get through it without disturbing the visibility. He didn't want to hear it. He was really upset. I thought this was more about losing access to Cocodrilo than the dive that morning. As the week went on, he had been getting moodier, often complaining about not being able to dive Cocodrilo. I decided it wasn't worth it to say anything else. It was one thing to be upset with the situation. It was another thing to direct the anger at us. I wasn't going to let him dampen our moods. It was that evening that Greg tore the large map off the wall back at the rental house. He remained in a raw mood the rest of the trip. Fortunately, we were near the end of the trip.

Unfortunately, the items we had squirreled away under the tree were no longer there when we surfaced from our dive. The other three had gotten out of the water and went to retrieve Greg's gear bag, but it was no longer there. Jose checked for his dive light, and it was also gone. There's not very much crime on the island of Cozumel. The Cozumeleños know the importance of tourism and are self-policing. They don't want to get the reputation of being riddled with crime and lose the tourism dollars that are spent there. Crimes of opportunity still happen, though. This was exactly what had happened. Someone must have been watching us getting ready for our dive and saw us tuck the items under the trees. Other than the dive light, they didn't get anything of value. Fortunately, I had brought the keys to the van into the cave in a watertight container. The tools were old and already rusting. David's ballcap was old and sweaty. Roger's eyeglasses were easily replaced when he returned home. He was due for another pair anyway. It just became inconvenient for the next two days.

Roger did have a second pair of eyeglasses with him. They were prescription sunglasses. They were fine during the day, but a bit out of place at night. Roger also had prescription lenses in his scuba mask, and I suggested he wear those indoors and at night. I was really looking forward to hearing how his passage through airport security went once we all got back home. He didn't take me up on my suggestion, though. David was probably the one most upset with his loss. That ballcap was his favorite. He had owned it for years and wore it everywhere. It was an AB Biller cap that he had gotten at a spearfishing event. For the next two and a half days we kept an eye out looking for someone who might be wearing an AB Biller ballcap, ready to tackle the person so David could have it back. Unfortunately, we didn't find it. That wasn't necessarily a bad thing, as we also didn't see the inside of a Mexican prison.

The four of us, less Jose, returned to Dos Coronas the next day. David and I brought full reels ready to do more exploration. I had seen more leads that I wanted to check out. I was prepared to empty my explorer reel again. I had looked at the map and noticed that the path from Dos Coronas II was only fifty feet shorter than the path from Dos Coronas I. Under normal circumstances that meant we shaved a minute off of our swim time. However, we lost that minute in trying to get through the restriction we had to pass entering from Dos Coronas II. So we headed in through Dos Coronas I this time. This was a better option for Greg and Roger, as well. We made our way to Winter Wonderland. This time it was David and me on one team and Greg and Roger on the other team. We didn't even begin our dives at the same time. After two failed attempts, we weren't going to try to stay together a third time. David and I also let Greg and Roger go first so they could have good visibility heading in. We caught up to them in Hades as they were heading back out. They had finally made it to Winter Wonderland.

I had a lead near the beginning of Winter Wonderland that I wanted to look at. It led to the right, away from where Ygor's team had been focusing their efforts. This tunnel almost immediately transformed from the light-colored rock we found with a smooth, white surface that we saw all throughout Winter Wonderland to a dark, almost black craggy surfaced rock. It resembled the hardened lava I had seen during a visit to Sunset Crater in northern Arizona a few years earlier. Only I didn't think Cozumel was a volcano formed island. I made a mental note to research this.

I had reloaded my explorer reel the evening before, replacing the line on it that David had used the day before to line the new passage we found. I emptied the reel of all of its line for the second time on that trip. As I was running line farther into the tunnel, David followed behind and marked a few leads off of the main tunnel we were in that he wanted to check out. I let out the last of the line on my reel and signaled to David to continue with his reel. We went about another three hundred feet before David came to a restriction. The ceiling had sloped down, so it was only about a foot above the floor. That, in itself, wasn't so bad. The bad part was that there were columns from floor to ceiling throughout this low area. If we were going to get through, we would have to figure out the best path between the columns.

David didn't feel comfortable going through first, so he handed me his reel. I took it and began heading into the low area of columns. It didn't take long for me to get wedged in there. I had to back up and remove one of my sidemount tanks so I could hold it in front of me. With a narrower profile, I was able to maneuver my body in between the columns. About thirty feet later I popped out into a taller room free of columns. I had also used the last of the line on David's reel. I tied the end of the line to a formation on the floor as David swam up next to me. After seeing me go through the restriction, he felt more comfortable doing it himself. I handed him his empty reel, finished tying the end to the formation, leaving a loop to tie into on our next dive when we returned to Cozumel. I had already decided more trips were in order. I considered extending the line a little more using one of my jump spools, but thought better of it. We were more than two thousand feet from the entrance and had to get back through the restriction we had just passed through. Further exploration would have to wait until the next trip. We both placed markers at the end of the line.

We begrudgingly turned around, and I surveyed what we had placed in the tunnel. It ended up being almost fifteen hundred feet of newly lined passage. The end of that line was slightly more than twenty-one hundred feet from the entrance. This was a great find! We were excited about it and wanted to go back to continue pushing the end of the line Unfortunately, it was the last dive of the trip. I would eventually learn that the last dive of each of my trips would often be the one where I had my biggest find.

We were sad our trip had come to an end. The tunnel we were in on that last day continued even farther back. According to the Google Earth overlay, it was heading toward a swampy area of the jungle. There could possibly be another cenote in that swamp. One we could access to reduce our travel time. With the end of the line more than forty-five minutes from the opening, another access point would be welcome. We would have to wait until our next trip to go back and push the tunnel farther to see if we could find evidence of a cenote. At least we had more exploration to do on our return trip. And we did plan on returning. In fact, before we even left the island to return home, David and I had already set the dates to come back four months later.

14

Weighted down in the Swamp Land

Four short months later...actually, it felt like four very long months...we were back on the island of Cozumel. This time it was just David, Jen, and me. I extended an invitation to Greg and Roger, but they weren't interested in returning so soon after the last trip. I think Greg was still upset about losing access to Cocodrilo. Roger had his job and couldn't take any more time off that year. One of the nice things about being a nurse is the schedule. David and Jen worked three twelve-hour shifts a week and I was per diem, meaning I only had to work four shifts per schedule. Shifts could be scheduled at the beginning and end of the pay period, which meant eight days off in a row for the full-timers. That made it easy to go to Cozumel for a week as often as we wanted, budget allowing.

With just the two of us diving, David and I had more flexibility in our dive plans. Jen was going to enjoy the beach for a week. Our plans included only diving Dos Coronas and, as I mentioned earlier, small caves aren't Jen's thing. Jen didn't mind. She was perfectly content holding down a beach chair in paradise.

Cocodrilo was still off limits. Not that we asked, but only four months had passed. Aerolito was a beautiful cave, one that I wanted to revisit at some point, but it didn't offer the same exploration opportunities as Dos Coronas. Besides, we had plenty of unfinished work to do in Dos Coronas. I wanted to get back to the end of the line we had placed on the last dive of the previous trip, and I wanted to check out all of the leads David and I had marked.

I made some changes to my equipment during the break in between trips. I originally went to Cozumel with the same harness and wing that I used in Florida. That was my trusty Armadillo sidemount rig. It was somewhat compact, at least by Florida standards, with an air bladder that had only thirty-five pounds of lift capacity. It could handle the heavier steel scuba tanks commonly used in Florida, so I knew aluminum eighty cubic foot scuba tanks wouldn't be an issue. The issue was that by Mexico standards, it wasn't that compact. I simply didn't need that much buoyancy lift for aluminum tanks.

At the time, one of the dive equipment manufacturers had introduced a trim inflation device in its product lineup. The purpose of this device was to counteract the knee drop that occurred when diving with heavier steel scuba tanks. One of the issues commonly seen in sidemount divers is leg heaviness. The trim inflation device was placed underneath the butt plate, which was positioned over your butt (hence the name), so it could be inflated when the feet were too low and deflated during ascent when the air in it expanded. With the relocation of the steel tanks from higher on the back in the backmount configuration to lower alongside the body in the sidemount configuration, the weight distribution also shifted. The tanks were no longer closer to center mass over the lungs, our natural buoyancy compensators. They were shifted closer to the feet and caused the feet to drop down. Sidemount buoyancy compensators were designed to counteract this, but they could only do so much. One of the dive equipment manufacturers came up with the trim inflation device as a solution.

The concept never took off. The problem was that the device added another buoyancy bladder to control. That meant an additional task for the diver who had to inflate it with air during descent, as well as release the air during ascent. This was in addition to managing the primary buoyancy device and drysuit which also required air to be inflated and exhausted to prevent suit squeeze and runaway ascents. Divers wanted things to be simple, not more complex. The trim inflation device was discontinued after about two years. I managed to buy a few before that happened, but not to use as intended. My intention was to use it as a primary buoyancy device that was low profile and could handle the buoyancy change that occurred with aluminum scuba tanks. Aluminum scuba tanks only have about a two-and-a-half-pound shift in weight from the beginning of a normal cave dive to the end. The trim inflation device had ten pounds of lift. It could easily handle the buoyancy shift of four aluminum tanks. It was perfect for my dives in Cozumel at the time. I built a simple harness made of two-inch webbing and stainless-steel hardware and attached the small device to the lower back area of the harness. I experimented with it in Florida, but this would be my first time putting it to actual use in the environment I intended it for.

As we drove around the island, to the Thirsty Cougar, the fill station, and the supermarket, we kept an eye out for David's lost AB Biller cap. It was gone but not forgotten. He was still lamenting over the loss of that thing. He had another ballcap, but it just wasn't the same. Every day as we drove from the house to go diving and back again, we looked at every ballcap we saw, hoping to find it. David and I were ready to jump out of the van and pounce on anyone who would dare to wear it out in public and flaunt it in front of us. It never made an appearance again. I did bring Jose a new dive light to replace the one he had lost. The four of us that were on the second trip pitched in to get him that light. He made out on the deal because the new light was brighter and more compact than the one he had hidden beneath that bush.

During our first dive, David and I headed into Dos Coronas to set up our safety tanks and connect the gaps in the lines with our jump spools. We used the Dos Coronas I opening. We had four scuba tanks each. We would come out with three each. The safety tanks and jump spools would remain in the cave for the duration of the trip. We were the only ones diving Dos Coronas and having everything in place made things much easier and more efficient during the subsequent dives. We could get in and out of the cave quickly and spend more time exploring. Having safety tanks in the cave also added an additional layer of safety. It was comforting knowing we each had an additional eighty cubic feet of air to breathe should we run into trouble.

The dive couldn't just be to leave safety tanks and jump spools in the cave, though. While it was a setup dive, we also intended to do some exploration. The lava rock area still had areas to be explored, but that would require a dive dedicated solely to that. I was more interested in what I considered the main tunnel that was to the left of that. This was the passage that contained most of Winter Wonderland and eventually transformed into the Swamp Land area.

* * *

Before I go on, let me address the lava looking walls, floor, and ceiling in the tunnel we had lined the last day of the previous trip. I did some further research and confirmed that Cozumel was not formed by a volcano, so it definitely wasn't lava we were seeing. One thing I noticed whenever I clipped a stage tank to the line and set it on the floor was that it sounded like a bell when the side of the tank hit the floor. Don't get me wrong. I wasn't slamming the tank into the floor. I just happened to notice the bell-like tone as the tank moved around in response to our movement through the water next to it. It was as if the tank was being hit with a hammer. I hadn't heard this sound in a cave before. This bell-like sound made me wonder if the formations hitting it could be some type of metal alloy.

The formations also tolerated contact very well. I'm not one of those cave divers that will break formations just to make a restriction bigger and easier to get through. However, sometimes formations break accidentally. Just a flick of a fin tip can be enough to tip over a formation. I've even seen a large formation fall from a wall with the force of the water being moved by a fin. The rock in the Lava Tube tunnel did not break, even with forceful contact. I rubbed it with my fingers, and it was solid. It was a very hard and durable substance. I did notice some areas where something white could be seen peeking out from beneath the black outer layer. I searched around for a broken piece. There had to be some broken pieces somewhere. The problem was this was a very hard substance and not prone to breaking. I finally found a broken bit and discovered the interior of the formations in this tunnel was indeed white. It appeared to be a white core with a black outer layer. The outer layer was about three to four millimeters thick, and it couldn't be scraped off. It was strange. I wouldn't discover what it was for a couple more years.

A few trips later, Jen and I visited the museum in Cozumel. We had gotten into the habit of taking the last day off to allow our wetsuits to dry before we had to pack them for the flight home. As we were walking through the museum, learning about the history of Cozumel and the reefs that surround it, I saw a display of coral that could be found around the island. The shape of the coral was extremely familiar. I hadn't seen it *around* Cozumel. Other than the reef outside the entrance to Dos Coronas I had not yet done a recreational reef dive in Cozumel. In fact, it was about ten years after my first trip, and more than twenty trips, before I did my first dive in Cozumel that was not in a cave!

I saw this coral display and it hit me. The coral looked a lot like the formations in the Lava Tube tunnel in Dos Coronas. That tunnel must

have once been exposed to daylight and had been a thriving coral reef
At some point, it became enclosed in the cave and the coral died
without any light to sustain it. The outer layer of the coral then turned
black. I'm no scientist and I haven't tested this theory, but I do believe
I may be onto something here. One day I might get in touch with
someone who can test it, and I can bring out a small, loose piece that
has already been broken off. I'd love to know if my theory is correct.

* * *

.

Back to our dive in the Swamp Land. We headed to the back of the
cave along what I was referring to as the mainline of the cave, set safety
tanks at the junction between Winter Wonderland and the Lava Tube,
and continued toward Swamp Land, looking for leads as we went.
David and I took turns taking the lead in these tunnels. Most of the
tunnels heading to the right looped back eventually onto the main line.
We had hoped that we would be able to connect to the Lava Tube
tunnel, and we did see evidence that it would eventually connect if the
passage was large enough. We weren't able to find anything at that
time, though. It was several years later, on a dive with a couple of other
former students, that I eventually found a connecting tunnel between
Swamp Land and the Lava Tube. It came out onto the guideline in the
Lava Tube where David had left a line marker to indicate a lead was in
the area. I don't know if we ever checked it out from that side or not,
but I had finally found it. Unfortunately, it wasn't that far into the Lava
Tube tunnel, so it didn't provide us with a shortcut.

David and I finally breathed through the air we had allocated for
the penetration part of the dive and began making our way out. We
hadn't found any major passages. Most of the tunnels we found didn't
go very far before ending or looping back to the Swamp Land line. We
were exiting with just under a thousand feet of line less on our explorer

reels (David had finally purchased one for this trip). We had survey data so I could add it to my map. David had been practicing line survey and did his first survey of newly laid line.

The new harness and buoyancy wing worked out great! Previously I had to remove my stage tank to get through the corkscrew and the restriction just before the Trash Room and the Devil's Throat. With this smaller, more streamlined rig, I no longer had to do that. Restrictions that I used to have to pull tanks off and push ahead no longer required that maneuver. I would glide through them effortlessly and then turn around to watch David struggling to get through with his larger Nomad while holding his stage tank out in front of him. I vowed to get David into a similar rig for our next trip.

The next day we returned to Dos Coronas to keep going farther back into the cave and continue looking for additional leads. Because we already had safety tanks in the cave, we were each able to carry two stage tanks with us and extend our dive time by another half an hour. Our dives were now exceeding the two-hour mark. We were averaging two and a half hours in Dos Coronas each dive. We also left close to fifteen hundred feet of line in the cave during that second dive of the trip. We headed to Wet Wendy's that evening to celebrate with a good meal and hopeful to catch Richard's rendition of *Gotta gotta got faith*. About fifteen minutes after we were seated, we saw the familiar face of Richard Ramirez walking up on stage to check the equipment. It was going to be the perfect ending to a perfect day!

* * *

The next day, we went back to the Lava Tube. I know it wasn't really lava, but it resembled it, so the name stuck. We headed back to the end of the line that I had placed on the last day of the previous trip. This was a bit more than twenty-one hundred feet from the entrance and just beyond the low area with lots of columns that required us to unclip one of our sidemount tanks and push it ahead as we passed from one side to the other. Even in my new streamlined rig, this was still necessary. The restriction was that small. If the Lava Tube continued much farther without us finding a cenote to access, it would require us to get stage tanks through that restriction. That would prove to be an interesting endeavor. One of us would have to remove the stage tank and leave it with the other, pass through the restriction, turn around and go back into the restriction so the stage tanks could be passed through to the other side. I've had to do this in a restriction in a Florida cave. It wasn't fun, but you do what you have to do to get the job done. As I was moving through the column restriction, I had flashbacks to that Florida restriction.

It was interesting going through the Lava Tube column restriction while running line from my explorer reel. It became a lot more interesting on this return dive. We arrived at the area about forty-five minutes after we had begun the dive and saw the restriction twenty feet ahead. Reaching back, I found the clip attached to my left tank and unclipped it from the D-ring on my harness. With the lower part of the tank free, I swung it around in front of me so I could pass in between the columns. I slowly proceeded into the restriction. Suddenly my movement was stopped. Something was preventing me from proceeding through the restriction. This was strange and unexpected. I had gotten through it during our dive there the previous trip when I was using my Armadillo sidemount rig and hadn't gotten stuck. How was I getting stuck with my smaller customized rig?

I tried to back up, but I couldn't move more than a foot. I tried to move forward and got stopped again. I thought I was wedged in there somehow. Maybe my right tank was trapped between a couple of columns. I moved to my left. I tried to move forward and backward again. I got the same result. I wiggled around while moving back and forth, trying to get unwedged with no success. It was no longer just a matter of not being able to move forward. I also couldn't move backward. I was stuck in this restriction twenty-one hundred feet from the opening. This wasn't the Crack in the reef, but I was definitely having flashbacks to that dive.

I thought about the situation I was in and looked at the restriction, trying to figure out what was keeping me from moving. There was nothing obvious. I shouldn't be stuck. I tried to move forward again and noticed the line moving with me. I placed my hand on the line and ran it along its length until I came to the cam band around the lower part of the scuba tank I was holding in front of me. I rotated my tank and saw that the line had gotten caught in between the weight I had on the cam band on the tank and the tank itself.

I'm a bit embarrassed to admit this. I used to place weights on the cam bands on my aluminum sidemount tanks. To be fair, this was back in 2012 and sidemount was not quite that popular yet. Many of us were experimenting with different configurations. Coming from a Florida cave diving background where we were accustomed to using heavier steel tanks as our sidemount tanks, adding weight to aluminum tanks seemed like the logical thing to do. A weight on the side of the aluminum tank made it feel and behave like the steel tanks we were used to diving back home in Florida. Many Florida sidemount divers were diving with aluminum tanks this way. Some still do.

I don't believe most of the sidemount divers living in Mexico were doing that, though. The majority of their experience was with aluminum tanks, and they had found better ways to manage the positive buoyancy that aluminum tanks take on as the air was breathed out of them. An aluminum scuba tank filled with air to 3000 psi remained slightly negatively buoyant. As the air was breathed from it, the tank became lighter. Typically, the bottom of the scuba tank began to float a little when the pressure dropped to 2500 psi. When this happened, the tanks were no longer in line with the body. This meant low restrictions were not as easy to get through. It also created more drag with a greater surface area being exposed to the forward motion.

One of the ways to counteract this was to adjust the point where the body of the tank was attached to the harness. The full tank starts off attached to a D ring or butt plate on the back side. As the tank gets lighter, the attachment point must be moved along the waist toward the front of the body to counteract the positive buoyancy. That could be done by unclipping the bolt snap from the rear attachment point and clipping it to an attachment point on the hip or in front of the hip. There were also sliding D rings that could be moved along the waist strap from the rear to the front. None of this was necessary with steel tanks. Most steel tanks tended to remain negatively buoyant throughout the dive.

I had limited experience using aluminum tanks as sidemount tanks at the time. All of my dives in Florida were done using steel scuba tanks. Besides a trip in 2008 to the mainland of Mexico and a few times in Florida, I only had the previous two trips to Cozumel in which I used aluminum tanks in a sidemount configuration. I was still learning and developing as a sidemount diver.

The weight on my tank caused me to find myself in a small restriction, holding the tank in front of me with the guideline I was following wedged beneath the weight. When I say it was wedged, I mean really wedged. It was tightly sandwiched between the weight and the body of the tank. I tried to pull the line out from under the weight, but it wouldn't budge. I pulled as hard as I could, but it wouldn't break free from its entrapment. It didn't help that the restriction was so small, I couldn't get my right arm in front of me to assist in removing the line from beneath the weight. I had to free it with one hand.

After several failed attempts, and David behind me wondering what was going on, I pulled open the buckle on the cam band and loosened the band so the weight was no longer being pulled in tightly against the surface of the tank. This was no easy task with only one hand available to do it while lying flat between a stony vise. With the cam band loose, the line popped out and returned to its place alongside the restriction. I was free. I tried to secure the cam band back onto the tank before I continued forward. The restriction was too small. I couldn't get the leverage I needed to force the buckle closed with only one free hand.

I decided to push the tank forward, holding onto the cam band, until I was on the other side of the restriction and back into a larger area of the cave. I slowly moved beyond the point where I had gotten stuck and popped out of the restriction where I could swing my right arm around. Once there, I thought about removing the weights at that moment and relocating them. I decided that twenty-one hundred feet inside a cave beyond a small restriction was not the place to do that. I took a moment to get the cam band back in place and cinched down in its proper position. I swung the tank back around and clipped it back onto my harness.

With the weight situation resolved, I checked to make sure David had gotten through the restriction with more ease than I had. He also had weights on his cam bands. Fortunately, he learned from my experience and avoided the same predicament. Once he was through the restriction, I turned back to the loop I had left on the end of the line four months earlier, grabbed my explorer reel from the D-ring on the back of my harness, and began to loop the ends of the two lines together. With the lines secured to each other, I moved forward, hoping to empty this reel as well.

It didn't work out that way. The tunnel led me around to the right and into a small corridor. It continued to get smaller, then turned to the left. At least it was heading in the right direction. About thirty feet later, the tunnel got too small to continue. I couldn't get through even if I pushed both tanks in front of me. It was much too narrow. I secured the end of the line to a formation and left a marker with my name on it. I backtracked, looking for a lead I may have missed. There was nothing in the small tunnel. David and I scoured the larger room, looking for anything that would allow us to continue farther into the cave. There was nothing there either. All that effort to extend the line by only another two hundred and fifty feet. You don't know unless you look. I was slightly more than twenty-four hundred feet from the entrance and on the other side of the road that connected the beach road and the highway. I was hoping to find a cenote in that area. I knew the area above me was swampy. Having a cenote there would mean a lot less swimming to start our exploration. I didn't find going cave or a cenote. You win some and you lose some.

At the end of the dive, while we were disassembling our equipment and stripping the cam bands from our tanks, I removed the weights from the tanks. I had learned my lesson. Being trapped inside a cave more than two thousand feet from the entrance in a restriction so small I had limited movement was a wakeup call. Weights don't belong on scuba tanks if you're going to be negotiating tight restrictions. They might work on the cam bands for others, but they certainly didn't work there for the type of diving I was doing. I relocated the weights to my harness for the next dive and adjusted the D rings on my waist strap so I could move the bolt snaps from one to another as the buoyancy of the tanks changed.

Even though we had the end of the Lava Tube tunnel, there was still so much unexplored cave passage in Dos Coronas to find. Most days we surfaced with empty reels and big smiles. We ended up doing five dives in Dos Coronas on that trip and put in another twenty-five hundred feet of line in the cave. We were fast approaching eight thousand feet of lined passages in Dos Coronas. We spent more than ten hours underwater in Dos Coronas that week and found unexplored virgin cave tunnels every day, but the long runs of tunnels seemed to be running out. It appeared we had lined the major arteries of the cave.

15

Heading into the jungle to meet Chechen and Chaca

It was another six months before we returned to Cozumel to continue our exploration efforts. It was just David, Jen, and me again. I invited Greg and Roger, but neither accepted. That was fine. David and I had started something that they wouldn't want to be a part of. Greg was focused on his art. Roger just enjoyed leisurely cave diving. Neither was that interested in becoming part of a major exploration project. My feelings weren't hurt. That meant more virgin cave for us.

This was the trip when I brought three thousand feet of gold line to replace the line in parts of Cueva Quebrada. This would be our first time diving Cueva Quebrada. David and I were both excited about this unique opportunity. We couldn't wait to see what was known as the longest cave beneath the jungle of Cozumel. The one unfortunate thing about this trip was the lack of the Richard Ramirez lookalike on the stage at Wet Wendy's. What made it interesting was that this trip took place about two weeks after the real Richard passed away. Hmmmm…maybe he was Richard Ramirez…

After waking up at two in the morning, barely awake, Jen and I drove four hours to the Hartsfield-Jackson International Airport in Atlanta, Georgia. We met David there. He had driven two and a half hours from his home in Alabama. We waited at the gate until we were allowed to board for our two-and-a-half-hour flight to Cozumel. We finally arrived in paradise shortly after noon. We had been traveling for almost eleven hours. All of our luggage arrived. It was always nice to see it coming out on the carousel. A delay in the luggage arrival would mean a day of cave diving lost. That was something we didn't want.

Jen and I could have driven to the Tallahassee or Panama City airports in Florida, which were both just an hour and ten minutes away. David could have driven to the Montgomery airport in Alabama. None of those airports offered direct flights to Cozumel. They directed us through Atlanta, Houston, or Miami, depending on the airline. Layovers meant more of a chance for misplaced luggage. Besides, an hour-and-ten-minute drive to either of those airports, followed by an hour flight to Atlanta, and a two-hour layover, actually took longer than driving to Atlanta from our house. The drive was long, but it was less stressful. It also offered us an opportunity to stop for a cup of coffee about halfway to the airport. The flights were also less expensive from Atlanta at the time.

Once in Cozumel, we headed for the Thirsty Cougar restaurant located on Melgar and overlooking the sea. We were always hungry after traveling for so many hours and had come across the Thirsty Cougar during our second trip. It had cold drinks, good nachos, and a beautiful view of the water. It quickly became our tradition to stop there the first day of every trip. We grabbed a table out of the sun and ordered our drinks as we looked out over the turquoise-colored sea and enjoyed the warm breeze. Once our drinks arrived, we talked about the plans for the trip. We didn't focus much on that, though. There was too much going on around us to ignore it.

We watched the cruise ship tourists walking by on the sidewalk, dressed in skimpy bathing suits and bikinis, carrying all sorts of Mexican souvenirs, like sombreros and brightly colored ponchos, to bring back only to be placed in a closet and long forgotten. We watched the local artist that bends and shapes metal into Mexican themed ornaments as he tried to entice the tourists to buy his wares. He ventured over to our table, but we kindly turned him away. He was talented, but we weren't the typical Cozumel tourists. We tipped the little girl who came along asking if we would like to buy some small trinkets she had on display. We let her keep her trinkets to sell to someone else. We watched the boats running up and down the coast leaving large wakes behind them. We were back in Cozumel.

The Thirsty Cougar played good rock'n'roll music, and the servers were attentive. There was always a server at our table with menus ready to take our drink order within seconds of us sitting at a table. The drinks came out a couple of minutes later and the food order was taken. The nachos and tacos weren't bad. Neither was the mango-flavored frozen margarita Jen always got and of which I had a couple of spoonfuls. It was the perfect setting to plan the week of dives in paradise.

After we had gotten bored with people watching and while we waited for our food, I began discussing the dive plans. Besides the one day we would be diving with Germán in Cueva Quebrada, our focus would remain on Dos Coronas. We might dive Aerolito one day just to change things up a little. It was a beautiful cave, after all, and I wanted to see more of it. We also needed to tie knots every ten feet into the gold line I brought with me. I knew at some point I would be surveying it and wanted to make that task easier. We had six days of diving planned. It was going to be a busy week.

With our bellies full of nachos, we paid la cuenta, and headed to the fill station to let them know I was back on the island and would be needing sixteen tanks the next morning. From there, we headed to Soriana's Supermarket to stock up for the week. It was conveniently located a few blocks from the house we rented for the week and frequented by locals more than tourists, meaning the prices were also local. It was amazing how much food we could buy for so little money. We finally returned to the rental house at about five. As much as I would have loved to lie down for a nap, I had too much to do to get ready for the next day. Jen sorted the groceries and then headed into the bedroom to lie down and catch up on the internet. She was passed out with the phone on her chest within minutes. I spent the next hour unpacking my dive equipment and getting it ready. The equipment needed to be organized, and batteries had to be charged. I was exhausted, but it had to be done. David was in the other bedroom doing the same. We had two dives planned for the next day. We were going to start out with a bang. With everything done, I took a quick shower to wash the travel ick off of my body. I finally crawled into bed around ten and fell asleep seconds after my head hit the pillow.

I was up bright and early the next morning, excited to get going. I checked my equipment once again as I caffeinated. As tired as I had been the night before, I wanted to make sure I hadn't missed anything. Everything looked in order. David and I went to the fill station to pick up the tanks we had reserved and then back to the house to finish caffeinating. We loaded the equipment into the car and the three of us headed straight for Dos Coronas. The first dive of the trip was a setup dive. We were going to close the gaps in the lines and place our safety tanks in the cave. That was all we had planned for that dive. We didn't even bring stage tanks with us.

We headed back to the Lava Tube. We had walled out the end of the passage, but there were still leads off of the tunnel closer to the front of the cave. We clipped our safety tanks to the guideline about fifteen hundred feet from the reef opening. We then slowly swam back out of the cave, taking our time and looking for more leads to explore in the future. We ended up finding a couple of small loops that we left line in as a bonus.

We exited the cave, surfaced, and set about packing up our equipment. With our tanks and gear in the van, we headed to Mega Supermarket to grab a pizza to go for lunch from their small food court. It wasn't great pizza. It certainly wasn't the pizza I was used to while growing up in New Jersey. But most any food after a dive is good!

After lunch we were off to Aerolito for our second dive. Usually we did two dives in the same cave, but a second dive in Dos Coronas would have taken too much time because we would have wanted to bring two stage tanks with us. We could easily do a single stage tank dive in Aerolito and have plenty of time to relax afterwards. We also wanted to see a little more of the cave and get to know it better. Two dives in a day wasn't the norm, but we were younger and had more energy back then. We headed into Aerolito with Jen tagging along this time and stuck to the main tunnel. We spent about an hour and a half in Aerolito just being tourists and learning the cave. It was a nice change of pace.

The next day we were back at it in Dos Coronas. We headed for the Lava Tube. We were hoping we might have missed the actual tunnel that would keep going farther beyond where we had ended up with the original push. There was almost always a tunnel that kept going. We slowly made our way through the Lava Tube checking out every dark hole we could find. This was no easy task. This tunnel was already almost black. Everything looked like a dark hole. David and I took turns keeping track of the line while the other swam away from it to look at what we thought might be another tunnel. Most of what we looked at didn't go anywhere. The shadows were playing tricks on our eyes.

We spent two days poking around the Lava Tube. We managed to find a couple of offshoot tunnels that did go for some distance. Both were on the left side of the passage, in between the Lava Tube and Winter Wonderland. Unfortunately, neither of them turned out to be a main artery. One tunnel went the wrong way, parallel with the Lava Tube tunnel but back toward where we had come from. Another tunnel did go in the same direction. I thought we had found the missing lead, but a few hundred feet later I came to another wall. We added about eight hundred feet of line on that dive, but our finds weren't that significant. On the way out, we grabbed our safety tanks and relocated them to Winter Wonderland. We were done exploring the Lava Tube, at least for that trip.

* * *

I had contacted Germán the day we landed and let him know I had the gold line with me. The plan was to get together a few days later to go and use it to replace the old line in the cave. We planned on meeting on our fourth day in Cozumel and doing two dives to get the line placed. The cave we were going to was Cueva Quebrada, a cave I had become familiar with from internet searches but didn't know very much about. I had pulled up quite a bit of information about Cueva Quebrada, including an old line map from the 90s. This map indicated that Cueva Quebrada had twenty-nine thousand feet of lined passages. More than five and a half miles. It wasn't the longest cave in Mexico, but it was the longest cave in Cozumel. We were looking forward to seeing it. According to the map, Cueva Quebrada also had nine cenotes. That was in addition to the sea opening at the Chankanaab National Park. Germán took us to one of the cenotes for our first dive in that cave. The name of the cenote was 1km; we called it one click. The plan was to replace about fifteen hundred feet of line that led from the cenote along the northbound tunnel.

On the morning of our fourth day on the island, we met Germán at the fill station. He arrived wearing jeans and a long-sleeved shirt. It was the end of June, the temperature was in the nineties, and the air was thick with moisture. I thought it was strange that Germán would dress like that with the almost unbearable heat and humidity we were experiencing. David and I were dressed in shorts and T-shirts and barely tolerating the heat. Maybe Germán just dressed like that all of the time. We grabbed the tanks I had ordered the previous day and followed Germán to 1km.

The trailhead, if you could call it that, was not easy to find. I wasn't sure how Germán found it, but he did. We parked on the side of the highway, unloaded our tanks and equipment, and placed everything just inside the edge of the jungle out of sight from people driving by. With the vehicles unloaded, we each grabbed a bag of dive equipment, and David, Jen, and I followed Germán deeper into the jungle. The path could barely be considered a path. It looked more like a game trail. There was a somewhat visible pathway through the thick jungle of trees and plants, but it wasn't very distinct. And it wasn't a straight path. If it were not for Germán, I wouldn't have been able to follow it. We had to wind in and out of the trees, duck under branches, and step over rock mounds. The jungle was so thick, it would be easy to get lost. The only thing that kept us oriented was the sound of vehicles speeding by along the highway to our west.

We meandered through the jungle, following Germán along this narrow, rocky path, trying to avoid tripping on rocks and stumps along the way. More than once we encountered areas where it looked like the path forked into two more paths. I wondered how Germán knew where to go but trusted him to get us to the cenote. Germán warned us to not use the trees to help us maintain our balance. They were not all safe to touch. Germán explained that there was a tree called Chechen, which is a hundred times worse than poison ivy or poison oak. If you get the sap on your skin, the resulting rash will be horrible. Not only does the rash itch, but it bubbles up and remains for several weeks. Once the rash is healed, you will be left with a scar to remember it by. Germán pulled up his pant leg and showed us his scar from an encounter with it a few years back. I finally understood why he was wearing jeans and long sleeves. David, Jen, and I treaded carefully through the jungle wearing shorts, T-shirts, and flip flops trying hard not to get any tree sap on our exposed skin.

Germán continued his story about Chechen and explained that there is one thing you can do to help relieve the itch and rash caused by the sap. There is another tree in the jungle by the name of Chaca. Chaca and Chechen trees can always be found close to each other in the jungle of Cozumel. If you get a Chechen rash, gather some nectar from the Chaca tree and apply it generously over the rash. The nectar of the Chaca tree will neutralize the sap from the Chechen tree. I have had a Chechen rash at least twice. It itches horribly and looks like the skin is melting off. The scars lasted for years. My scars are now just faint enough that they are difficult to see, but they're still there. I was never able to find any Chaca nectar.

The Mayan folklore behind the Chechen and Chaca trees goes something like this. There were two brothers, known as Kinich and Tizic. They were both great warriors but with different personalities. Kinich was gentle and kind while Tizic was arrogant and ruled by hatred. Both brothers happened to fall in love with the same woman, named Nicte-Ha. The competing love of the brothers led to a long and brutal battle between them. The battle was fierce and lasted a long time. During this period, the skies were covered by clouds and the moon refused to appear. The battle didn't end until both brothers died in each other's arms. Their deaths also led to the death of Nicte-Ha, who had become overwhelmed with grief by the brothers fighting over her and eventually died.

In the afterlife, Kinich and Tizic begged forgiveness from the gods that had punished them and asked to be returned to the world of the living so they could see Nicte-Ha one final time. They were unaware of her death. The gods granted their wishes and returned the brothers, Kinich as the Chaca tree and Tizic as the Chechen tree. The brothers can be found throughout the Yucatan Peninsula as the two trees, standing watch over beautiful, white flowers that represent Nicte-Ha.

It's a nice story. I love to tell it to my friends when they join me on a trip to Cozumel for the first time. And maybe it's even true. But it doesn't make the rash and itch from Chechen sap any easier to deal with. I haven't yet figured out how to extract nectar from the Chaca tree. It would be useful information to know for the next time I get the Chechen rash. And I'm sure there will be a next time.

David and I carefully followed Germán as we made our way through the narrow path hoping that none of the trees surrounding us were Chechen trees. Jen begrudgingly tagged along to see this hidden jungle cenote. We had seen cenotes on the mainland, and even been diving in them. We also saw the Aerolito cenote. But this was different. It was a cenote in the wild. The cenotes on the mainland were frequently visited by snorkelers and divers. Some of them had grand docks and steps leading to the water. Most had restrooms readily available for a fee of five pesos (fifty cents at the time). All had parking lots with attendants and access fees of about one hundred pesos ($10 USD) at the time. Aerolito was free and didn't have any of the manmade amenities, but it was frequently visited by tour guides and their cruise ship tourists. Cenote 1km was rarely visited. The path we were on was a testament to that. The absence of trash was another testament. Jen was concerned about the Chechen, but she also wanted to see this cenote in the wild. We all tried our best to avoid any contact with the trees around us.

Finally arriving at a small clearing in the jungle, Germán dropped his equipment bag and told us to follow him even farther into the thick growth surrounding us. We placed our equipment bags next to his and continued along another path that was even smaller than what we had just walked. We would not have been likely to notice it. I carefully pushed branches and leaves aside, hoping none of them contained

Chechen sap. About fifty feet later we came to a small cenote nestled in the middle of the lush, green jungle. The water was tannic and muddy. There was a tree that had fallen into the water many years earlier. We could just make it out about an inch beneath the surface. Jen looked at me and said, "Have fun diving this toilet!" as she quickly walked back toward the clearing.

The appearance of the cenote wasn't the worst part of it. If that was it, we wouldn't have thought twice about it. Jen might have even considered diving with us. After all, we had been diving in Cocodrilo during our first trip to Cozumel. Cenote 1km didn't appear much different than Cocodrilo other than the jungle was thicker at 1km because there were no groundskeepers keeping the foliage trimmed. The worst part of it was the smell. The odor emanating from the brown and tannic water in the cenote in front of us smelled like rotten trees and mud and old carcasses all mixed together. The odor was so strong we began smelling it as we walked from the clearing where we had dropped our bags. The mud below our feet was black and thick and I could feel it mushing over my flip-flops onto my feet and oozing between my toes. I had no clue what we were getting into and hadn't worn proper footwear, not only for the mud but also for the jungle.

On the other hand, maybe flip-flops, or chanclas, as they are more commonly referred to in Mexico, were more appropriate than sneakers. At least chanclas were easy to rinse off and it wasn't a big deal if they got wet. They hadn't been very comfortable to wear while walking on a rocky and stumpy uneven jungle path while trying to avoid Chechen sap. However, in the mud and water, they seemed to be the better choice of footwear.

David and I looked at each other. Jen had already walked back to the clearing to get away from the smell. We both silently communicated with the looks on our faces and asked each other what we had gotten ourselves into. We looked at Germán and all seemed normal. This was no practical joke. We were going to submerge ourselves in that most unwelcoming, foul-smelling, puddle of mud.

16

It feels like I'm swimming in piss!

We had come all this way. I had brought three thousand feet of gold line with me. David and I had spent the past three evenings tying knots every ten feet onto the gold line. That was three hundred knots! With that task came the realization that it was a lot easier to tie knots onto the thinner cave line we used on our explorer reels and jump spools than it was onto the thicker gold line. David and I found a rhythm doing it, but it still took a few hours to do. After all that, there we stood in the middle of the jungle, near a most fetid, unwelcoming leech pool, contemplating bowing out to head back to one of the cleaner caves. But Germán needed help replacing the line in Cueva Quebrada, particularly in that muddy, smelly water hole we were staring at. What the hell! I had gone into a brown cenote after seeing a small crocodile retreat into it. What could happen at this cenote?

Crocodiles! I quickly scanned the small shoreline surrounding the water, looking for the tell-tale signs of a crocodile in the vicinity. We were a bit far from the sea, across two roads, one a major highway. I hadn't seen any other bodies of water in the jungle, so seeing a crocodile at this cenote was unlikely. I was no crocodile expert, though. This was only my fourth trip to Cozumel, so I wasn't that familiar with crocodiles.

I had lived in the Florida panhandle for more than six years at that time. I was very familiar with alligators and their habits. I encountered a few alligators on the Florida rivers heading to and from springs that led to caves. I learned what to look for along the shorelines of the rivers. Crocodiles couldn't be that much different. They were cousins after all. I scanned the ground around the cenote looking for a smoothed-out trail leading into the water. A commonly used trail would be evident. I would see large gouges and sliding marks in the dirt, typically with a narrower line in the center where the tail was dragged through the mud. An occasional use entry point might only have flattened plant growth from the weight of the crocodile as it moved over land into the water. Fortunately, I didn't see either of these things. That left our only concern being the removal of the stench that was sure to stick with us once we exited the water after our dive.

We returned to the vehicles that were still parked on the side of the road. The smell of the cenote seemed to follow us. Could it be so thick that it was already embedded into the threads of our clothing? Jen informed me from a distance that she would be waiting in the car with the air conditioning on while we finished carrying our tanks and equipment from just inside the jungle to the clearing. She had also worn chanclas and wasn't about to walk the path again. She was only supportive of my endeavors to a point.

With the tanks and equipment spread out around the clearing, Germán moved his truck to a pull off about half a mile down the road. He didn't want to give away the location of the path to anyone driving by. I wasn't sure how anyone would see the path even with the truck parked right in front of it. Jen left to go to a beach club and enjoy the cool, clean seawater that didn't have a rotting smell. She would be back to pick us up in about two and a half hours. We were planning on a ninety-minute dive with time to set up and break down equipment on either end. I wasn't sure if she would let us into the car for the ride to the next cenote. If not, I hoped the next cenote wasn't too far from this one.

German, David, and I headed back into the jungle to the clearing to set up our equipment and get ready for our dive. While the appearance of the cenote wasn't all that appealing, and the odor was even less appealing, I was still excited to see a new cave. I had never been in Cueva Quebrada, but I had watched an old documentary about some of the exploration that had taken place there. The documentary included videos that showcased the beauty of the cave passage. The purpose of the documentary was to present information about an artifact mound in the cave which contained Mayan pottery, coral, and skeletal bones that had been sacrificed to the Mayan deities centuries earlier. There was no longer a cenote above the artifact mound, and they concluded that it must have filled in over the centuries. We wouldn't be seeing the artifact mound on this dive. I didn't even know where it was in relation to 1km, but it was still exciting to know it was somewhere in the same cave.

With the cam bands and regulators set up on our tanks, we moved them to the cenote. I carefully stepped into the water with my chancla-clad feet. The water was warm. That didn't do anything to ease my trepidation about diving in this cesspool of a cenote. Warm water bred bacteria and other nasty critters. I wasn't too concerned about getting it on my skin, but I would eventually have to submerge my head in the muck. I could almost feel the ear infections that most certainly would follow. My stomach grumbled at the thought of coming down with Montezuma's Revenge later that evening. I took small steps toward the center of the cenote, testing each foothold carefully. German had told us there was a shelf that extended about a third of the way across the cenote. The shelf just ended, and the bottom of the cenote dropped down to about twelve feet of depth. The entrance was located below the edge of the shelf and went beneath us and the clearing where we set up our equipment. I stopped when I got about one quarter of the way across the cenote. I didn't want to step beyond the edge and drop into the water with my clothing on. Jen would definitely not let me back into the car if that happened.

I set the tanks on the ledge with the valves leaning on the tree trunk that disappeared into the murky water. The trunk had a branch sticking up above the surface, so I clipped the top clips of my tanks to each other around the branch to prevent them from slipping down the ledge into the cenote without me. There are some that think those top clips are not necessary and shouldn't be used, but they were proving very useful in this instance. The ledge was a bit slippery and slimy, and I could feel my chanclas slipping on it with every step I took.

Once my tanks were in the water, I returned to the clearing to get out of my clothing and pull on my wetsuit. As warm as it was, I wished I had my drysuit with me so that I wouldn't have to have that malodorous water touching my body. A full-face mask wouldn't have been a bad thing either. But I had neither of those. We suited up and packed our clothes and other items that were not coming with us into our bags. Phones were placed into airplane mode so they wouldn't make any noise. We weren't using them away from wi-fi anyway. We disappeared into the thick jungle to stow the bags in the thick brush hidden from anyone who might happen to wander into the clearing while we were diving. It wasn't likely anyone would come across our things. I doubted they could even find the path. There was also no evidence of anyone having been around the cenote in a long time. There would be empty bottles, cans, or some other type of trash. None of that was at Cenote 1km, but it was better to be safe than to come out to find our belongings missing.

We walked back to the cenote and stepped into the water again. The odor was even worse. With the three of us walking into the water and stepping in the mud along the perimeter, we had disturbed the force and released even more putridness into the air. All I wanted to do was get my tanks clipped on and disappear into the water where I would hopefully no longer be able to smell whatever it was that was producing the odor.

We spread out as much as we could on the ledge, which wasn't very far apart because the ledge wasn't that big. The diameter of the cenote was about sixteen to eighteen feet, and we only had about one sixth of that. Even though the shelf took up about one third of the surface area, half of that was covered with branches from the trees surrounding it The three of us barely fit in that small space at the same time. We secured our tanks to our harnesses, and Germán reviewed the plan for the dive. He would be leading and setting the gold line while I followed and moved the line markers from the old line to the new one. David would begin to remove the old line behind us.

Germán secured the end of a jump spool to the tree branch I had leaned my tanks against and disappeared into the murky pool. I watched as his dark form completely disappeared only inches below the surface, replaced by a burst of bubbles from his regulator appearing where he had just been. Along with the burst of bubbles came a shot of odor. It was like one of those air fresheners that shoot out a scent every so often. Only this wasn't freshening anything.

I prepared myself to follow the line into the darkness. I shook as much water out of my regulator as I could and placed it into my mouth, hoping no microorganisms had attached themselves to it while we suited up in the clearing. I would pull it out of my mouth and rinse it in the saltwater once I arrived at that layer. I waved at David and descended into the dark void behind Germán, holding onto the line that he had trailed behind him. I couldn't even see the illumination from the dive light I was holding in my left hand. When I reached a depth of ten feet, the light finally began to penetrate through the darkness. It was still being muted by the detritus in the water, though. I couldn't see Germán. The brackish water was too dark and too blurry. I continued to follow the line that would help us get through this darkness back to the surface somewhere above.

A moment later I saw David's light above and behind me. He had followed closely. The visibility in front of me began to clear but maintained a bit of blurriness. We were transitioning from the brackish water layer above into the saltwater layer below. Maybe this wouldn't be so bad, I thought to myself. The visibility continued to lose the tannic hue it had and became clear. It was clear of color, but not clear as far as visibility. I was still in the halocline mixture, and it looked like I was swimming in gasoline. I hoped that wasn't what I had been smelling above the surface. I didn't think bad gas would take on such an odor, but I wasn't certain.

I finally saw Germán just ahead. He had stopped and was securing the gold line we had brought onto a formation. Then he would have to secure the jump spool line that led back to the surface onto the gold line. The visibility was still very blurry, but at least I could see his light and his outline. When Germán finished securing the gold line to the formation, he moved to the left. I moved with him, descending farther into the cave. A few seconds later, I finally broke through the halocline and found myself in the saltwater layer. I immediately pulled the regulator out of my mouth and swished it around, hoping to rid it of anything that might have taken up residency inside of it in the nasty water above. I noticed that the water temperature had increased by a couple of degrees in the saltwater layer, although the difference felt much more significant.

The temperature change reminded me of a video I had seen years earlier that was taken by Dr. Richard Pyle. Dr. Pyle, an ichthyologist, was gathering specimens in the South Pacific off the coast of Christmas Island. He and his assistant were diving rebreathers because they were doing deeper and longer dives. They were diving to depths in the four-hundred-foot range, so they had helium in their scuba tanks. This made them sound like Alvin and his chipmunk brothers when they spoke. Pyle and his assistant descended into the warm waters surrounding Christmas Island. The surface temperatures were in the mid-eighties so all they were wearing were shorts and T-shirts. At some point during their descent, they passed through a thermocline. A thermocline is similar to a halocline in that there is a difference in the water layers. Only with a thermocline, the difference isn't salinity. The difference is temperature. The temperature can vary depending on where you are and what the currents are doing.

I've experienced thermoclines. The first time was in Lake Pleasant located northwest of Phoenix, Arizona. It wasn't a distinct thermocline in the lake. It was more of a gradual change. As you got deeper, the water got colder. We had as much as a twenty-degree Fahrenheit difference in that lake. The first time we experienced a distinct thermocline was off of the coast of Mexico in the Sea of Cortez. We were in San Carlos, Mexico with a group of clients, and we had headed out to do a couple of dives on San Pedro Island, an uninhabited (by people) rocky outcropping several miles off the coast that was known for its sea lion population. We were descending along the sloped wall when Jen and I saw the water shimmering below us. As we approached the shimmer, we felt an instant drop in the temperature. The water in this pocket was several degrees colder. Fortunately for us, this was only a thermocline pocket. We kept descending, leaving the shimmering water behind, and returning to the warm eighty-two-degree waters we were expecting. We saw a few more thermocline pockets during that dive and did our best to avoid going through them. The temperature difference had been a bit of a shock. The thermocline pockets were indeed a unique experience; one we've never encountered since.

Another experience with a thermocline was when we were diving on a couple of shipwrecks off of the coast of Nags Head, North Carolina, including one of the famed U-boats that was sunk near the coast during World War II. Rather than a thermocline pocket, this was an actual thermocline layer. The Gulf Stream and Labrador Current both converge along the coast of North Carolina. The Gulf Stream, coming from the south, contains warmer water. The Labrador Current comes from the north and is much colder. Oftentimes, the temperature difference is twenty-five degrees colder than the Gulf Stream. Usually the Gulf Stream is shallower than the Labrador Current. That was the case during these dives. Foolishly, Jen and I hadn't bothered to bring our drysuits with us. I had called the dive center prior to traveling to the area and was reassured that the water temperature was in the eighties, so we only brought 3mm wetsuits with us. The water was eighty-two degrees...on the surface! The Labrador Current temperature was fifty-five degrees! I toughed it out the first day, but nearly froze. Jen toughed it out long enough to drop down to the U-boat, then ascended just above the thermocline back into the Gulf Stream. She patiently waited there, watching me as I explored the submarine. The next day we rented 7mm wetsuits from the dive center. I wondered if the employee I spoke with was clueless or if he was just trying to set us up for having to rent wetsuits after we got there.

Back to the Christmas Island story – When Pyle and his assistant descended through the thermocline into the colder layer, Pyle immediately began to comment on how cold it was. In addition to using rebreathers, they also had full-face masks so they could communicate to the surface support on the ship above them. Pyle started by simply saying, "It's cold down here." This was in that helium induced chipmunk voice that one gets when they suck in the contents of a helium-filled balloon and start to immediately speak. Before long Pyle was emphasizing just how cold it was with some choice expletives. Yet rather than stopping and ascending back into the warm water, he continued the mission and descended even deeper into the cold water! The temperature of the water he was in was fifty-five degrees. He was only wearing swim trunks and a T-shirt! The video only lasted seven minutes, but the dive lasted well over an hour. Pyle and his assistant were in the fifty-five-degree water for a much longer period of time than seven minutes.

Once they had collected the specimens they encountered, they began their ascent. This is how I know the dive was much longer than seven minutes. First, helium requires a slow ascent and decompression stops to prevent decompression illness, otherwise known as the bends. When breathing a helium mix while diving, the possibility of getting the bends during the dive during the decompression stops is much higher than when breathing an air mixture without helium. The bends are more likely to occur when breathing air after a diver has surfaced. With helium, on the other hand, the bends can occur while the diver is still underwater and ascending. That's never a good situation.

Another issue that necessitated a prolonged ascent was the specimens they collected. Specimens found at those depths must be allowed to equalize as they are brought to shallower depths. If they aren't allowed to equalize, they will essentially explode, ending their usefulness to an ichthyologist like Dr. Pyle. This meant they had to stop before they ascended to two hundred feet of depth to allow the specimens to equalize and then again for one to two minutes every ten feet. It took them well over twenty minutes to ascend above the thermocline.

When they finally reached the thermocline and passed back into the tropical eighty-six-degree water, Pyle immediately let out a sigh of relief and commented to his assistant, "It feels like I'm swimming in piss!" Again, this was in his best Alvin Chipmunk impersonation. Pyle let out sighs of relief almost continuously and repeated this phrase several times. To this day whenever I move from a colder layer of water into a warmer layer, that sentence pops into my head. And even with only a two-degree difference, it certainly does feel like I'm swimming in piss!

17

A swim through the past

It felt really good to be out of the warm, murky, rank water, through the colder freshwater layer, and into the clear, eighty-two-degree saltwater layer. I hoped that being in this water for an hour and a half would wash away the stink of the cenote we had just entered. Sadly, we had to exit through that same cenote, so any cleansing would be quickly undone. Maybe I could get to the surface and rush out of the water before it was on me for too long.

I was immediately mesmerized by the beauty of the cave we had descended into. It was different than anything I had yet seen in the caves of Cozumel. Cocodrilo was a large, dark, spooky looking cave with fallen and broken formations throughout. It almost looked like there had been an earthquake that had caused many of the formations to lean or fall over. I think part of this was because the cave was so shallow, and the tunnels I had seen passed under the highway. The layer of earth above our heads was so thin we could hear the cars moving overhead. There was also some type of quarry to the east of Cocodrilo. The tunnels of Cocodrilo passed right beneath it. As we got closer to the quarry, we could hear the steady, low hum of the large machinery above our heads. This hum lasted for several hundred feet of passage. The three times I was in that cave I fully expected the ceiling to come crashing down around me.

Dos Coronas was a smaller cave with the first six hundred feet of tunnels under the rocky beach. It was also a true to life sea cave with lobster, cowry, cleaner shrimp, and more. The amount of life in that cave was amazing. After that it transformed into the snow-like covered Winter Wonderland and then into the tannic ceiling ponds of Swamp Land. There was also the Lava Tube tunnel with its strange, coral-like formations. There was so much variation.

Aerolito was a combination of the two. It had sea life residing in it, and it had large tunnels much like Cocodrilo. Except the Aerolito formations weren't falling over like those in Cocodrilo. They were all intact and stood as proud sentries overlooking us as we swam between them. This was probably because all that existed over Aerolito was jungle. There were some roads above it, but those sections of Aerolito were a bit deeper than the tunnels in Cocodrilo. At sixty feet deep, I doubted they were affected by traffic rumbling overhead. I had been in one such tunnel in Cocodrilo that was sixty feet deep and all the formations at that level were intact and nothing could be heard rumbling above.

Cueva Quebrada, on the other hand, seemed to have some of the features found in all of the Cozumel caves I had been in. It was on the large side with tall ceilings and wide rooms. Broken formations could be found scattered about. They weren't as large as the ones in Cocodrilo and had a different appearance. They were also not as common. There were enough broken formations that I could understand why it was named Quebrada, the Spanish word for broken. Although the word quebrada also has other meanings that would be fitting for the cave. Its other meaning was ravine or gully. I would eventually see the main tunnel coming from the sea entrance. It felt much like a ravine running through the tall desert mountains of southern Arizona that I had explored when I was in the army and stationed on Fort Huachuca. I understood why the cave had been named Quebrada. Cueva Quebrada also had dark areas as well as light colored areas. There weren't definitive zones, though. It seemed random. It was a very diverse cave, and I was only seeing a small part of it on this dive.

David and I followed behind Germán as he secured the gold line in place next to the existing guideline that had been there for many years, maybe even decades. I removed line markers from the old line and held them in my hands. I examined the markers and looked for the names or initials written on them by those who had placed them there. I searched my memory of cave diving history to try to put initials together with names of the better-known explorers. I thought about the original explorers who had first discovered this cave and wondered how they must have felt swimming through these passages, running line, and rarely coming to a dead-end. They had found and lined twenty-nine thousand feet of tunnels. We were two cenotes in from the main sea entrance according to the map I had studied and there were several more even farther into the jungle. Exploration had begun from that sea opening. What must it have felt like to swim along in a dark tunnel and suddenly see the sun's rays penetrate the darkness in the distance ahead? I longed to have been a part of that team and to have experienced their excitement and emotions.

I had my own exploration project ongoing in Dos Coronas and it was certainly fulfilling. I doubted it was anything like what the original explorers of Cueva Quebrada must have felt. I was coming to the end of passages. I was walling tunnels out. This is a phrase used to describe when a cave explorer comes to the end of a tunnel and finds nothing but solid walls. I felt that I was almost at the end of the exploration of Dos Coronas after only a couple dozen dives. In Cueva Quebrada, we were three kilometers from the sea entrance and there was still so much more cave beyond our location.

I placed the markers onto the gold line as close to the original position on the line as they had been on the old line that we were going to remove. As I pulled the markers off, I noticed how brittle the line was. It was literally disintegrating in my hands. Even when I wasn't removing the line markers from it, I would tug on the line and watch it snap and crumble. The line broke into countless pieces and slowly fell to the floor. I understood why Germán wanted to replace the old line. It wasn't safe!

Germán had mentioned how harsh the environment was for the cave line. He told us some of the line he had placed in there only lasted two to three years. I thought he might be exaggerating a bit. A couple of years later I would see firsthand that it was not an exaggeration. I thought that the line we were replacing might have been the original exploration line, but it was not. It was not nearly that old. Although, I would find some of the original exploration line in other areas of the cave years later.

I followed Germán and tried to remove the old guideline from where it was wrapped around formations as best as I could, letting it drop to the floor a couple of feet below. The plan for the exit portion of the dive was to spool the old line onto the large spool that David and I had put the gold line on. It would be empty at that point. I glanced back and noticed David was already gathering some of the line and had started to create a large ball with it. Maybe we could display it somewhere in Cozumel as an attraction. We could bill it as the largest ball of used cave line in the world. Tourists from all over would come to see it. Maybe not...

We swam farther into the cave until the last of the gold line was secured in place. Germán tied the end of the gold line to the existing cave line that continued into the darkness beyond and turned around. I wondered just how strong the line he had tied it onto was. I was surprised it hadn't disintegrated when he tied the loose end to the gold line. We turned around and Germán took the lead again and collected the old line that David hadn't gathered. I brought up the rear and decided to survey the gold line we had just placed.

As I mentioned, David and I had spent the previous three evenings tying knots in the gold line every ten feet. I did it because I believe all cave line should be knotted. I also knew it might be useful should I ever return to this cave. It ended up being useful on that very first dive. We made it back out to the beginning of the line, which was not far from the opening. My focus was on surveying the line, so I didn't pay much attention to the cave at this point. Once we were back where we had started, we began our ascent into the murky, malodorous cenote above. I was not looking forward to surfacing in that muck. It had to be done, though. As much as I would have liked to, I couldn't stay underwater forever.

I moved in front of Germán so he could retrieve the line from the jump spool he had run into the cave from the surface. I followed this line to the right and arrived to where it was tied to a large branch on the floor and angled up into the tannic layer. I looked up and could see daylight. I had been so busy looking down and searching for Germán when we descended into the cave that I hadn't noticed the light penetrated all the way to the floor. The daylight had a red hue to it from the tannins in the water. It wasn't clear or very bright, and it wasn't a large area. Most of the light was swallowed by the murkiness of the surface. There was some light, though. I was thankful we had run a line from the surface. An errant flick of the fin could have easily stirred up the sediment on the floor and obliterated the already diminished visibility.

I surfaced in the cenote a few seconds after David. Germán was not far behind. David held a ball of old line about the size of a basketball. Germán surfaced about a minute later, spooling up the guideline he had set at the beginning of the dive. He then unclipped the large spool, which was one of those orange extension cord spools that can be purchased from Home Depot or Lowes. I had purchased two of them so we could wrap the thicker gold line onto them to make it easier to deploy. They worked great! The spool was about half full of old line. Some of the line had small pieces of coral and sponges on them. We were not that close to the shoreline, maybe a kilometer straight line distance (that was probably why it was called 1km), but there was still sea life this far in. It was incredible to think about.

We unclipped our tanks and set them near the perimeter so we could retrieve them once we brought our other equipment into the clearing. We exited the water back into the thick jungle path. Once in the clearing, I ducked into the jungle brush to get the bags we had hidden. I tossed them to David and crawled out from the dense brush into the clearing. We quickly stripped out of our stinky wetsuits. They were definitely going to need to be rinsed that evening! The dive was over, and we had a fantastic time. But there was still work to be done. We had to carry the tanks and equipment back through the jungle to the road and load up the vehicles. We would grab a quick lunch and head to the next cenote to continue the job of line replacement. It was going to be a long day.

I brought a GPS tracker with me and got the coordinates to the cenote before we left. I would use those coordinates to overlay my map in the correct location on Google Earth. It was only fifteen hundred feet of line. There were twenty-seven thousand five hundred feet of line left to survey in the cave. But it was a start. The start of the biggest cave exploration project of my life.

18

Chupacabras, haloclines, connections

David and I hauled the tanks and our equipment back to the edge of the jungle near the highway while Germán walked down the road to get his truck. Jen was already at the trailhead waiting on us. We loaded the vehicles, drove back to the road pull off and had a quick roadside picnic, thanks to Jen. I was also thankful that Jen allowed David and I to get back in the car after having been in Cenote 1km. We were doing a second dive in Cueva Quebrada that afternoon, only this time we were accessing it from a cenote named S1. Cenote S1 wasn't far from Cenote 1km, but it was on the other side of the highway and through another jungle trail. The map I had obtained of Cueva Quebrada, just a simple line map from the early 1990s, indicated two cenotes right next to each other at this location. They were named S1 and S2. I've never been able to determine the significance of the names. Maybe someone thought cenote was spelled with an S. Or maybe it stood for sinkhole.

We finished our lunch and followed Germán down the road to the trailhead. It was much like the trailhead to Cenote 1km. It couldn't be seen from the road. You had to know its location and walk several feet into the jungle before you found the small and narrow trail leading to the cenote. We unloaded the vehicles and again placed all of our tanks and equipment just inside the tree line, out of view from passing traffic. Then we each grabbed a bag full of equipment and began our trek along the jungle path.

This trail was a little better maintained than the trail to 1km. It was more of a medium sized game trail, but we still had branches to duck under and rocks to climb over. The trail to Cenote 1km wasn't straight. The trail to Cenote S1 was even less straight. There were times I felt like we were doubling back on ourselves. There was a lot of meandering back and forth to get around thick copse of trees and plants. At one point we came upon a large body of water to our right. I got ready to drop my bag thinking this cenote was a lot closer to the road than Cenote 1km. Except that body of water wasn't the cenote!

Germán told us it was just a low clearing that flooded whenever there were heavy rains on the island. It was a mud pit. There was no access to the cave. There wasn't even a vent. We just happened to be there during the rainy season. We continued past this faux cenote, our spirits being brought down a couple of notches at the fake out. We continued to follow Germán, careful to not touch the trees or trip on the rocks. A couple of minutes after walking past the mud pit we heard a noise to our left. I looked in the direction of the noise and saw a dark shadow moving quickly through the brush about fifty feet away from where we were. It appeared to be heading toward the highway. I immediately proclaimed it to be a chupacabra. After all, what else could be out in the middle of the jungle in Cozumel scurrying about? David thought it looked like a monkey. He had seen a long tail sticking up above the low jungle brush. I didn't think there were monkeys on Cozumel. Germán confirmed this. We agreed that it was probably a coatimundi. I had seen coatimundi in the Arizona desert and the size of what we saw in the jungle that day, along with the long tail matched the description. Or maybe it was a chupacabra. I think I'll stick with the chupacabra story and claim we barely made it out of there alive. It's a much more interesting tale.

The rest of the hike was uneventful. We had no more wildlife sightings. We eventually arrived at a much smaller clearing than what we had at Cenote 1km. About fifteen feet beyond that was where the true cenote was located. Not only was Cenote S1 smaller, but the area around it was not as flat as the area around Cenote 1km. We had to step down the sloped path to get to the level of the water's surface. Germán advised us to continue a few more feet beyond this clearing. There was more room around the cenote to set up our equipment.

Cenote S1 was oval in shape, about twelve feet wide and fifteen feet long. The water wasn't clear, but it wasn't as muddy as 1km. We could see the bottom about three feet below the surface near the edge. S1 also didn't smell quite as bad as 1km. Although, there was a little bit of an odor to it. The stench was not so bad that Jen was disagreeable to diving there at some point. She would sit out on this dive because it was a working dive, and she didn't want to interfere with the line replacement.

The surface of Cenote S1 had two sections to it. The main section, and also the one where the entrance was located, was to the left of the trail we had taken. There was a much smaller overflow area to the right that measured about three feet across by five feet long and the depth was measured in inches. There were probably some vents that came up from the cave beneath the jungle in the overflow area. We weren't sure because they weren't big enough to see. The surface of the two areas was connected by a narrow strip of rocks and dirt making it shaped like an asymmetrical number eight. It resembled a snowman with a large body and small head. The narrow bridge was only about a foot long and easy to get across.

We stepped across the narrow strip of rocks and dropped our bags on the edge of a small clearing between S1 and S2. The closest edge of Cenote S2 began about fifteen feet from the edge of Cenote S1. It was a long and narrow cenote, measuring about four feet wide by fifteen feet long. It looked dark and murky. The jungle grew right up to the water's edge at this cenote. We had a narrow point of access where we could stand over it to look down into the water. The opening to the cave appeared to be on the opposite bank under a ledge. It was dark and small and difficult to see from where we stood. I wasn't sure it was even big enough for someone to fit through. It wasn't somewhere we wanted to enter.

Germán told us the two cenotes came out in different passages in the cave. The interesting thing about the cenotes was that they were so close to each other on the surface. The two openings were no more than twenty feet apart. However, beneath the jungle, they had a few hundred feet of tunnels between them. I made a mental note to look for the Cenote S2 opening from inside the cave at some point. It would be good to know where it was so it could be used as an emergency exit should the need arise. It was always good to have options.

We turned our attention back to Cenote S1. There was a slope just to the side of the narrow strip we had walked across that provided easy entry into the water. The cenote was shallow and there were no ledges, so we didn't have to worry about walking off the edge or losing a scuba tank in the water. We finished our reconnaissance of the cenotes and headed back to get the rest of our equipment and the tanks. This path was longer and not as direct as the path to 1km, so it took us a little longer to get to the smaller clearing from our staging point just inside the jungle's edge. Once we were packed in and ready to begin setting our equipment up, I sent Jen off again with instructions to return in about two-and-a-half hours. She was going to go hold down a beach chair at a different resort during this second dive. Because Cenote S1 didn't have the smell of the dead rising from it, I wasn't too concerned about being let back into the car after this dive. I returned to the clearing, and we set up our equipment and suited up, ready to see a new part of Cueva Quebrada.

The plan was the same. Germán would set the gold line while I followed and moved line markers from the old guideline to the gold line. David would bring up the rear and gather up the old line whenever he could. Germán again secured the end of the line from one of his jump spools to a tree trunk. This trunk was still alive and was growing out from in between a couple of rocks on the edge of the cenote just to the left of the entrance to the cave. He dropped below the surface and headed toward the far end of the pool. I descended behind him, holding onto the line. Even though the visibility in the cenote wasn't bad when we arrived, that was no longer the case after the three of us had stood in the basin clipping our tanks onto our harnesses.

Cenote S1 wasn't that big, and the floor was covered in a thick sediment of mud, branches, and leaves. Three divers standing in the cenote while we put on our fins and clipped sidemount tanks onto our harnesses stirred all that muck up quickly. Visibility in the cenote became non-existent forcing David and I to blindly follow Germán's line into the cave once again. It only took a few seconds before the conditions changed. The entrance to the cave was under a large shelf at the end of the cenote. The permanent line in the cave was tied to the wall beneath that shelf about five feet deep and less than ten feet from the edge. The guideline led to the right. There was another line leading to the left.

Germán removed the old guideline from the protrusion coming out of the wall and replaced it with the gold line. He looped the jump spool line to the gold line, securing it in place, and then took off to the right through the halocline layer. Visibility had gone from seeing nothing in the cenote, to getting a glimpse of perfect visibility just inside the cave, to blurry as we followed Germán through the halocline layer. The tunnel we were in was very shallow. We were only about eleven feet deep. The halocline was also at that depth, so it was impossible to not disturb it. Because we were so shallow and had to swim in the brackish water, visibility was distorted enough that we didn't have a clear view of the ceiling above us. Most of the time, I couldn't tell exactly how close to the ceiling I was. The floor had an alternating topography. It allowed us to get into the saltwater below just long enough to warm up a bit before forcing us back into the colder brackish layer above. The Richard Pyle video kept looping in my mind. I didn't see much of the cave during those first two hundred feet. It was too blurry. I maintained contact with the line as I couldn't see it either. I also repeated the phrase, "It feels like I'm swimming in piss," several times during that five-minute swim.

We managed to finally get under the halocline for a few minutes. The ceiling also sloped down, and I could finally see it just above my head in the clear visibility. It felt nice to be in the warmer saltwater layer for more than a few seconds. That didn't last long. As we continued beyond an intersection of lines where the other line headed to the right and almost back where we had come from, I noticed a hazy layer above my head. It was much like being out on a gloomy, overcast day. The layer was only a foot above me. I poked my finger into the haze and watched as the two waters mixed together giving the appearance of oil mixing with water. We were soon forced back up into the colder, brackish water and the hazy, blurry visibility. It was a bit of a gentle roller coaster ride moving through that tunnel. It was almost like one of those kiddie coaster rides that can be found at traveling fairs. I wondered if the entire section of cave in this area was like this. I hoped it would eventually get a little deeper so we could see the cave.

What I could see despite the diminished visibility was that the tunnel in this part of Cueva Quebrada was even larger than what we had seen in Cenote 1km. The walls were wider apart. The floor to ceiling height in some areas, where I could see the ceiling, was much taller. There were areas on both sides where the floor dropped a little deeper. In one section to the right, at least ten feet deeper than where we swam, I could see a silty floor and a couple of white lines tied to formations. Those lines disappeared into the darkness under the ceiling that dipped down to my right. The passages in this part of the cave seemed to be much larger.

I moved line arrows from the old line to the new line, reading names and initials as I went, trying to place the initials with the names of the explorers on the original map. I recognized a few initials. I saw a few of Germán's line arrows. He had been one of the original explorers in the cave. I felt honored to be able to do my first two dives in this cave with one of the original explorers.

After about thirty minutes, Germán stopped and secured the gold line to a formation rising up from the floor. He cut the line leaving some remaining on the large orange spool. He had mentioned that there were a couple of tunnels where he wanted to place the gold line in this part of the cave. The northbound tunnel, which we had just gone down, got about twelve hundred feet of line, and the other tunnel, which was westbound, would get the remaining line.

We turned around and repeated the process from earlier in the morning. I took up the rear and surveyed the gold line that we had just placed in the tunnel. We got back about two hundred feet from the opening when Germán stopped at a line intersection. This was the first one we had passed where the other line headed almost parallel to the line we had come in on. There was a white guideline tied onto the same formation as he had tied the gold line. The white line was heading into the hazy brackish water to the west.

Germán tied the end of the gold line that remained on the spool onto the gold line below us. He turned and headed to the left at about a one-hundred-and-twenty-degree angle from the gold line that he had placed there only an hour earlier. This had us heading somewhat back in the direction of the opening. The floor rose up forcing us through the halocline and into the brackish water where we remained for a couple of minutes. The line began to curve to the left, taking us away from the southwest trajectory we had been making. I could see the floor to our left gently sloping up but couldn't see where it met the ceiling through the haze. To the right was nothing but a dark, hazy void. I had no idea how large this room was. It felt big. Fortunately, the floor began sloping down about a hundred feet later and we found ourselves back in the clear saltwater layer. We continued through a light colored, rock tunnel with the walls only about twenty-five feet apart from each other. The ceiling was also visible as it was now deeper than the halocline layer. There was no more brackish water for the time being.

About eight minutes later, Germán let the last of the gold line off the spool, cut the existing line, and tied the end of the gold line to the free end of the line he had just cut. We turned around to exit. I surveyed the line back to the intersection, then continued my previous survey to the opening. This time I didn't dread surfacing as much as I had at Cenote 1km. This cenote wasn't nearly as rank as the other one. We could see the daylight streaming into the dark cave when we were still about fifty feet from it. It wasn't well defined because we were in brackish water, but it was much more visible than what we had experienced in Cenote 1km. We arrived at the cenote where all of the silt and debris we had stirred up at the beginning of the dive had settled back to the floor during our ninety minutes away.

We surfaced with another basketball sized ball of old cave line. More than half of the line we had removed ended up in that ball because there was still gold line on the spool when we swam back to the intersection. We knelt in the cenote slowly removing our tanks, talking about what we had just experienced. Cueva Quebrada was truly a special cave, and I was thrilled to have had the opportunity to dive it, not once, but twice. Not many people can claim that. After changing out of our suits and hauling all of our tanks and equipment back through the jungle to the road, Jen took some photographs of the three of us standing on the side of the highway with the balls and spools of old line from the two dives at our feet. These would be used in an article I was going to write for the quarterly journal printed by the training organization that donated the gold line. We hoped the thicker, more durable gold line would last much longer in the harsh environment of Cueva Quebrada.

Later that evening, I plotted the survey data I had obtained during our two dives. I finished entering the data into the mapping program, then I overlaid the map using the coordinates I had waymarked at the cenotes. That was when I saw it. That was when I realized why Ygor's team was so intent on pushing the leads to the left in Dos Coronas. The tunnels in Dos Coronas were very close to the tunnels we had just relined in Cenote S1. In fact, the closest tunnels were only two hundred feet apart. The lines in Dos Coronas that came closest to Cueva Quebrada were lines I had placed during the previous trip. They were lines in the Winter Wonderland/Swamp Land area.

I hadn't yet surveyed anything besides the gold line we had just placed in Cueva Quebrada. I had noticed the white lines on the floor ten feet below us to the west when we were relining the northbound tunnel. Those lines seemed to be heading toward Dos Coronas according to my maps. Ygor's team thought the tunnel in Dos Coronas was heading west and that the tunnels to the left would connect to the tunnels we were just diving in Cenote S1. What they didn't realize was that the main tunnel in Winter Wonderland was actually on a northeast bearing and all of the tunnels they were lining were heading northwest back toward the sea. They were heading away from Cueva Quebrada. Suddenly, my objective in exploring Dos Coronas changed. We were no longer just looking for unexplored virgin passage. We were looking for a connection to Cueva Quebrada!

19

A tannic lake and an underwater chupacabra

We had two days of diving left after our day of diving the cenotes with Germán. We used those days to explore Dos Coronas with one objective in mind. We wanted to find the tunnel connecting Dos Coronas to Cueva Quebrada. I studied the maps the evening before and determined the area I wanted to focus on. That was the area where the two caves came the closest to each other according to the overlays I had created. That had to be the area where they connected. We arrived at Playa dos Coronas the next morning eager to get into the cave and find the connection. The maps indicated that the Swamp Land was the closest area to the Cenote S1 tunnels that had been relined with gold line. We headed there and began searching for leads we might have missed. Previously, our focus had been to extend the line along the main tunnel and head east toward the center of the island. We thought Dos Coronas was its own independent cave, so we looked for the main artery to try to extend it as far as possible. We wanted to know where the cave led. The Winter Wonderland/Swamp Land tunnel was heading in an east and northeast direction, so we were always looking toward the east when we were looking for leads. That was a mistake.

While we did extend the line in that tunnel just over two thousand feet from the reef opening, the tunnel kept getting smaller and the leads we were finding were looping back around to tunnels we had already lined. We weren't getting much farther into the cave. That was a shame. If the tunnels did continue east, we would eventually run into the tunnel of Cueva Quebrada, that is if they were at the same depth. With information about a possible connection to Cueva Quebrada, we changed our focus and started looking to the northeast, where the closest passages we knew about in Cueva Quebrada were located. We quickly began finding small restrictions that led to larger tunnels. Those holes had been there all along. We just hadn't looked that way. We never noticed them because our focus had been to explore and push the ends of the lines of an independent cave. We had been pushing the big tunnels. Overlaying the two maps on Google Earth helped me to see the error in our ways.

During the next two days, we emptied the line from our explorer reels. We had missed that much unexplored cave by being so focused on the wrong thing. But how were we to know? I'm sure we would have eventually found the passages we were lining, but it would have been after several more dives. This discovery changed the way I explored Dos Coronas. It also had an impact on how I explored any cave. I no longer focused on one objective. I simply looked for leads using the maps I had as guides to where I wanted to maintain my focus. I looked everywhere, not just in the direction where the main tunnel was going (at least what I thought was the main tunnel). I would enter the cave with an objective in mind and an area targeted to spend as much time as our air supply allowed. This new technique led to many great discoveries over the years.

One of the discoveries I made in Dos Coronas was of a large room that I named the Stadium. The room measured about one hundred and twenty feet across, fifty feet wide, and forty feet from floor to ceiling around the perimeter. It wasn't the biggest room I had been in, but it was the biggest room in Dos Coronas and deserving of such a name. It was somewhat oval shaped and had two narrow access points from the main passage in the Swamp Land. The ceiling had a tannic layer of water about ten feet tall. This was Swamp Land on steroids. The tannic layer was more of a lake than a puddle. I ventured up into the tannic lake to find the ceiling. It was too dark and red to see the ceiling from the clear water below. There could have been a giant cenote above our heads and we wouldn't have known it. Sadly there wasn't. I searched the ceiling hoping to find a small opening. There wasn't one of those either. There was also no evidence of any jungle debris in the room. The depth at the ceiling was four feet though. We were right beneath the jungle floor. At some point, the earth above our heads could collapse and form a new cenote. With that thought I moved to the perimeter of the room.

I searched the outer areas of the Stadium and found some offshoot tunnels, but nothing that went very far. One such tunnel was only about sixty feet long. I generally wouldn't leave a guideline in such a short passage, but the tunnel led me deeper to a floor that was seventy-one feet deep. This was the deepest part of Dos Coronas by close to thirty feet, so it became significant. Prior to this finding, we hadn't come across anything deeper than forty-two feet.

At one point, David and I separated and went our own ways in the Stadium. The Stadium was big, and we spent forty-five minutes swimming just to get to it. We had to use our time and resources wisely to effectively explore it. We met back at one of the line intersections about twenty minutes after going our own ways. Neither of us had found any promising leads. We had managed to line the perimeter of the room, though. Unfortunately, it was time to begin our way out of the cave. We had one day left to search the Stadium area.

The next day we returned to Dos Coronas and headed straight for the Stadium. It was such a large room I knew I had missed something the day before. David and I planned to get there and split up again so we could divide and conquer. This time I decided to ascend into the

183

tannic water and follow the wall around the perimeter. Maybe there was a tunnel in the tannic layer that I hadn't been able to see the day before. I started in the middle and went in the direction away from where we had entered the room. It was dark and murky, and I could only see about five feet in front of me. I got to the far wall and continued following it to the left as it curved around. A few feet later the wall disappeared. Actually, there was an opening in the wall. A rather large opening that continued away from the Stadium. The only reason I knew I had swum out of the Stadium was because there was now a floor directly beneath me. The floor in the Stadium was anywhere from fifteen feet to thirty feet below the tannic layer. The tunnel I found was only about seven feet from floor to ceiling and the tannins permeated the entire area.

I followed this tunnel through the tannic water for fifty-five feet. I must admit it was a bit spooky swimming through blood red water with diminished visibility into unchartered territory. What normally should have taken me a minute to swim took me three or four as I slowly made my way farther into the tannic tunnel. The line I was deploying from my explorer reel was the only thing providing me with a reference to where I was. I could see the wall to my right, but I had no idea what was to my left or ahead. I kept expecting the boogey man to jump out at me. Or maybe a chupacabra.

I continued through the tunnel, wrapping my line around small protrusions from the floor every time I changed direction. There wasn't much in the way of formations in this area. The floor had more of a pocked surface to it with bits of it sticking up. About seventy feet after I had started into this tunnel I broke out of the tannic water into clear water. I hadn't changed depth. I simply swam out of the reddish-brown murkiness. It was very strange.

Usually, tannic water is located in shallow areas of the cave. It's caused by the tannins from the tree roots in the jungle floor above.

The ceiling was at the same depth as it had been. The only way I could explain the sudden clear water was that the tannic water must have been intruding from a porous area in the Stadium and there was so much of it that it penetrated into this offshoot tunnel. Either that or there weren't as many trees in the jungle above this area. I had a general idea of where I was from my overlay and Google Earth did show the jungle above me to be fairly thick. My first theory had to be the correct one.

Either way, I was back in clear water. What was even more remarkable was that the cave passage I was in looked a lot like the cave passage I had seen in the S1 section of Cueva Quebrada. Granted, at this time I had only done one dive there, but I had seen enough to recognize the similarity in features. I knew I had found the connection between the two caves! Unfortunately, I didn't have enough air in my tanks to continue exploring this new area. It was time to turn and start heading back. The really bad news was that this was the last dive of this trip. The next day we were taking a surface day to dry our equipment and wetsuits and then we were flying out the day after that. Once again, I found myself with a big discovery on our last day.

During the last dives of the previous two trips, I made big discoveries in Dos Coronas. It gave me something to look forward to on the next trip, but the anticipation of returning was almost too much to bear. Finding what I thought was the connection between Dos Coronas and Cueva Quebrada was an even bigger discovery. I had only known about the possibility of a connection for a couple of days, but it was already consuming me. Just the thought of this new area being here, so close to Cueva Quebrada, and me not being here to explore it was already too much to bear. Being back home in Florida, even with my exploration projects there, was going to bother me! There was nothing I could do that day, though. It was time to turn and head back out. I was more than two thousand feet from the entrance, and I had to survey the line I had just placed. We also had to retrieve the safety scuba tanks we had placed in the cave on the first dive of the trip.

With my shoulders slumped, mixed spirits over the excitement of the discovery, and the realization that I wouldn't be able to do anything with it for some time, I turned and started to survey my line as I headed back into the tannic tunnel. About a minute after entering the blood-red water I saw a chupacabra coming toward me. It had two small, bright red eyes that stared directly at me. They were slowly moving toward me. I thought, that's it, the chupacabra we had heard the day before found its way into the cave and was coming for me. I didn't know chupacabra could swim or even hold their breath, but here it was only thirty feet away. The chupacabra had revealed itself as the grim reaper and had finally shown its face. It knew I was close to connecting the two caves and the reaper wasn't going to let that happen. This secret portal would remain hidden for all of eternity.

Thirty seconds later, I recognized the form of a diver behind those two red eyes. It was David. He had a small light on each side of his mask, and he had them both turned on. The lights appeared red in the tannic water, and from a distance, they looked like evil chupacabra/grim reaper eyes. Relieved that it was David, we regrouped, and I finished surveying the line I had just put in. We then made our way out of the cave, collecting our safety tanks, sad that this was the last dive of the trip. When we surfaced, I excitedly told David about the tunnel I had found that looked like the passages in Cueva Quebrada. He hadn't gone far enough to break out of the tannic tunnel into the clear water, so he hadn't seen the distinct similarities. I went on and on about this new area, excited about the discovery. Then an idea came to me.

"Do you want to come back in a month?" I asked David.

"Sure, let's do it!" He responded with a huge smile on his face without pausing to think about it.

We moved toward shore and Jen helped us get our tanks out of the water. I told her about my discovery and our plans to return in a month. Fortunately, she didn't dissent. She had fallen in love with Cozumel and was more than happy to return so soon. We packed up our dive equipment, loaded it into the car, and headed for lunch. We didn't waste a lot of time as we were anxious to get back to the rental house so we could check on flights and the availability of the rental house as well as work schedules. It would be a short trip, but we could get three days of diving in. And if we hit it hard, we could do two dives each day. Jen always accompanied me on these trips and lovingly served as our shore support. She didn't mind and she knew how much this exploration meant to me.

Jen is also a cave diver, but she doesn't dive small caves. She prefers to visit the caves as a tourist. Exploration isn't her thing. She's been diving in the caves of Cozumel, but mostly she spends her time holding down a lounge chair at one of the beach clubs while we're off exploring the caves beneath the jungle. We're both happy with the arrangement.

We returned to the house and I sent off an email to the owner of the house where we were staying. He had a unit available in four weeks. We reserved it and a rental car after making sure there were flights available. We paid a premium for the airfare, but we were positive we would be able to connect the two caves when we returned and that would make it worth the expense. With all the plans and reservations taken care of, leaving the island wasn't going to be so bad. We would be connecting the crowns four weeks later.

20

Connection? Or disappointment?

We returned to Cozumel exactly one month after we had arrived on the previous trip. We were certain we were going to connect Dos Coronas to Cueva Quebrada. Cueva Quebrada was originally explored in the late 1980s and early 1990s. The only existing map of the cave claimed it had twenty-nine thousand feet of lined passage. No one had done any recent exploration there until we started poking around. Very few people had even been diving in Cueva Quebrada. The logistics didn't make it very appealing to most cave divers. I was certain we would eventually find unmapped passages in Cueva Quebrada.

We learned on a subsequent trip that there was a couple, Steve and Judy Ormeroid, who were both part of the original exploration team. They had begun to explore Cueva Quebrada again. This was a few years after I first started diving there. After running into each other on the trail, we met at a taqueria to discuss our respective exploration projects and coordinate our efforts. Neither of us wanted to interfere with the other's efforts. Steve and Judy were concentrating on a different section of the cave than we were, so we didn't have to worry about stepping on each other's toes. Their efforts resulted in almost five thousand feet of line being placed in previously unexplored cave passages, as well as a new cenote that they named Sac Be. Surprisingly, the passages they had pushed didn't require sidemount configuration. They had simply been overlooked by the original team. More on that will come later in this series.

I believe Steve and Judy have since retired from cave diving. It's been a few years since I've seen them in Cozumel. The last time I was in contact with them they had taken a break from their exploration. They were already pushing seventy when we met them and were still hauling scuba tanks and dive equipment into the jungle at that time.

David and I arrived in Cozumel ready to go. We checked into our rental house and headed to the Thirsty Cougar for some nachos and frozen margaritas. This was our fifth trip to Cozumel and the Cougar had established itself as a tradition on the day of arrival. With the exception of one trip that I've organized, we've eaten at the Cougar at the beginning of every trip. The one time we didn't was because they were closed for renovations. I'm not superstitious, but I was a little concerned that breaking tradition might affect our exploration that week. Thankfully it didn't.

After filling our bellies and enjoying the warm breeze blowing in from the sea, we headed to the fill station to place our order for scuba tanks for the next morning. It was only two of us, but we had two safety tanks that would be placed in the cave during the first dive and removed during the last dive. We carried four additional tanks each during our dives. I also got a couple of extra tanks in case there were any issues with valves leaking.

The scuba tanks in Cozumel are abused. Cozumel is one of the prime destinations in the world for scuba diving. Thousands of scuba divers are there every day during the busy season. I'd venture to guess that there are more than a million scuba divers on the island each year. So the scuba tanks see a lot of action. The tanks are moved around the fill station, loaded on trucks, delivered to the various dive boats at the marina, jostled around the boats, dropped by divers, not rinsed properly allowing saltwater buildup. You get the picture. The fill station does the best it can considering the conditions the tanks are exposed to. Only so much could be done. It was more common than not that we would find leaks in the valves.

The scuba tanks were fine for diving on the reef where there was unimpeded access to the surface. The leaks were small, and the loss of air was minimal. But even a small leak was unacceptable when you had a hard ceiling above your head and had to swim a couple thousand feet before you could surface. The air in those tanks allowed us to breathe and stay underwater. If it leaked out, we wouldn't be able to breathe it. Small leaks could also turn into big leaks. We were vigilant to eliminate, or at least reduce, the amount of leaks that we found. After a couple of years of visiting the island, I became good at field repairing scuba tank valves. Occasionally, I would encounter a valve that couldn't be fixed. By occasionally, I mean daily. Those tanks were set aside. That's why we always ordered two to three additional tanks each day.

With the tanks ordered, we set out to organize our equipment. Excitement didn't describe the feeling David and I had over this trip. Even though we had been awake since two in the morning, sleep was the farthest thing from our minds. We would have gone diving that first day if we didn't think it would be too risky because we weren't fully rested. We had to maintain some sensibility. Besides, Jen wouldn't have allowed it. We resigned ourselves to having to wait eighteen more hours and kept our minds occupied by preparing equipment and looking over the maps.

This would be the culmination of all of our exploration in Dos Coronas. We only discovered the possibility of a connection between Dos Coronas and Cueva Quebrada a month earlier, but we knew we were going to connect them during this trip. We had put a lot of work into exploring Dos Coronas. I was very familiar with that cave. It was going to happen. Making the connection also meant adding another eighty-three hundred feet of passage to Cueva Quebrada, bringing the total to more than thirty-seven thousand feet. This would be an exciting discovery. It would make Cueva Quebrada the fifteenth longest underwater cave in Mexico.

Early the next morning, we ate a quick breakfast, picked up the tanks, and headed to the dive site. We only had three days of diving and we had two dives per day planned, each lasting two-and-a-half to three-hours. We couldn't waste any time. While we were hoping we would find the connection the very first dive, we weren't leaving anything to chance. Jen came along and waited on the beach while we were in the cave. About an hour and a half after we submerged, she took off to get lunch for us to eat during our surface interval. This allowed us to expedite things and get back into the water quickly. Fortunately, the caves were shallow, the deepest being about thirty-five feet, except for that one area that was seventy-one feet deep, so we didn't need much time on the surface. Just enough to swap out tanks and eat a couple of slices of pizza or a sandwich.

Our first dive in Dos Coronas lasted just over two hours. We left our stage tanks in their usual location on the shelf before Hades. We continued in with safety tanks and placed them about fifteen hundred feet in from the entrance. We still had some air left in our sidemount tanks and continued to the Stadium to take a quick look around. I immediately headed to the tannic tunnel I had found a month earlier. I had named the area beyond it Quebradita, or little Quebrada, because it looked so much like the cave passages I had seen in Cueva Quebrada. Once at the end of my line, I secured the line from my explorer reel and started farther into the tunnel. Unfortunately, I only got to put a few hundred feet of line in during that dive. Because of the safety tanks, we only used one stage tank and that shortened the dive. I checked my tank pressure gauges and noticed I had breathed them down to turn pressure. I reluctantly tied the line onto a formation, cut it, and turned to exit. I surveyed the new line I had just placed in the tunnel.

We told Jen we would be on the dive for about two and a half hours. She was waiting on the rocky beach for us with a couple of hot pizzas and some cold drinks. We surfaced and ravenously ate and rehydrated while we swapped out the bands and regulators from the used scuba tanks to the full ones she had waiting for us in the rental van. Less than an hour later, with full bellies and tanks, we headed back into the turquoise-colored sea and swam toward the entrance to Dos Coronas. This time we had two usable stage tanks, ready to continue our search for the connection.

This was the hardest part of the dives. At a normal swimming pace of fifty to sixty feet per minute, it took us about forty-five minutes to get to the Stadium. That was a long time spent just traveling each dive. Because we had the additional stage tank, we would have about thirty to forty minutes of exploration time before we had to turn around and head back. We arrived at the end of the line I had placed a couple of hours earlier and I tied onto it. David took off to explore another area while I was laying line in this area. Divide and conquer became our new motto. I started into the tunnel, pushing it until I arrived at a location where I couldn't go any farther. It walled out.

We searched high and low for the connection. We placed a lot of additional line in the cave, but none of it led to Cueva Quebrada. Everywhere we went, the cave pinched down or walled out. I was beginning to feel like Juan Ponce de Leon in his search for the Fountain of Youth. I had been so certain I was going to find the connection between Dos Coronas and Cueva Quebrada the first day back on Cozumel that to say I was disappointed was an understatement. I wasn't ready to give up though.

I surveyed the line I had placed on that dive back to where I had started, looking for additional leads as I went. Eventually I reached my turn pressure again and had to start making my way out. David and I had met up with each other by this point. We exited about two and a half hours after we had started the dive. That two-and-a-half hour dive resulted in thirty to forty minutes of exploration. It would have been nice to be able to spend more time back there, but that meant either bringing more tanks or using rebreathers. We were already pushing the limits of the restrictions with the four tanks we were bringing through them. A fifth tank would have not only slowed us down at the restrictions, but it would have also slowed down our swimming pace. So why didn't we just use rebreathers?

21

Was it time to start using rebreathers?

Rebreathers were all the rage at the time I was writing this book. Everyone seemed to be buying a rebreather. Sidemount rebreathers were the most popular. Purchasing a rebreather and paying for the training necessary to get certified on it often required upwards of $10,000. There might even be some travel involved to find an instructor that taught on a particular brand and model. Rebreather prices began in the $5,000 range. The average price was $8-10,000. Training ran anywhere from $1,200 to $2,000. That was just for the first module. Additional modules of training were priced equally as expensive. Then there were the consumables, travel costs, etc. Once that was all done, the newly certified rebreather diver did dives that could much more easily be done using plain old scuba tanks.

There are those who argue against this logic. They argue that rebreathers give you all the time in the world to sort through issues on a dive and get safely back to the surface. Rebreathers allow you to stay underwater almost indefinitely. Rebreathers are safer because of the additional time it buys for the rebreather diver. Those are valid arguments, but they neglect one important factor. They fail to consider that the issues that most commonly come up during a rebreather dive wouldn't be issues if the diver wasn't using a rebreather.

A rebreather is actually a simple device. The air you breathe when diving a rebreather remains inside of a closed-circuit loop. That air is breathed over and over (rebreathed) throughout the duration of the dive. There are a couple of scuba tanks, one with oxygen and the other with air or helium and air, that replenish the air in the loop when necessary. This is usually done so the oxygen content remains at a life-sustaining level. The amount of oxygen and air required to make these adjustments is very small. The tanks are typically less than a tenth the volume of the scuba tanks normally used during a dive.

When all goes well, a rebreather diver can remain submerged much longer than if diving only with scuba tanks, or what we call open circuit. A diver can remain underwater for up to four hours using a rebreather and two small tanks while it takes an open circuit diver many more tanks, depending on the depth of the dive, to remain in the water for that amount of time. It seemed like it would make sense to use rebreathers for the diving we were doing in the Cozumel caves. Employing rebreathers should allow us to go as far back into the cave as we wanted without having to worry about how much air we had left in our tanks. A small six cubic foot tank would last for several hours when used with a rebreather.

The problem was that dives must be planned as if something will go wrong so if it does, we are prepared to handle the issues that arise. I admit that rebreathers can be very efficient and allow divers to stay underwater for much longer than is possible breathing from open circuit scuba tanks alone. I say alone because scuba tanks are still needed with rebreathers, both for the gases that are necessary to allow the rebreather to function properly and for bailout tanks in case the rebreather or the diver malfunctions. Yep, divers can malfunction as well.

There are a few considerations to keep in mind with rebreathers. First, the absorbent that allows the rebreather to do its job isn't infinite. As exhaled air passes through the rebreather circuit, the absorbent gets used up and eventually will no longer scrub carbon dioxide out of the air. Most rebreather scrubbers are only rated for about four hours before the efficiency of the absorbent is diminished below acceptable standards. There are divers that push their rebreathers beyond the limits. Some of them push them more than double the recommended time. They are taking a huge risk when they do that.

In our dives in Dos Coronas and Cueva Quebrada, we were already doing three-hour long dives. One additional scuba tank would allow us to stay underwater for four hours, and much more safely than if we were using rebreathers. So the $10,000 price tag didn't make sense. Consider the other argument that rebreathers allow divers to stay underwater longer so any problems that are encountered can be dealt without having to have the immediate concern of breathing through all of the air in the scuba tanks. The issue with this is that the problems which occur are usually related to the rebreather itself. One such issue is a carbon dioxide hit.

A carbon dioxide hit can result from a few different causes. The diver can be working too hard and breathing faster than the scrubber can handle. This is one of the diver malfunctions I referred to earlier. The air circulating around the rebreather loop isn't being properly scrubbed of the carbon dioxide in the exhaled air. A higher level of carbon dioxide is being inhaled and that will eventually cause the diver to lose consciousness if not addressed soon enough.

Another issue that can cause a carbon dioxide hit is channeling. This is when the exhaled air finds channels through the absorbent where it can pass through the granules with less resistance and doesn't spend enough time in the scrubber to have the carbon dioxide removed as efficiently. While the risk of channeling can be minimized by properly packing the absorbent into the canister, it's still a possibility.

A third issue that can cause a carbon dioxide hit occurs when the mushroom valve in the rebreather loop gets torn or folded over. The mushroom valve functions as a check valve ensuring the air in the rebreather loop only moves in one direction. If the mushroom valve is compromised, the air is no longer prevented from moving in the opposite direction. In this situation, the same air in the rebreather is being breathed over and over, much like breathing into a paper bag. That air isn't being scrubbed of carbon dioxide.

Regardless of the cause, the result is the same. Carbon dioxide hits occur when the body gets too much of this exhaled gas. Respirations are driven by carbon dioxide. When carbon dioxide levels are high, the body attempts to release the excess by increasing the respiratory rate. The respiratory rate can be increased enough that breathing through a rebreather will only worsen the condition because the air moving through the scrubber doesn't have sufficient exposure to the absorbent to be scrubbed of the carbon dioxide. The only way to counteract this is to breathe from an open circuit scuba tank. Breathing from a rebreather loop only exacerbates the issue. When a person takes a carbon dioxide hit, the respiratory rate doesn't just increase by ten or twenty percent. It increases four- or five-fold or more. That's four to five hundred percent. At that point, breathing from the rebreather is no longer an option. Instead of taking twelve breaths a minute, that person must take fifty to sixty breaths a minute. The rebreather can't keep up with the high respiratory rate and will not function properly. The diver must bailout to open circuit and breathe from a regulator connected directly to a scuba tank.

Here's where it gets interesting, or at least as interesting as it can get. Scuba tanks hold a finite amount of air. We plan our dives according to this and plan on turning and heading back out with at least two-thirds of our air supply left in our tanks. That allows us one third for exiting and one third for emergencies. Planning air management with rebreathers is a little more difficult, especially inside of a cave. If you have direct access to the surface, you simply ascend. In a cave, there must be enough air in the bailout scuba tanks to exit the cave from the farthest penetration planned so you can get to the surface. That means if the planned penetration is three thousand feet there must be enough air to swim out from three thousand feet inside of the cave. At fifty feet per minute, that's one hour of swimming, as long as we have no issues during that swim. Based on the rule of thirds, which is what we live by in cave diving, one and a half times the amount of air required to swim that distance must be available. The depth of the cave tunnels also has to be accounted for. If it takes us two hours to breathe a full tank empty on the surface. At thirty-three feet of depth, it would take only one hour to breathe through that same tank. The change in atmospheric pressure means more air is necessary in order to fill the lungs the same amount. This is valid at a normal breathing rate.

If a carbon dioxide hit occurs while using a rebreather and the breathing rate increases by four times, that hour of air at thirty-three feet of depth becomes fifteen minutes of air. Four full scuba tanks would be required just to get back out to the surface after a carbon dioxide hit at maximum penetration. Using the rule of thirds, that means six tanks are required. That's six scuba tanks in addition to the tanks used for diluent and oxygen. That brings the total to eight tanks necessary just to swim an hour into a cave thirty-three feet deep, which is the average depth of Dos Coronas. An hour and a half penetration, the penetration we were making, would require nine bailout tanks. Woah! We were already swimming an hour and a half before turning to the exit and we only needed four tanks to do that! Why would we use rebreathers and have to have seven additional tanks?

There are some that will argue that so many bailout tanks aren't needed. They argue that the possibility of having a carbon dioxide hit is very small and the possibility of having it at maximum penetration is even smaller. I'll give them that. But there's still a possibility of it happening. If it does happen, I want to be able to survive it no matter where I am in the cave. I'm not increasing my risk simply because the possibility of something happening is small.

Another issue with using rebreathers on these dives involved the larger physical profile that we would have. We were already having to unclip two scuba tanks to get through the first three restrictions we encountered. We would stage the first tank we breathed from several hundred feet in and then go through another restriction where we still had to unclip two of the three scuba tanks we had left. We could have brought bailout tanks into the cave on the first day and staged them in the passage. If we were there for several weeks that would make sense. But we weren't there for several weeks. Our shortest trip involved three days of diving and our longest one ten days. We didn't want to waste a day on each end to set up the bailout tanks and remove the bailout tanks, especially on the three-day trip!

Carbon dioxide hits also take a long time to recover from. Bailing out to open circuit scuba tanks won't resolve the issue and restore normal breathing within a few minutes. That's not the way it works physiologically. Once your body has increased its respiratory rate because of too much carbon dioxide, it takes hours to recover from and decrease the demand for air. The bailout scuba tanks will be empty long before breathing normalizes. I've treated patients in the intensive care unit on ventilators with high concentrations of carbon dioxide in their blood. Even under those conditions, with the assistance of a computerized mechanical ventilator, it took hours, sometimes days, to treat. That was in conjunction with administering intravenous medications to assist the transition. Granted, an intensive care patient is typically not healthy, but neither is a rebreather diver who just took a carbon dioxide hit. That diver will breathe through all of the air in the bailout tanks before getting back to the surface. That leaves only one outcome.

I almost lost a close friend to a carbon dioxide hit years ago due to a folded over mushroom valve. He wasn't in a cave, but he did have a decompression obligation that kept him from ascending directly to the surface without risking decompression illness. Decompression illness is more desirable than drowning, but it can lead to paralysis or death. Fortunately, my friend didn't have to make that decision. He encountered another diver on the ascent line just as he was taking his last breaths from his bailout tank. The diver had just finished his decompression obligation and fortunately understood my friend was in trouble. He left him his bailout tanks to complete his decompression obligation. My friend was able to make it to the surface a bit out of breath but uninjured. It took him another hour before his respiratory rate returned to normal. If he had been in a cave, he would have breathed through all of his air long before he was back at the surface.

After careful analysis, David and I decided rebreathers simply weren't practical for the dives we were doing. They would only complicate the logistics and increase the risk. We continued to do our dives using regular old scuba tanks. It was simpler and safer.

22

Stuck in a virgin (tunnel) in Cueva Quebrada

After being unable to find the connection during our two dives in Dos Coronas that first day, I decided we should go back to Cueva Quebrada and search from that end. We had only been in Cueva Quebrada through Cenote S1 once previously. The tunnels we were finding in Dos Coronas were not leading us to anything promising. The farther we went, the less they resembled Cueva Quebrada. Maybe we would have better luck exploring from the other side. Maybe we just needed a fresh perspective.

We headed to the fill station and swapped out tanks. Because we were having to haul the tanks through the jungle path, we only had one dive planned in Cueva Quebrada. We were crazy, but not crazy enough to do two dives that day! It was a lot of work hauling the tanks and equipment through the jungle while narrowly escaping the attack of a rabid chupacabra!

Back at the house, we pulled the tanks out of the rental car and tested the valves for leaks. We were able to park close enough at Dos Coronas that we didn't mind carrying the scuba tanks to the water to test them. We didn't have that luxury at the jungle cenotes. We didn't want to carry eight tanks several hundred feet through a narrow path and wait to test them for leaks in the cenote only to have to carry the leaky valved tanks back to the car to swap them out with the extra ones I had gotten.

A couple of the tanks leaked, and I did a quick field repair to stop one from leaking air. The other tank was not repairable and was set aside. With the tanks tested, I settled in to plot the survey data we had obtained during our two dives earlier in the day. We had added more than one thousand feet of line to the cave. The tunnels we found were heading toward Cueva Quebrada. We had to be missing something.

The next morning we arrived at the Cenote S1 trailhead and quickly unloaded the tanks along with the rest of the dive equipment, setting everything on the path just inside the edge of the jungle. Because we had multiple trips in and out of the jungle carrying everything, I told Jen to give us four hours before returning to pick us up. This was before any of the mobile phone providers offered free international plans and charged exorbitant fees just to send and receive text messages. I'm glad those days are over. Although, looking back at it now, I probably should have paid the extra fees and not been so stingy. David and I carried our equipment through the jungle. We heard our chupacabra rustling around in the brush a couple of times but didn't get any glimpses of it this time. We kept an eye out just in case. It took us half an hour to get all of the equipment to the clearing next to the cenote and another half an hour to set it up and get in the water. We descended and made our first unguided trip into Cueva Quebrada. Based on the map overlays, the tunnel to the west looked like the best option. It would bring us the closest to the area we had been exploring in Dos Coronas. We headed that way and focused our efforts on the south wall.

There were so many potential leads. We spent two and a half hours poking our heads into each one. Most of them didn't pan out. They were nothing but short runs into dead-ends. There were a couple of tunnels that seemed promising. Both were small and low. The first one didn't get as small. I put about six hundred feet of line in it before coming to a dead-end with no viable leads. It was unlike Dos Coronas where we would end up at the end of a tunnel and find several cracks and holes. The end of this passage was surrounded by smooth walls There was no way I had missed a lead there.

The second tunnel I found did a few things that made me think it would be where I found the connection. It gently sloped down away from the main tunnel, bringing us from the eighteen feet of depth we had in the main tunnel to twenty-six feet of depth at the end. It was also located between the other tunnel I had just found and lined and Dos Coronas, putting us about forty or fifty feet closer. It wasn't just curved smooth walls. There were possible leads in this tunnel. The floor continued to slope down to the right along with the ceiling The crack between them was filled with sand. I wondered if that could be the connection. Nothing else jumped out at me.

The one issue with this tunnel was a section about a third of the way in that we had to pass through. It was a low, nasty section with less than a foot of clearance from floor to ceiling and nubs jutting out from the top and bottom of the passage. There wasn't a layer of sediment on the floor, but there was a dusting of it. Visibility was quickly diminished. There was no way to get through this section without making contact with both floor and ceiling. It was heading in the right direction, and it appeared to open up about forty feet later. If it weren't for those two things, I probably wouldn't have gone into it. However, because I saw a potential for going passage beyond it, I had to have a look. David followed. I wondered if he would have followed if he had perfect visibility going into the passage.

We both made it through, although with some difficulty. It wasn't a straight shot through. There was some backing up and repositioning required before I was able to find the right path through the nubs. On the way back, I tried to get David to exit first, but he insisted I lead the way. Maybe he didn't want to see how small it was in there. I couldn't blame him. I was also not all that disappointed to be leading.

Remember that rule about the larger diver leads on the way in and follows on the way out? I proceeded into the low area and as I got about halfway through, I came across a jump spool. It was one of mine. Apparently, it had come loose from my harness when I went through the restriction the first time. We made it to the end and began our way back to the cenote.

Three hours after we had started the dive, we surfaced. We had left nine hundred and two feet of new line in the tunnels we had found, but we hadn't encountered anything that screamed to me that it was the connection. I was still pleased with the results. It was a good feeling to find unexplored virgin cave passage in Cueva Quebrada. There had to be more. In addition to that, something about that twenty-six-foot-deep tunnel kept gnawing at me. I felt we were onto something in that area.

We stripped off our equipment and the tops of our wetsuits while drinking water and discussing what we had found, or rather, hadn't found. This trip wasn't turning out the way I had hoped it would. We were finding virgin cave and adding line, but we weren't doing what we thought we were going to do. We weren't connecting Dos Coronas to Cueva Quebrada. We hauled our tanks and gear back to the edge of the jungle near the road. I had told Jen not to park near the trailhead. We would watch for her and flag her down. We didn't feel comfortable with her waiting for us alone on the side of the road. She didn't speak Spanish and if one of the local cops stopped, she wouldn't be able to explain why she was parked there.

As I got to the edge, I looked through the branches at the passing traffic and saw Jen drive by. I hurried out and tried to wave her down. She didn't see me. I knew she would be driving around to the coastal road and coming back. At that time, the coastal road allowed two-way traffic. I waited just inside the jungle's edge and tried to get her attention when she came back around. I wasn't fast enough. I would have called her and sucked up the roaming charges, but I knew she had her phone on airplane mode.

We waited just inside the tree line and tried to time her travel around the loop. We didn't want to stand on the shoulder of the road and draw attention to ourselves, so we tried to stay hidden until we knew she was coming. My command of the Spanish language had improved since that first trip two years earlier, but I wasn't sure I could adequately explain to the Mexican police what two ragged looking men were doing in the jungle. We decided to play it safe and not invite trouble, even if we weren't doing anything wrong. Jen drove by two more times without seeing us. Finally, David had the idea of placing one of our water bottles on the shoulder of the road. Maybe she would notice it. Fortunately, the water bottle worked. We had frozen the water, and the bottle still had some ice in it. Jen noticed the condensation on the plastic. Thankfully she was paying attention! She knew we were there and sending her a signal. She pulled over and parked in front of the trailhead.

We quickly loaded the tanks and our equipment into the van. We were ready to get some food in our bellies and I was ready to plot the data I had collected during that dive. In addition to the survey data from the nine hundred feet of passage I had found, I also surveyed some additional line that had been in the cave. I had almost twenty-one hundred feet of line surveyed. That brought my total survey data for Cueva Quebrada to five thousand feet, forty-one hundred feet of that from existing line. Only twenty-four thousand and nine hundred feet to go to have the entire cave surveyed.

The next day we returned to Dos Coronas. It was our third and final day. The pressure was on. We had to find the connection that day. If we didn't, it would be at least four months, maybe longer, before we could return to the island to continue looking for it. I had a good feeling about the dives planned for the day. We were heading back to the Quebradita section to poke around some more. I was certain I had missed something back there.

We entered the water and waved goodbye to Jen. She was going to hang out on the beach, enjoying the sun, and cooling off in the water while we were diving. In about two hours, she would take off to go get lunch and cold drinks for all of us. I was so thankful that she was not only there with me, but that she was so supportive of our efforts. Not only in a manner of supporting my endeavors, but also assisting with logistics. There was no way we would have been able to do two dives each day in Dos Coronas and accomplish what we were doing without her.

We made our way back through the cave, moving quickly through the restrictions, the low bedding plane with the old turtle remains, to the shelf where we removed and left our first stage tanks. We had enough air in our tanks to keep them with us a little longer, but the upcoming restrictions were a bit tight for four tanks, and the effort required to bring those tanks with us wasn't worth it. It was also comforting knowing we had a little extra air in the tanks waiting for us on the way out. We bumped our way through the baffles of the Devil's Throat, trying to be careful and disturb the silt as little as possible, but knowing it was an attempt at futility. The tunnel was small and any movement through it resulted in dust flying everywhere. I popped out at the end of the Throat and moved several feet into Winter Wonderland.

Back in Wonderland, I turned around and watched David's light through the hazy visibility as he emerged from the Throat. Once in Winter Wonderland, he secured his stage tank onto his harness, and we continued our way farther into the cave. About eight hundred feet later we came across the safety tanks we had placed in the cave two days earlier. I opened the valves briefly and checked the pressure gauges. The tanks had 3000 psi of air in them. I closed the valves and

ROB NETO

made sure the tanks were still secured to the line. We moved on, eager to get back to the Quebradita section.

It was a long swim. It would have been nice to have dive propulsion vehicles, commonly referred to as scooters, to propel us through the tunnels faster and get us to our intended destination sooner. Scooters are long watertight tubes that hold motors and batteries and pull the diver through the water. Unfortunately, we didn't have any scooters in Cozumel and didn't know how we would be able to get any there. It was difficult enough traveling with all of the scuba equipment we had to bring down to cave dive. My scooter in Florida also used a rather large lithium battery that was prohibited on airplanes.

Even if we could get scooters onto the island, Dos Coronas wasn't the best cave to use them in. It was challenging enough to get through the restrictions with multiple stage tanks. We would probably lose the time gained by using the scooters to the time lost having to maneuver them in front of us along with our stage tanks through the restrictions. So we continued at the slower swimming pace, trying to breathe less so we'd have more time to explore.

We arrived at Swamp Land, the area with the tannic ponds on the ceiling, and continued the slow swim. We passed our friendly neighborhood spiny lobster along the way. It was still in the same area and came out to greet us almost every time we passed through. We reached our usual staging area where we left the stage tanks we were breathing from. I checked the gauge on my stage tank, and it was right at turn pressure. Time to switch to one of the sidemount tanks and leave the stage tank clipped to the line. With our stage tanks removed and the valves closed to prevent an accidental loss of air while they were unattended, we continued our journey deeper beneath the jungle.

We had crossed under the rocky shore and the coastal road long before we made it to the first staging area, right before the cenote and the Devil's Throat. At this point, we were pretty far into the jungle that separated the coastal road and the main highway on Cozumel. For some reason, the rainwater didn't seep through the ground into Winter Wonderland. This didn't happen until we were about fifteen hundred feet in from the reef entrance. It was a cool effect to see the dark reddish-brown clouds of fresh tannic water suddenly appear above our heads. I looked around the cave again hoping to see signs of a cenote nearby. This was usually indicated by the presence of leaves or branches. Sadly, I saw neither. The tannic water was seeping in from the jungle floor through the stone layer overhead. We would have to keep doing this swim if we were going to continue to explore the area around the Stadium.

We finally made it to the to the location where we had to leave the guideline we were on and go through an offshoot tunnel to get to the Stadium room. I left my jump spool in place two days earlier, knowing we would be back on the last day. I planned on retrieving it during the last dive. I doubted anyone else would be diving this cave, especially this far back. We were more than two thousand feet from the reef opening. Just in case, I always removed the jump spools at the end of the trips because I didn't want to make it easy for anyone to find the area we thought might connect to Cueva Quebrada.

We marked the jump line with our non-directional markers and continued through the fissure crack that led to the Stadium. Rather than going back toward Quebradita, there was another area, on the other side of the room, that I wanted to check out. That side didn't hold the resemblance that Quebradita did to Quebrada, but it was still heading toward Quebrada, and I had come up empty in the other area. It was a smaller tunnel, so during our dive briefing David and I planned a separation. He went to look elsewhere while I swam toward the crack I had seen two days earlier.

I found the marker I had left on the line, indicating where the crack I wanted to explore was, and secured the end of the line from my explorer reel to it. I swam about ten feet and wrapped the line around a protrusion so it wouldn't place tension on the line in the tunnel I had just come from. I looked into the crack. It appeared a little smaller than I had remembered, but it was still big enough for me to pass through. I slowly entered the crack, careful to minimize contact with the cave. The walls were almost black and uneven and had lots of protrusions from floor to ceiling. It held a faint resemblance to the Lava Tube tunnel. The floor and ceiling had lots of protrusions as well. It was more of a narrow tube than a crack. I slowly made my way through, pushing farther into the tube as I spooled out line from my explorer reel. The tunnel continued to get smaller and tighter until I could no longer continue to move forward. I had penetrated it about two hundred feet.

With this ending up being another bust, I wrapped the line a few times around a fist size protrusion in front of me and cut it. I didn't bother leaving a loop on the end. I could clearly see there were no leads at the end of this tunnel. I tied the end back on itself, placing one of my directional markers at the end of the line to mark it as my find. I formed a loop on the end of the line coming from my explorer reel and tied a knot in it then reeled the excess back onto the reel and secured it in place. Once the reel was stowed, I pulled out my wetnotes. This didn't end up connecting to Cueva Quebrada, but it was at least a couple of hundred feet long. I wanted to get it surveyed for the map, mainly so I would know it had already been explored. I wrote down the heading and depth and tried to turn around. The crack was too small for that to happen. That was fine. I had been in smaller. I could back up. Visions of the Crack of Death flashed in my mind.

Fortunately, there wasn't any sediment in this tunnel, so the visibility wasn't disturbed. I slowly backed my way up to where I had secured the line at the last corner, counting knots as I went. I wrote down the distance between stations and took the next depth and heading readings. The fissure was still too small to allow me to turn around, so I continued to move backwards while counting knots, occasionally getting A-framed by my sidemount tanks and having to adjust my position to be able to keep moving. I had more flashbacks of my second dive around the Dos Coronas reef. I quickly pushed them aside. I didn't need those kinds of negative thoughts more than two thousand feet inside of a cave.

Eventually I reached a wide area of the crack and decided to try turning around again. I pulled my knees into my chest as I attempted to rotate my body around so I could be facing out toward the direction from where I had come. I was able to rotate myself about a third of the way before I got stuck. My legs and fins were jammed beneath me, my head cocked to one side by the wall. I tried to wiggle around to continue rotating, but I couldn't move. I tried to rotate back the other way figuring I would continue to back out until I reached a larger area. I couldn't turn that way either. I had gotten myself into a jam...literally.

23

A Charley Horse and the Horse Trails

I managed to get myself free from that fissure crack that I had found along the perimeter of the Stadium. It took some doing. I had to contort my body as well as pull my fins off of my feet. The added length of the fin beyond my toes wasn't helping matters. One of the fin tips got stuck in the rocks as I was trying to rotate my feet around. With the fin trapped in a small crack, I wasn't able to move the foot that was wearing it. Once I pulled my fins off, I completed rotating my legs around and finally stretched out my body. I accomplished that just in time! I was on the verge of getting a charley horse in my right leg from being in that contorted position. Stretched out more comfortably, I rubbed my hamstring and worked out the tension that had built up while I was bent and twisted like a pretzel. Once the muscle was relaxed, I put my fins back on and continued my way out of the crack, this time headfirst.

With no luck in the small fissure crack, except in finally getting myself unstuck, I decided to go back to Quebradita. I made my way there, through the tannic passage into the clear water of little Quebrada. Though the larger tunnels in this area resembled the cave passages in Cueva Quebrada, there were also smaller tunnels beyond them that resembled the fissure crack I had just come from. The walls were dark gray and black and had lots of protrusions. They weren't exactly like the Lava Tunnel. The appearance was different The resemblance was there, though. What amazed me was how the cave transitioned so quickly from a light-colored, smooth-surfaced passage to dark-colored, craggy-surfaced walls and floor. It was as if an interior decorator had come in and said, "We'll do this room in a light color with soft furnishings and this room right next to it in a dark color with sharp furnishings." I don't know much about interior design, but I don't think the two would complement one another, even in different rooms. They certainly didn't look like they went together well in the cave.

I headed into one of those dark, craggy tunnels. I had explored them and left line in them two days earlier, but I hadn't been anxious to get back to that area because they didn't look like Quebrada. The stark change in appearance made me put them lower in priority because I didn't think they would lead to a connection. Maybe I was overthinking it. The quick transition in appearance could also happen on the other side. Maybe it was just a vein of this dark craggy rock going through the lighter colored smooth walls found in Quebrada and Quebradita.

I swam to the end of the line I had placed in this tunnel two days prior and tied the line from my reel onto the loop I had left at the end for that purpose. I had a couple of options to choose from. I went for the larger tunnel, not wanting to get stuck again. I moved forward, spooling out line from my reel. I expected the tunnel to get smaller, much like the last tunnel where I had gotten stuck. My awareness was elevated, and I fully expected a repeat performance. I pushed forward anyway. After all, I was able to get myself unstuck once. I could do it again. Fortunately, the tunnel didn't get smaller. The walls got wider apart and the ceiling a little higher. I relaxed as I continued farther into this unknown territory.

The passage zigzagged around a bit, but mostly went in the same general heading curving toward the right. I eventually came to a sharp turn to the left and followed the tunnel. It continued to loop to the left until I ended up in a small, round room. I looked around to see if there was anywhere I could continue beyond this area. I found a small restriction on the other end from where I had entered. As I moved across the room toward the restriction, I pictured the path I had taken. I was pretty sure this restriction was going to loop me back onto the line I had placed in the tunnel I had just swam through. I carefully squeezed through the restriction, hoping for different results, but not expecting them. Then, below the shelf, I found a bright white, new line. It had to be the line I was expecting to see.

I secured a non-directional marker on the line in front of me and backed up a few feet. I chose one of dozens, maybe even hundreds of protrusions sticking out of the floor and wrapped the line around it a few times. I cut the line and tied the end back onto itself, placing a line arrow pointing back the way I had come. I backtracked along my line, surveying as I was going, as well as looking for a hole that I might have missed. When I got back to where the tunnel had taken a sharp left, I found a smaller tunnel heading in the other direction. I looked down the line leading out and saw my non-directional marker fifteen feet away. I swam to it, looked to my right and saw the end of the line I had tied off. I removed the line arrow and placed it back on the line, pointing the other way, toward me, this time. That was the shortest distance to the opening after all. I replaced the non-directional marker with another line arrow on the line I was next to, also pointing toward the exit.

I swam back to where the tunnel I was in intersected with the perpendicular tunnel I had just come from. I placed a directional marker on the line, pointing toward my exit. Even though there was a line arrow only fifteen feet behind me, I was about to create a new intersection, and that called for another arrow. I tucked my survey notes into my pocket and looped the end of the line onto my reel around the marker. I followed the smaller tunnel that headed to the right until I came to a wall. I looked to the right and to the left. I had viable options both ways. This area was turning out to be a maze of tunnels. The question was whether any of these tunnels would eventually connect to Cueva Quebrada. I wasn't sure which way to go. I had an idea of which way the tunnels of Cueva Quebrada were, but I had made a few turns to get to where I was, and my sense of direction had been lost a few turns back. I might as well have flipped a coin, if that could be done underwater.

I decided to explore the left side first. It seemed to be the way to go. About two minutes later, I came to a sharp hairpin turn to the right. The tunnel had me going back in the direction from where I had just come. About two minutes later I came to a dead end. Unless I had missed another lead somewhere along the way, I had chosen incorrectly. I had lined another three hundred feet of passage in the cave, though. I tied the line off, placed a marker on it, and turned around. Another good thing was this tunnel allowed me to turn around without having to contort my body. Getting stuck once during a dive was enough. I pulled my survey notes out of my pocket, got out a clean sheet, and surveyed the line on the way back.

Once back at the spot where I had decided to go left, I put the survey notes away, grabbed my explorer reel, tied it to the line at that turn, and continued straight. This was the direction that would have been to my right earlier. Almost immediately, I was forced to turn left. This tunnel was a little longer than the last one and was fairly straight. At least it didn't have any sharp turns. But it ended in another round room. I scanned the room and saw some small restrictions. I poked my head inside a couple of them. I could tell immediately that they went nowhere. At least not anywhere that I could fit. The walls came together too quickly. They weren't even as large as the Crack of Death. There was one restriction that was a little bigger, but it looked like it ended fifteen feet or so away from where I was positioned. It was also a bit small. It wasn't quite as small as the Crack of Death, but I could see myself getting stuck in it. Flashbacks to my experience only twenty minutes earlier appeared in my mind. I decided to tie off the line, mark it, and let it be. It didn't look like it went anywhere anyway. I was also getting close to my turn pressure and didn't think it would be smart to enter a small restriction without more air in my tanks.

As I was surveying on the way back, I found another hole in the wall to my left. I checked my pressure gauges and saw I still had some air left. It was at least enough to check out a standard size tunnel. I placed a marker on the line pointing toward my path out and once again looped the line from my reel onto the marker. As I prepared to put more line into the cave, I thought about the fun I was going to have trying to decipher my survey notes later in the evening. I think I was on my fourth set of notes. I wasn't sure as I had lost count. I hoped I would be able to understand all of the sets of notes a few hours later.

I started into this new tunnel, taking a sharp right then a sharp left. If the picture of the cave map I was forming in my head was correct, I was heading back toward another tunnel I had already lined. That picture ended up being spot on. I found new, bright white cave line in a tunnel perpendicular to the tunnel I was in. I tied my line off a few feet from it, this time using a non-directional marker since I wasn't absolutely sure of where I was. I left enough line on the end to tie it onto the perpendicular line on my way out if I was correct. The reason I didn't tie the two lines together at that moment was because I didn't want to create an intersection where I couldn't place a line arrow with certainty of the closest path to the exit. It was better to leave the gap than to create a confusing intersection.

With that done, I turned around and prepared to exit. I had just created a maze of lines and now had to find my way back out to the opening twenty-four hundred feet away. I had gone left and right, back and forth, and looped back on my own line a couple of times. It can get confusing, and if I were only relying on my memory to make it back out to the Stadium and then back to the cave opening, I might not make it back before breathing through all of the air in my tanks. It's like driving into a new neighborhood without GPS, making several turns, and becoming completely lost. The difference is that when cave diving, we bring line markers with us. We have both directional line arrows and non-directional line cookies, circle shaped markers.

I've mentioned placing line markers on the lines a few times during my account. Those are the breadcrumbs we use to find our way back out of the cave. Anytime I arrived at a navigational decision, I placed either an arrow or a cookie on the line that would lead me out of the cave. I used a line arrow if there were no other arrows on the line. I used a line cookie if there were arrows on the line so I could indicate the direction from which way I came. That would also be the way I would go to exit the cave.

The line arrows placed on the lines are supposed to be pointing toward the closest opening. If there were multiple openings, that might not be the opening that was accessed for that dive. Unless you *planned* on exiting from another opening, you always exited from the opening you entered, even in emergency situations. You do this because you never know when that other line may be compromised, or the tunnel may be blocked, and you won't be able to proceed toward the other opening. It might sound a bit confusing, but it's simple and works as long as you don't second guess yourself and you trust the markers. This is especially important if you have to exit in diminished visibility and navigate by feeling the shapes and positions of the markers relative to line intersections. I've had to do that a few times.

With my notes in hand, I started swimming and collecting more survey data. I eventually made it back to the non-directional marker I had just placed on the line. I swapped that out for a directional marker and tied the additional line I had left to the perpendicular line since I was certain of the correct path to the exit. A couple of minutes later I was back where I had started. My explorer reel wasn't quite empty of line, but most of it was gone and remaining in the cave. I estimated about one hundred feet of line left on the reel. I had also breathed my tanks down to the point where it was time to start heading back out of the cave. I had close to an hour of swimming before I would see daylight again.

The exit was uneventful. David had been exploring another area while I was exploring the black, craggy tunnels. He hadn't had any luck either. We both almost emptied our explorer reels, though, so it was still a successful dive. We encountered each other in Quebradita; this time David was beyond the tannic water and not impersonating a chupacabra. We began our exit, retrieving our stage and safety tanks as we went. A month earlier we had been certain we would find the connection. We had just completed our fifth dive and we didn't think we were any closer to finding it than we had been three days earlier. It had been a good trip with very good dives. But our failure to find the connection left us a little deflated.

Back at the rental house I sat down at my laptop to try to make sense of the survey notes I had taken. The first dive's notes were straightforward, and I plotted them quickly. I then organized my notes from the second dive and started to enter them into my mapping program. Fortunately, the data made sense, and I was able to produce a map of the area I had just spent forty-five minutes exploring and lining. It looked like a galloping horse. At least, that's what it looked like to me.

The first line I placed in that section, that came from Quebradita, made the rear legs. It kept going, curving to the left, and transitioning into the horse's back. This horse was a bit sway-backed as you can see on the following page. After passing the saddle area I arrived at an intersection of tunnels and had to decide whether to go right or left. The tunnel with the hairpin turn was to the left and made the shape of the head. To the right were the front legs. The bottom of the body was made by the last tunnel I lined where I tied it back on to the first line. The other line that looped back on itself was the tail. Because the outline of the tunnels resembled a horse and also because the tunnels reminded me of trails on which I had ridden horses as a teenager, I named this section the Horse Trails.

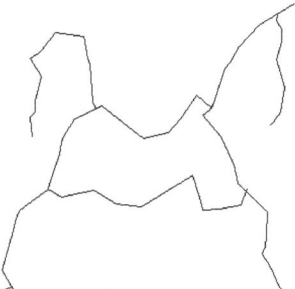

The Horse Trails

The disappointment of not finding the connection between Dos Coronas and Cueva Quebrada on this quick return trip was numbing, but that's how things go. I was certain it was in that area. I had to be missing something. We still got a lot done in the caves, and I would keep looking, but I felt let down. I tried to push that feeling aside. I tried to make myself confident that we would find the connection at some point. Unfortunately, a mix up in my files threw us off course for several dives.

24

Cueva Quebrada and the Grinder

We didn't return to Cozumel for another six months. It pained me to be away for so long, especially after failing to find the connection between Dos Coronas and Cueva Quebrada, but schedules wouldn't permit a return trip any sooner. I spent a lot of time thinking about our exploration and looking over the maps I had created. I was anxious to get back to Cozumel and back into Dos Coronas to look for the connection again. When we did finally return, we headed straight to Dos Coronas and did a nice, easy dive the first day back. We only brought one stage tank with us and spent ninety minutes in the cave looking for new leads. We didn't go back to the Stadium. We had spent a lot of time there already. Instead, we swam along the Winter Wonderland/Swamp Land line and concentrated on looking to the left. I was certain we had missed something. We scoured that passage, poking our heads into every single crevice we could find. We came up empty. Unfortunately, our reels did not.

The next day we decided to head to Aerolito for the day. David and I had only done three dives in there so far. We thought a change of scenery might do us some good. We headed into Aerolito and went back to Wonderland. This was just plain, old Wonderland rather than Winter Wonderland, although there was absolutely nothing plain about that area of the cave. It is one of the most decorated sections of Aerolito with lots of stalagmites, stalactites, columns, and drip formations. It was nice to swim around and take it all in and just be a tourist diver for the day. It was also nice to be able to find the main guideline on the first try. I did manage to do some survey in Aerolito that day. I couldn't help myself! I saw potential for exploration in Aerolito as well. The main guideline didn't have any knots, so David swam in front of me, running line from my explorer reel alongside the guideline, while I followed and surveyed the line. We left the explorer reel clipped to the line while we went to check out Wonderland. I spooled the line back up on the way out.

After a relaxing dive in Aerolito, we returned to Dos Coronas the next day ready to hit it hard. We brought in two stage tanks with us and spent almost two and a half hours in the cave. We swam to Winter Wonderland and started our search for missed leads in the area where we had begun to exit two days earlier. We found some short loops, left a little line in the cave, but again, we found nothing of significance. We were discouraged to say the least. I was beginning to think that the two caves weren't connected after all, at least not through a tunnel that was large enough for a diver to get through. The water probably moved from one to the other, but that would be the extent of the connection. As disappointing as it would be, sometimes it was how things went. We decided it was time to turn our attention elsewhere.

We had spent a lot of time focusing on Dos Coronas during our previous trips to Cozumel. We had put a lot of new line in that cave. The total length was up to eighty-three hundred feet, more than sixty-five hundred of that being placed in the cave by David and me. We weren't finding anything of significance in there. I wasn't quite ready to give up on the notion, though. We decided we should focus on Cueva Quebrada for the rest of the trip. We had only done three dives in Cueva Quebrada. It was time to spend more time in that cave. I would have preferred to find the connection from the Dos Coronas side. We had dedicated so much time to it that it just seemed more appropriate, but we hadn't had any luck there. If there was a connection, maybe we could find it from the other side.

We had three more days of diving, and they would all be spent at Cenote S1. We had only spent one dive looking for the connection in Cueva Quebrada prior to this trip. Even if we didn't find a connection, it would be fun to dive and become familiar with a new cave. We headed to Cenote S1 early on the fourth day of the trip with four tanks each ready to hit it hard. The tunnels in Cueva Quebrada were a bit shallower than those in Dos Coronas. We didn't have as far to swim to get to the area where we wanted to explore. I also wanted to begin resurveying and working on a new map of Cueva Quebrada. I already had fifty-one hundred feet of passage surveyed in the cave, I might as well continue surveying it. There was a tradeoff between the two options. We could either swim the extra distance underwater in Dos Coronas to get to the area we wanted to explore, or we could haul our gear several hundred feet through a narrow, winding jungle trail while narrowly escaping the advances of the elusive chupacabra. We opted to risk a chupacabra encounter.

On the first dive back in Cenote S1 we headed to the section where I had found a couple of low tunnels that were heading toward Dos Coronas. I wanted to take another look at one of them. The second one I found was more promising. It was shorter but it was in between the first one and the passages in Dos Coronas. We headed directly there. Fortunately, we didn't have an hour of swimming to do to get there. It was closer to twenty-five minutes. I still had plenty of air in my stage tank to continue breathing from it, but the tunnel we were about to enter was low and would have required me to unclip it and push it in front of me. This was the tunnel with less than a foot of clearance. Rather than push my stage tanks in front of me, I left them on the guideline. One of them was partially breathed and the other one was still full. I also had full sidemount tanks. I would save the air in my stage tanks to look around the cave later. Besides, the tunnel wasn't that long or that deep.

I marked the line with a line marker even though my stage tanks were clipped to it. I tied my jump spool line onto the main guideline. I then swam across the tunnel in the direction of the beginning of the low tunnel I had found during my previous dive in Cenote S1. My line was tucked back around a corner and out of sight. It was impossible to see from the tunnel we came from and would have been very difficult to happen upon accidentally. I didn't know if anyone was diving this cave, and I didn't want to take any chances. I found my line and secured my jump spool to it, leaving a line marker on it. I followed the line one hundred and sixty feet to the beginning of the low passage. I looked at the little nubbins that poked up from the floor and down from the ceiling. They looked like fat fingers just waiting to grab anyone who dared to enter. And the fingertips were almost touching each other. One of those fingers had grabbed my jump spool from my harness the last time I went through that passage.

I took inventory of my spools and began my way into the passage. It was not easy to get through. In most areas, the clearance between nubbins was only about eight inches. In some areas, it was even less. Our scuba tanks had a diameter of seven and a quarter inches, and we had to choose our path carefully so they wouldn't get wedged between nubbins coming out of the floor and ceiling. I followed the line. It seemed to have moved since the time I had placed it there during the previous trip. It was also possible I had positioned myself differently. I tugged at the line to move it to a more favorable route. I had to wiggle myself through, backing up several times whenever I got wedged in between the floor and the ceiling. I would back up so I could reassess the fat, stubby fingers and decide on a new path to take. I would pull the line toward me or push it away, depending on what the nubbins dictated. I kept pushing forward.

Normally, I don't like to make contact with the cave. I prefer to maintain my distance from the floors and ceilings. However, sometimes, for the sake of exploration, it was a necessary evil. I wasn't breaking anything in the cave, but I was scraping against its surface. I kept going because I knew there was a bigger passage on the other side of this low restrictive area. I believed the connection could be somewhere in that larger area.

I finally got through and popped out into the larger tunnel. At least compared to where I had just come from, it was a decent size. I turned to watch for David. There was no silt or sediment on the floor, but visibility was slightly reduced from the dust on the surfaces. We could still see each other, though not clearly. David popped out of the restriction and looked back at it shaking his head. I felt like it had gotten smaller since the last time we went through. Either that or we had gotten bigger. It was a tight place, and we had to go through again in order to get out of the cave. At least we had approached it more slowly this time and now knew the proper path to take.

I continued for another three hundred feet before arriving at the end of the tunnel and the end of my line. This tunnel was different than the one to the east of it. I looked around for any lead I might have missed the first time I was in the tunnel. The only possible connection I saw was the sand trap to the right. I wondered if that could be the connection. If it was, even if we could dig it out, we would never fit between the floor and the ceiling. The hard stone floor and ceiling came too close together. I turned away from the sandy crevice and we spent several minutes swimming back and forth in the tunnel between the restriction and the end of the line. We found nothing new and finally decided to make our way back through the restriction.

I got to the restriction and prepared myself for going through it again. It started off better than expected with the new line placement. Then about halfway through the restriction, I came across a jump spool on the floor. This time it was one of David's. One of the fingers had snagged it from his harness. I smiled as I picked it up. I continued through the rest of the passage. Once I was on the other side of it, I stopped and waited for David. He popped out about thirty seconds later and handed me one of my line arrows. I traded him his jump spool for it. That was when I decided the name of this restriction – The Grinder. We spent the rest of the dive poking around looking for new leads and surveying more line. We hadn't come any closer to finding the connection, but I had a good amount of passage in the cave surveyed after that dive.

The next day we decided to head in a different direction than we had done during the previous two exploration dives in Cenote S1. The main tunnel in this area split into two, one went south and the other went west. Germán had put the longer run of gold line in the southbound tunnel. We had been working in the westbound tunnel. We decided to start poking around the southbound tunnel to see if there were any leads there. The connection was somewhere in that quarter slice between the two tunnels. Maybe we were looking in the wrong place. Maybe the connection was coming in from a different direction. As we swam along the line heading south, we focused our efforts on the wall to our right. I had seen some white lines to the right in a deeper section when we were in there with Germán, and I wanted to look at them more closely. We checked those lines first. We extended a couple of the lines, and I got survey data on them, but there was nothing significant in that area. One of the lines looped back toward the main tunnel that we were in. The other one joined up to the westbound tunnel where we had previously looked.

We left those behind and continued southbound, beyond the end of the gold line. I had to replace the old white line Germán had tied into because it was just as brittle as the line he had replaced. I didn't know how he had been able to tie the gold line into the old line without it breaking. I used most of the line on one of my explorer reels just replacing the old line during that first dive beyond the end of the gold line. We kept pushing farther south. Not only was it a little far from where I thought the two caves might connect, but the cave transformed along this tunnel. The features I had seen from the Dos Coronas side that looked like Cueva Quebrada were no longer present. Instead of the smooth, sediment free floor we had seen in Dos Coronas and along the westbound tunnel from Cenote S1, we were swimming over floors with a thick layer of mud. We breathed the first third of the air in our stage tanks and had to keep carrying them because there was nowhere to leave them without disturbing the sediment on the floor. We didn't want to clip them to the line and allow them to fall into the sediment, leaving indentations where the valves came to rest.

As we continued south, something kept gnawing at me telling me we must have missed something in the westbound tunnel. We kept pushing south anyway because we hadn't been lucky enough to find anything to the west. Sometimes things just weren't what they seemed. This could be similar to that transition in Quebradita in Dos Coronas. A few hundred feet after I began replacing the old line with new line, the tunnel became very wide. I couldn't see the wall to my right. The ceiling also sloped down a bit, but not so much that it was unpassable. It was just much lower than the ceiling where we had been in the middle of the tunnel. I saw what looked like a lead to the right. Something about that area told me to go toward it. That was also the direction we should be taking to get closer to Dos Coronas, although at this point, I thought we had swum too far to connect to it. I came across a medium-sized rock on the floor, wrapped my line around it to hold it in place, and turned toward the lead. Another hundred feet and I came across another line that was running parallel to the line in the tunnel we had just come from. This area was low and wide and more of a room than a tunnel. There were very few features in it. It was like a desert underwater. The floor was a smooth layer of brown sediment. The ceiling was smooth rock. There were no formations in sight. The transformation was eerie.

I tested the new line that I had encountered and surprisingly found it to be sturdy. It was at least sturdy enough to not break if we had to follow it out in diminished visibility. With the sediment covered floor in this area, losing visibility was very possible. David and I were both good divers with excellent control of our buoyancy and trim, so it wasn't very likely, but why take chances. A piece of the ceiling could suddenly be released and drop to the floor because our exhaust bubbles forced an existing crack to finally break free. The result would be a mushroom cloud of silt in the cave. I wrapped the line from my reel around the line, tied a knot, and cut it so I could take my reel with me. David was right behind me. There was a large rock just below the line. It was the only feature in sight. I looked up at the ceiling above it and saw where it had once resided. This reinforced my concern about a possible loss of visibility. It wasn't a huge rock, so I wasn't too concerned about a cave-in. Sometimes pieces of the ceiling fell. It wasn't unusual to see. The rock was large enough that we could balance the stage tank valves on it without disturbing the silt. With a third of the air breathed from them, the bottoms of the tanks were positively buoyant and would float, staying off the floor. We decided to leave the stage tanks clipped to the line at this spot.

We continued swimming along the line until we came to another line intersection about a hundred and thirty feet later. We could continue on the line we had been following and go to the right or turn onto the new line and go to the left. Dos Coronas was to the right, so we went that way. About a hundred feet later we were back in a smaller tunnel and heading to the right again, toward Dos Coronas. I had no clue whether Dos Coronas was this far along or if we had already swam beyond its reaches. I thought the latter was more likely. We were seeing new cave though, so we continued to follow the line into the tunnel.

I followed the line and came to a third intersection of lines. The guideline I was on intersected another guideline that was perpendicular to it. We placed markers on our guideline, tested the sturdiness of the new lines. The line going straight was tied to the wall a few feet ahead and ended abruptly, but the tunnel didn't. That tunnel seemed to be heading toward Dos Coronas. The line heading to the left went into a larger opening. I decided to push forward into the smaller tunnel. David indicated that he would check the tunnel to the left. We were once again splitting up.

All divers are taught in their basic open water scuba courses that the buddy system is of the utmost importance and that you should never dive alone. Solo diving is simply too dangerous. One of the reasons is that as a recreational open water diver, you have one scuba tank with you. Should something happen with that tank or your regulator, you need to share air with your dive buddy. The other option is to do what's called a controlled emergency ascent to the surface.

As more experience is gained, some divers begin wondering about diving solo because it's not always easy to find a reliable buddy. The training agencies have even acquiesced and developed scuba courses for such activities. One agency calls it self-sufficient diver. Another calls it solo diver. Even the big agency finally came out with a course called self-reliant diver. None of the training agencies encourage or promote solo diving at the technical diving level, which cave diving is considered to be. However, solo diving is much more common at the technical and cave diving level than at the recreational diving level. The training agencies just can't acknowledge or sanction it because it isn't allowed by their lawyers and insurance adjusters.

That said, it's not uncommon for underwater cave explorers to separate during a dive. I've mentioned David and I going our own ways a few times. We're in the caves looking for unexplored, virgin passages. Sometimes the tunnels we have to go through to find those types of passages are on the small side. Going through them solo is actually safer than going through with a buddy. This is especially true if you know the visibility is going to be diminished or eradicated during the penetration half of the dive. The second diver in line isn't likely to see anything anyway.

We also go separate ways so we can divide forces to conquer the cave, something we did in the Stadium the last couple of dives there. Very few explorers want to be the second in line behind the guy running the reel into virgin passage. It's simply not as exciting or invigorating. That is unless you've already done it a bunch of times. I've often handed off my explorer reel to a buddy diving with me so he can lead the way into an unexplored tunnel. I've found and lined more than twenty miles of passages in underwater caves. I can let others have some fun too. In fact, I just did that during a recent trip to Cozumel. I got more joy out of watching my good friend, Jose, running that line into the tunnel I had found than I would have had I been running the line myself. Don't get me wrong. I still get a lot out of being the first person in a cave passage. I don't always give away the reel.

So I went west, and David went south. The tunnel I was in not only continued to the west, but it also began to get deeper. I started to get excited. I might have just found the connection!

25

At peace in the darkness and more lost equipment

The tunnel I decided to explore kept getting deeper, but it also got smaller the farther I went. I was glad David had followed the other line rather than following me. I began to see some formations – stalagmites and stalactites. This looked promising. It might be the connection. I did manage to find thirty-four feet of depth, which matched up to the depth of the tunnels in Dos Coronas, but it got too small to continue. I peered through the three-inch-tall space in front of me, trying to see if it opened up on the other side. At this point, I would have been content seeing line I had placed in Dos Coronas on the other side. Unfortunately, the twisting and turning and small mounds of mud didn't allow me to see very far. If there was line on the other side, there was no way I would ever see it. I pulled my wetnotes out of my pocket and opened them to a blank page so I could survey the line I had just placed in the tunnel. I got the depth and compass heading at the end of the line and turned to follow it out as I counted knots. About ten minutes later I was back where David and I had separated with one hundred and sixty feet less line on my reel.

I looked around but saw no sign of David. I shielded my light beam in an attempt to see the illumination from his light somewhere in the distance. We never turn off our lights because we don't want to flip the switch again only to find out they won't turn on. Hovering there in the dark I felt at peace as I waited for my eyes to adjust to the blackness surrounding me. I hovered there, weightless in the water. Enjoying the solitude of being in a cave devoid of any visual distractions. I became a part of the cave. About a minute later, or maybe five (I lost track of time), after still not seeing any sign of David, I reluctantly removed my hand and let the light escape, cutting through my dark surroundings. The sudden illumination was almost shocking as it broke through the peacefulness I had enjoyed for the past few moments. I checked my pressure gauges. I still had lots of air in my tanks.

David hadn't returned yet. Maybe his luck had been better than mine and he had found a tunnel that continued. I started swimming along the line David had followed. Three minutes later, the line intersected with another line. It was old and brown and obviously had been there for a while. Even though I knew David would have checked, I tested its durability. It didn't crumble to my touch and held sturdy when I gently pulled and put some tension on it.

David had placed a non-directional line marker on the line before the intersection, but there was no indication of which way he had gone. There usually wasn't. I placed my own marker on the line and went to the right, or westbound, because that was where we were focusing our efforts. It made sense that David would have gone that way. About two minutes later, I came to another intersection of lines with David's marker on the line I was following. One line went toward the south and the other toward the north. I waited there for about half a minute trying to decide whether I should choose a line to follow or wait for David. The westbound decision was easy. This one not so much. If I chose wrong, I might miss David completely. David would see my markers but that didn't mean he would stop and wait for me. We were also getting close to having to begin our exit from the cave. I checked my dive computer. We had been separated for fifteen minutes.

Although the temptation to continue exploring was there, I decided it was better to head back rather than choose a line and miss David. I turned around and retrieved my marker as I made my way to the area of the cave desert. I arrived at our point of separation, and I waited another minute. When David still didn't appear, I got bored and decided to go poke around some more. I would retrace our path slowly to see if there were any other leads I might have missed. I pulled out my wetnotes and found a blank page. I jotted a quick note to David, telling him I was slowly heading back to our stage tanks while poking around. I folded the sheet and hung it over the line like a tent, securing it in place with one of the clothespins I carried to mark some of the line intersections I encountered.

I slowly swam toward our stage tanks looking for more leads, searching, but not finding anything. I made it back to the tanks. Still no sign of David. I decided it was probably best to retrieve my stage tank. David and I had been separated for more than thirty minutes at this point and I wanted to have as much air with me as possible in case he needed an additional tank. Hopefully that wouldn't be the case. I went back to where I had left the note. Still no sign of David. Where the hell had he gone? I've been known to head off into a tunnel and not reappear for quite some time because I found a lead. It was different being on the other side of it. I also felt responsible for David. Not only had I invited him on these trips, but he was my former student.

Bad thoughts started to go through my head. Was David stuck? Had he gotten bad gas and passed out? Flashbacks to the dive with Brendan flew through my mind. We always analyzed our tanks for carbon monoxide, but anything was possible. What would I do if David didn't come back out? I pushed those thoughts out of my head. He was fine. I had confidence in his ability. I had taught him after all. He was a levelheaded person, and I trusted his judgment. I wouldn't have invited him on these trips if I had any concerns. David was just following a lead and lost track of time. I've done that myself plenty of times.

I swam past the note I had left on the line and into the tunnel where I had last watched David go. I found the first line intersection, his marker still in place where it had been the previous time. I went to the right to where I had seen his other marker. It was there but still no David. He must have found something. Maybe he found the connection to Dos Coronas. This time I decided to continue a little farther. I chose to go to the right. This passage got shallower so I didn't think it would end up connecting to Dos Coronas. We were already about fifteen feet shallower than the tunnels of Dos Coronas that we were attempting to find. I continued for about a minute anyway because that would be the logical way to go based on the overlaid maps. Maybe it got deeper again.

The tunnel didn't get deeper, but it started to get smaller. I decided it wouldn't do either of us any good to have two divers in a space this size, especially with the thick layer of sediment on the floor. I carefully turned around so as not to disturb the silty floor and backtracked. When I arrived at the intersection, I went the other way. A few seconds into the swim I saw the line laying loosely on the floor of the cave. It wasn't intact. David wouldn't have gone this way without replacing it with new line. I turned around and headed back. I gathered my line markers from the two intersections and arrived at the note I had left. I decided to wait there for a few minutes. I still had plenty of air in my tanks, so I wasn't in a rush. I covered my light again and hovered in the darkness waiting for David, hoping to see him soon. I let the blackness absorb me. I cleared my mind to match the void that surrounded me. I didn't think about anything. For a brief moment all thoughts of exploration were gone from my head. It was just me hovering weightless in a dark void. I couldn't have been more at peace.

About a minute later David's light disturbed my moment as it penetrated the darkness from around the corner. It was moving slowly and methodically. All was okay. He had simply been exploring the cave, looking for that elusive connection. I waited in the darkness and watched the slow movement of David's light as he got closer. Another minute and a half and David appeared behind his light, his attention focused on his compass and survey notes. I didn't know if he had found the connection. We would have more survey data to add to the map, though. I unshielded my light when David was only fifteen feet away. He glanced up and shook his head. He hadn't found a connection. He wrote down the final numbers of his survey and we headed toward the exit. It was still a good dive.

The next day, our final day of diving, I decided to go back to the area of the Grinder. There was something about that area that was calling me. I was certain I had missed something. We headed straight there, and I checked the longer tunnel first. I hadn't been in it since I first discovered it and placed line there. We swam the six hundred feet to the end of the tunnel and found the same thing. We were surrounded by solid rock. There were no leads that we had missed. We turned around. I kept looking anyway. I was that convinced that the connection had to be in that area. I had been surveying on the way out the last time and could have missed something from that angle. Indeed I had. I found another lead heading east. This lead looked very similar to the Grinder. Actually, it looked smaller. I was determined to check it out anyway. I grabbed my explorer reel and looked at David and pointed at the lead. He shook his head in a way that let me know he wasn't following. He wasn't about to go into that restriction. I shrugged my shoulders and turned toward it.

I proceeded into the restriction. It was even tighter than the Grinder. I wiggled my way through, pulling with my hands and pushing with my heels. There wasn't much water current in this area, so the visibility was significantly affected. The thin sediment flew up into the water column. It spread out in front of me and extinguished all signs of light. I closed my eyes and pushed on, feeling my way over the nubbins as if I were reading Braille. I got stuck a couple of times. I had to back up a few feet and change the angle of my body. The floor to ceiling clearance was even less than in the Grinder and the nubbins felt longer. I found myself thankful David had opted out of following me into this restriction.

About twenty feet later, I emerged into the Grinder. This was nothing more than a cross passage between the two tunnels I had found the first time in this area. I tied the line to one of the fingers near the perpendicular line in front of me and turned around to head back toward David. I somehow managed to get survey data for those twenty feet of line even with the visibility almost completely obliterated. Normally, I would have pulled the line out, but I needed it to get me out and felt it was safer to leave it in place than to try to reel it back onto my explorer reel while negotiating the restriction. No one else would ever be back in that area anyway.

I regrouped with David who was hovering in the big tunnel shaking his head. He was beginning to learn that there wasn't much I wouldn't try to go through. We headed back to the other tunnel and to the beginning of the Grinder. After what I had just gone through, the Grinder was going to feel like the Lincoln Tunnel connecting New Jersey to Manhattan. I might have been a little too confident. I still had to pick and choose my path and back up one time to be able to get through it. The fingers kept reaching out and grabbing at me. I felt them tugging at me, reaching up from the floor and down from the ceiling to grab my harness and hold me in place. At one point, I had to push hard to get past one of the fingers that had gotten a tight hold on me. I finally managed to get it to release its grip, but something felt off. About two-thirds of the way through I saw the line I had just placed from the other tunnel to my left, the Little Grinder. I saw the silt I had stirred up still hanging in the water. Not that it was a better option, but at least now we had a couple of paths out of this area of the cave.

Options were always good, even if they were small ones, literally.

I emerged from the Grinder and turned to wait for David. I took inventory of my spools and reels and accounted for all of them. David came out of the Grinder and handed me my wetnotes. I had tucked them inside my waist strap after I had last used them. The Grinder's fingers had stolen them from me. I took the wetnotes and tucked them into my pocket this time. We continued to the end of the line, searching for something we had missed. We didn't see anything new. Nothing was jumping out at me. We turned and began to head out, almost despondent. Another dive trip completed and still no connection. We made it back through the Grinder. I found another one of David's jump spools on the way out. The Grinder was determined to steal all of our equipment from us each time we passed through it. We were going to have to be more aware the next time. And there would be a next time. I still felt we were missing something.

26

Chankanaab, new overlays, and another visit to the Grinder

We were back less than five months later to continue our exploration efforts. After arriving in Cozumel, having our first traditional meal at the Thirsty Cougar, and picking up our tanks for the first day, we settled in to set up our equipment and get a good night's sleep. I had a new approach this time. I wanted to check the positions of my overlaid maps to make sure they were in the correct location on Google Earth. Maybe the coordinates were off, and the caves came close together in other tunnels. David and I headed to S1 prepared to survey the jungle path to the cenote.

I found the entrance to the path using Google Street View. There were enough manmade landmarks to get me in the right place. I knew the GPS numbers to the cenote, but those didn't always line up properly on maps. The numbers had to be worked a little to get the map to settle in the correct location. I had enough experience trying to coordinate GPS with maps that I knew a set of numbers could be as much as a couple of hundred feet off. I took measures to minimize the error, but there was only so much that could be done. I hadn't gone to the Chankanaab entrance of Cueva Quebrada yet, but I knew where it was in relation to what I had already surveyed. I had a map of the entire cave system that I scaled to the map on my screen. I then made it a bit translucent and overlaid that map onto my Google Earth overlay. I knew where Cenote S1 was on both maps, and I knew where the

Chankanaab entrance was on the original map. The Chankanaab entrance was also very easy to find on Google Earth. What I didn't know was precisely how accurate the original map was.

The first day back, we headed into Cueva Quebrada through Cenote S1 with the objective of finding the Chankanaab entrance and surveying that passage back to the cenote. Jen dropped David and me off at the trail to Cenote S1 and went off to one of the beach resorts. David and I carried our equipment through the jungle to the cenote. I could swear over the previous five months the trail had grown longer and narrower. At least it felt that way. The mosquitos were horrendous this time. We were in Cozumel during the rainy season, and it had rained most of the night. Fortunately, the clouds broke before we left the house. The only moisture we had to deal with was from the obtrusive humidity that permeated the air. By the time we had our equipment set up and were ready to strip and get into our wetsuits, our clothing was soaked through in sweat. It was a welcome relief to step into the cool eighty-degree Fahrenheit water of the cenote, even if it did smell a little ripe. Or maybe that was us.

We descended into the murky water and headed toward the clear water inside of the cave, happy to be back in Cozumel diving beneath the jungle again and happy to be out of the humid heat above. We easily found the tunnel heading toward the Chankanaab opening. The line in it was in terrible shape. It was broken in several places and the line that was still intact disintegrated with a light touch. It had been years since anyone had been down that passage. I emptied almost an entire explorer reel replacing the old line. As we neared the opening we began seeing signs of sea life. First, we saw a spiny lobster crawling around in the cracks below. Then we came across a ray trying to blend into the rocks. When I shined my light on the ray, it started to slowly move off, trying to find a better place to camouflage itself. I continued along the passage, letting more and more line off of my reel. Sections of the old line remained intact, but most of it was broken and lying on the floor of the cave. I decided to run a continuous line from my reel all the way to the opening. David gathered up as much of the old line as he could. After about thirty minutes, my reel almost empty, I saw the sharp, straight outline of a manmade object ahead. Even though it was encrusted in coral and sponges, it held its distinct shape. As I got closer, I recognized the familiar shape of a stop sign. We were almost at the entrance.

I approached the stop sign and swam around to the front.

STOP! UNLESS CAVE TRAINED
We Care

This was one of the common signs found at the entrances to various caves around the world. It warned untrained divers to not go beyond it into the cave. I shielded my light and looked around. I could barely make out the rays of sunshine penetrating the darkness in the distance. This sign was quite far inside of the cave. It might have been better to locate it closer to the entrance. We continued toward the daylight, reaching the opening about one hundred and twenty feet later. We hovered in the water, scanning the shape of the openings. There were three windows to the sea, side by side. They measured at least one hundred feet across. They had columns about fifteen to twenty feet wide between them. It was an amazing sight. We remained there taking in the beauty before us for a few moments.

We decided to venture out beyond the openings a short distance. We didn't go far and didn't surface. The Chankanaab National Park had banned diving at that entrance. Even though we had come from inside of the cave and were probably within our rights, we didn't want to put the ban to the test. I heard that if they caught anyone diving there, they would confiscate the dive gear. We certainly didn't want that to happen. After a minute looking up at the surface and around the large sea pool formed by the current coming out of the cave, we returned into the darkness. I placed my explorer reel on the floor near the center opening and surveyed the line back to the stop sign. I returned to my explorer reel, pulled in the line back to the sign, and secured it to the post. I hadn't seen any markers on the original line to relocate to the new line I had placed. My line wasn't the first line in that passage, so I didn't leave one of my markers. I continued to survey the line as we made our way out of the cave.

After we surfaced and got our tanks and dive equipment back to the rental car, David and I headed back into the jungle to survey the path. Even though I had the survey data from the Chankanaab entrance to Cenote S1, and I was confident in its accuracy, I still wanted a verification that the map was overlaid in the correct location. I hadn't brought my tape measure this time, so we used a jump spool with knotted line. I counted knots as I moved along the path and took headings back toward David at each turn in the path. We did this from the street to the cenote. It took about twenty minutes. There were several survey stations. Unfortunately, that included very few long stretches of straight path.

With the new survey data from inside the cave, I had more than sixty-five hundred feet of surveyed passage from Cueva Quebrada. A bit over fifteen hundred feet of that was new line David and I had placed. Only twenty-four thousand feet more to survey. I overlaid my partial map of Cueva Quebrada using the Chankanaab entrance as my starting point. The map only shifted millimeters. I had been close. I also overlaid the jungle path from the road to Cenote S1. My underwater map was perfect. The jungle path overlay ended right where Cenote S1 was located on my map of the cave. I now had certainty that my Cueva Quebrada map was properly positioned.

At the end of the previous trip, I had David hold the end of the line on my primary reel and I swam out to the entrance to Dos Coronas. That line was knotted as well so I was able to get an accurate distance to the opening from the shoreline. I then measured the distance from the road to where David stood. The road was permanent. The shoreline depended on the tide. This gave me the distance from the road to the opening. That was the easy part. The hard part was determining where the opening was along the length of the road. Google Street View came to the rescue once again. There were enough unique manmade landmarks along this road as well. I was able to determine exactly where the opening lined up by taking a Street View stroll along the road. My confidence level regarding my overlays increased even more.

With the positions of both caves updated on my overlay, I looked over the maps. They had only shifted slightly. The closest the caves came to each other was still in the same place. I asked myself what we were missing. We had scoured the passages on both sides and came up empty. Maybe there wasn't a connection. Maybe all this effort was for naught. Even with those doubts creeping in, I wasn't ready to give up.

We decided to go look in Dos Coronas again. It had been a while since we were in there. We ended the last trip with three dives in Cueva Quebrada and started this trip with the first two days back there as well. During the last dive in Dos Coronas, we had scoured the east wall of the Winter Wonderland and Swamp Land passage and found nothing new. Maybe we had missed something. With five months away and five dives in Cozumel looking at different tunnels, maybe we would have a fresh enough perspective and see something we hadn't seen the last few times. We went in with two stage tanks in addition to our sidemount tanks. We didn't bring safety tanks this time because we weren't planning on going to the end of any lines. Our maximum penetration would be about two thousand feet.

The surge from various storms had broken the line in several places.

I had to run the line much farther in from the opening than I had been doing on previous dives. I had only used a hundred-foot spool this day, like I usually did. That didn't quite get me to the intact line. I had plenty of spools on me, so I grabbed another one and closed the remaining ten-foot gap. I would have to use a hundred-and-fifty-foot spool from now on. We made it past the restrictions, through Hades and the Devil's Throat and arrived in Winter Wonderland about twenty minutes after we had entered the cave.

It was still as amazing as I remembered and almost took my breath away. After a moment of appreciating the beauty of the passage, we pushed forward with our focus to the east again. David and I spent almost two hours in that section poking our heads into every dark hole we came across. None of it went anywhere. We ended up finding some small tunnels that looped back to the main one, but nothing extensive. We didn't even leave any line in the cave. Nothing we found was worth the trouble. An hour and a half after we had entered the cave, we turned to start making our way back. We didn't stop looking, though. We were hoping to see something we had missed from a different angle. All we did was rediscover the small loops of tunnels we had found on the way in. Disappointed, we retrieved the jump spool we had put in at the beginning of Winter Wonderland and headed into the Devil's Throat. It was another bust.

The next day we were back at Cenote S1. There was still a little bit of hope holding on. I don't know why, but it was there. The plan was to head straight toward the Grinder. We took a short cut that I had discovered the day before as we were exiting. This shaved about five minutes from our swim and gave us more time to explore the cave. We arrived at the location where I had to install a jump line to the line leading into the Grinder. A few minutes later I was staring into its bowels mentally preparing myself to go through it. I could almost imagine the floor and ceiling in a peristaltic movement just waiting to grind us up as we passed through. It had become easier to negotiate the restriction during the last trip because we had gone through it a couple of times. I also had the experience of the Little Grinder. Five months away from Cozumel made it seem like we were about to go through it for the first time. I felt a bit of anxiety knowing it would be easy to get stuck. I wondered if I had gained any weight while I was away. It wouldn't take much to make a difference in the Grinder. I think the memory of the Little Grinder was more responsible for the anxiety than the thought of going through the Grinder.

Some might wonder why I would expose myself to such feelings. Why would I go through a passage that induced anxiety? There was always a bit of anxiety when I went cave diving. It presented itself at different intensities. It was always there regardless of whether it was a simple sightseeing dive or if it was a deep cave dive into tight restrictions in unfamiliar territory. Being in unfamiliar territory actually reduced the anxiety because my focus was on exploration. My mind remained occupied with the task of searching for some hidden passage that others may have missed. When there wasn't a distraction, my mind allowed me to feel anxiety. I've told many people, including my cave diving students, that the day I stopped feeling that anxiety, the day I stopped asking myself what the hell was I doing in the cave, was the day I needed to stop cave diving because that was the day I had become complacent. And complacency in an underwater cave will get you killed.

The anxiety made me a safer cave diver. It allowed me to accurately and responsibly assess the risk and determine if it was worth taking. If I wasn't feeling anxiety, then I had become complacent. That was dangerous territory. When you became complacent, you made mistakes. Those mistakes could be deadly, especially in an underwater cave. So the anxiety was a good thing. It wasn't so strong that I wasn't ready or willing to go through the Grinder. It was strong enough to keep me in check. I took inventory of my equipment, making sure everything was clipped where it should be, hoping to eliminate, or at least minimize, the loss of any equipment in the Grinder. I had learned my lesson the previous times I had gone through it. I moved forward into the tight restriction, looking at the fingers, and searching for the path that gave me the most clearance. I followed that path slowly, pulling myself through one foot at a time. There was no finning in the Grinder. It was too small for that. My fingertips touched the fingertips of the cave, and I pulled myself past them.

About halfway through, I got stuck. Something was tugging on my midsection. Maybe I had gained a couple of pounds. It felt like the stainless-steel buckle on my waist strap had been grabbed by one of the fingers on the floor and was being held back. I pulled harder but didn't budge. I tried to back up, but I couldn't move that way either. There must have been another finger below my buckle preventing movement in that direction. The cave literally had me in its grasp and was refusing to let go. I located a large thumb-like protrusion at arm's length in front of me and grabbed it with my hand. I pulled even harder. I felt myself move forward an inch. I located another large protrusion and grabbed it with my other hand. I pulled hard with both arms. I felt like I was rock climbing, only I was horizontal instead of vertical. The cave began to lose its grip on my buckle. I managed to anchor my heels on the ceiling, and I pushed with my legs. The cave finally let go and I moved forward. Something felt different though. Something felt off.

I continued through the Grinder and made it out on the other side with no further issues. Things still felt odd. I had a lot more space around me to figure things out so I could take a moment to check my equipment. I felt around my harness with my hands, taking inventory of my spools and reels while tracing the straps. I came to the buckle, and it hung loosely below my belly. It appeared the cave had managed to unbuckle it, and the waist strap had slid out. I looked back at my waist and saw that my conclusion was not correct. The buckle was hanging from the right side. If it had let the free end of the webbing go, it should have been hanging from the left. The buckle had not come open. It was still closed on the two-inch webbing.

I opened the buckle and slid it off the strap to examine it. With it in front of me, I noticed that the bar between the slots where the webbing had been weaved was broken on one end. The bar was still there, but it was bent out and had allowed the strap to slide off. The Grinder had broken a stainless-steel buckle. Luckily, I was able to rig it to work for the rest of the dive. I slid both ends of the straps through the buckle and closed it over them. It was a tight squeeze, but it held. I checked it often to make sure the pressure of the two straps didn't pop it open. I had a Delrin belt buckle back at the house as a spare that I would have to use for the remainder of my dives that week.

What could have possessed me to even go into the Grinder in the first place a couple of trips back? There was no line in it so no one else had been through there. The tunnel wasn't all that inviting when you looked at it. From one end of the Grinder you couldn't tell for certain that it opened up on the other end.

I knew I could fit. I couldn't see an ending to the tunnel. And my map overlays told me that going that way meant going toward Dos Coronas. I had to have a look. It was no different than Jacques Cousteau exploring the depths of the ocean with the minimal equipment that was available at the time.

Submersible pressure gauges that indicated how much air was left in a scuba tank weren't available when Cousteau first began diving. Instead, tanks were fitted with a mechanism called a J-valve. The air in the tank was breathed until the pressure dropped to a certain level. When you took that last breath and got no air, you reached back and pulled the handle on the J-valve, flipping it open, and allowing the remaining air, usually about 500 psi, to be breathed. As you pulled that J-valve handle, you hoped that it hadn't already caught on something and been pulled open. If that was the case, there was no air left in the tank. The only option was to swim for the surface as you exhaled whatever little amount of air was left in your lungs. Usually that wasn't much because your last breath had been cut off. Some people still dive tanks with J-valves. They call themselves vintage divers. I call them crazy, but in a respectful way.

There are those that call me crazy for the stuff I've done. I guess it's the perspective. For my part, it's all a calculated risk. Several years earlier, after first getting trained and certified to dive in underwater caves, I would never have attempted to go into a tunnel like the Grinder. I probably would have thought there was no way I could fit. These days, there aren't many restrictions I don't think I can pass through. Perspective changes with time and experience. Things look different. I've gone back to restrictions that I passed up years earlier. The first time they looked too small. On my return, the restrictions didn't look small enough to give me pause. The anxiety might still be present. I'd still think about the possibility of getting stuck. I'd try though. I've been in enough situations in which I know what I'm capable of and I know my limits. I also know I can get myself out of most anything I get myself into. Experience has taught me that.

Most importantly, I always have lots of air to breathe. I would never go into a restriction like the Grinder for the first time during the tail end of a dive. That was a restriction meant for full tanks so if I got into trouble, I had plenty of time to get out of it. Consequently, the Grinder wasn't a restriction that a diver on a rebreather would be able to fit into. There simply wasn't enough room for the rebreather and the tanks needed for the rebreather.

I continued along the guideline in the tunnel beyond the Grinder looking mostly to the right. That was where my maps told me I should be looking. Not far after the Grinder the tunnel got much wider. The wall on the right side curved to the right and there was a triangular shaped room about thirty feet long at the base, where I had run my line, and about forty-five feet from the base to the tip. I looked at that area and placed a marker on the line. I wasn't sure how I hadn't noticed that during my previous dives in this tunnel. I must have been so focused on the area near the end of the line that I wasn't paying attention near the beginning. I looked around the area. There was a manhole size depression in the floor about forty feet away. It was such a small hole and difficult to tell from that distance if it was actually a hole or just a depression in the floor. I would check it on the way back. I wanted to go to the end of the line first.

The wall to my right curved back about thirty feet later. Or rather, the ceiling dipped down toward the floor to my right. The floor also sloped down. I knew it had to be sloping down to the lower section of Dos Coronas. My overlays told me this was the closest the two caves came to each other. Even with the adjustments made to the overlays, it was still the closest. There had to be something I was missing. The problem was that sand filled the void between the ceiling and the floor to my right. Even if I could dig out the sand, the space between floor and ceiling was too narrow for me to fit. Even if I had smaller diameter scuba tanks, my body would not fit in that crack. Could it be that the connection simply wasn't large enough to be passable by a person? I wasn't ready to give in to that idea.

27

A lost map goes down the Drain

I reached the end of the Grinder about five hundred feet later. As before, on every other dive I had done back to this area, the tunnel simply ended. There was a solid wall of rock in front of me. The floor wasn't even sloping down on the right like it had been. That crack had ended several feet back. There was nowhere to go except back toward the Grinder. But dammit, the maps indicated Dos Coronas was so close! It was less than one hundred feet away, closer to fifty feet. Why did I keep coming back when I knew what I would see? I wasn't expecting to see anything different. I wasn't expecting there to be an opening where there wasn't one before. I was hoping I had missed something. I was hoping there was some hidden hole that had escaped my notice. Sometimes it's right there in front of you and you just don't see it. So I kept returning and hoping that I would finally see what I hadn't seen before. This persistence has worked for me in the past.

I turned around and signaled David that it was time to head back out. Time to get back to the Grinder and pick up any equipment that we had lost on the way in. It had broken my buckle so, even though I had taken inventory, I wouldn't be surprised to find something waiting for us in the grasp of its fingers. David turned around and I began following him out. We reached the marker I had left to remind me of the manhole. It was a good thing I had placed it there. I had momentarily forgotten about it. I signaled David. He stopped and looked back. I communicated that I wanted to go check out the hole. I grabbed a jump spool from my harness. It was only about forty feet to the hole so I wouldn't need the thousand feet of line on my explorer reel. A one-hundred-foot spool would do. I released the end of the line and wrapped it around my marker, passing the spool through the loop, securing it to the permanent guideline. I turned to my left and started heading toward my target. My expectations weren't high, but everything had to be checked.

I reached the depression in the floor and looked down. It was indeed more than just a bowl in the floor. It was a hole. It extended down about five feet while sloping to my left, heading toward Dos Coronas according to the overlay. How had I missed this? How had I not looked at this during any of my previous dives to the area? I stuck my head in the hole and looked to the left. The small tunnel continued, but I couldn't see much. I pulled myself farther down into the hole, trying to get a better look at where this drain would take me. I thought the Grinder was bad. The Drain was much worse. I felt like I was crawling into a kitchen sink drain and into a garbage disposal. I hoped no one flipped the switch and started the blades spinning.

There were protrusions sticking out all around the perimeter of this hole. They were much bigger than the fingers of the Grinder. They were also more defined. The fingers in the Grinder were smooth and easy to slide past compared to the fingers in the Drain. These fingers had sharp edges. If the walls spun, I would most certainly be chewed up and spit out as if I had gone through a garbage disposal. I couldn't move an inch without one of these fingers hooking my gear and trying to keep me out of it. I persisted and kept pulling myself deeper into the hole. I could only imagine what I looked like to David with my body positioned head down vertically in a hole and only my legs and fins sticking out.

I finally got my head in as far as the tunnel would allow. I hadn't removed either of my tanks. They were wedged against the sides of the hole. If I was going to go through this hole, I would need to remove at least one of the tanks and push it in front of me. I shined my light beam down the horizontal tunnel in front of me hoping to see another line at the other end. I didn't see a line. I did see that the tunnel appeared to get larger. It looked like it opened into a room. I considered pushing forward through this tunnel but thought better of it. I had previously been through restrictions that opened into small rooms and led nowhere. After going through the Grinder, I wasn't mentally prepared to go through something even smaller. I was also fairly certain I knew the area in Dos Coronas where this might connect if it did connect. Access from that side of it might be easier than it looked to be from this side.

Instead of pushing forward, I tied the line I was holding, the line from my jump spool, around one of the fingers below me. I tied it in a position where I knew I would be able to see it coming from the room at the end of the small tunnel I was looking down, if I could find it from the other direction. It would be more fitting to make the connection from the Dos Coronas side anyway. We had done many more dives in Dos Coronas and spent countless hours exploring and creating the map. We had placed more than a mile of new line in tunnels that had previously been unexplored. Dos Coronas had, and still has, a special place in my heart. The connection would wait until I could hopefully find it from that side.

I wiggled my way backwards, back up to the room where I had left David. At least where my upper body had left him. Being wedged in the hole from all sides didn't allow me to turn around. The fingers didn't make it easy to back out either. I reaffirmed that this restriction was much worse than the Grinder. At least the Grinder was wide and allowed me to turn around if I had to. The Drain was small all the way around. About ninety seconds later, I finally popped back up into the room from where I had started. David was there shaking his head at my antics. He was going to get whiplash if he kept doing that. Even he thought I was a little crazy. Maybe I was.

I pulled my notes out of my pocket so I could survey the forty or so feet of line that I had set from the permanent guideline to the Drain. It was a straight shot from one to the other so all I had to do was get the compass heading, depth, and distance. I also had to survey a few stations on the permanent guideline so I would know where to add the new line to the map I had saved on my laptop. Back at the Grinder, I jotted down the last of the numbers and tucked my notes into the pocket of my wetsuit so I wouldn't lose them. I would hate to get through the Grinder only to have to go back to retrieve my survey notes. I let David go first and followed closely behind. On the other side of the Grinder, David handed me a jump spool. Apparently, the Grinder had stolen it from me on the way in and I had once again missed it in my inventory. I wasn't surprised because I tended to carry lots of spools.

Later that evening, back at the rental house, I plotted the survey data I had recorded of the forty feet of line to the Drain. I overlaid the map onto Google Earth. The maps were even closer to each other, but there was still a space about a hundred feet long between them. We had gotten closer, but not close enough. I studied my maps. Something wasn't sitting right. I had a feeling I was missing something. I pored over the maps and my notes. Were we not looking in the right place? I continued examining the maps and trying to figure out what was eating away at me.

It suddenly came to me. I made a realization. Over the past two trips I had been working with an old map of Dos Coronas. One important section was missing from that map. I bought a new laptop between the previous two trips. Google Earth overlays didn't transfer from one computer to the other. You had to share your favorite places by emailing yourself the file. I had the KML files (Keyhole Markup Language) I used for Google Earth overlays on my laptop, so instead of emailing myself the files, I simply opened them and saved them to Google Earth. I had inadvertently opened the wrong Dos Coronas KML file and had an old map overlay. I hadn't been using the proper map for my exploration plans during the previous trip or the trip we were on. I had done three dives in Dos Coronas and five dives in Cueva Quebrada using an old map. The old map was from before I had found the Horse Trails. Somehow, the period of six months between trips had allowed me to forget the Horse Trails existed. Without seeing them on the overlay, they had vanished from my memory as well. That led me to focus on other areas of Dos Coronas. We hadn't even gone to the Horse Trails during the previous trip or the day before. We never even made it back to that area.

I searched my laptop and found the correct file with the most updated map. Thankfully, it was still there! I converted it to a KML file and opened the file in Google Earth. The new overlaid maps showed the two caves almost touching. I had to zoom in to see that the two lines weren't actually connected. They were just millimeters apart from each other on my screen, which meant they were just feet apart from each other beneath the jungle. The end of the line that was almost touching one of the lines in Dos Coronas was the line I had just placed inside of the Drain. I made sure I saved Google Earth with my updated KML file. I also made a new rule for myself. Every map I made would include the date of the update to the file name. This way I would always know I was working with the most recent and up-to-date map. I was kicking myself for this error. How could I get the files mixed up? I had spent the entire last trip looking for the connection without having complete maps to plan the dives.

We changed our plans and decided to head back to Dos Coronas the next day. We were going to the Horse Trails for the first time in almost a year!

28

Back in the saddle – Never give up

With the realization regarding the mix up in the files and not having used a map showing the Horse Trails, plus the discovery of the Drain the previous day, I was excited to get back into Dos Coronas. I knew this was going to be the day. We were about to connect the two caves. The only question I had was whether I would be able to fit through the connection. It would be nice to swim to the room where I suspected the connection would be and to see the line I had placed down inside of the Drain. However, I would prefer to be able to tie the two ends together. Even better than that would be if I could get through the restriction and pop out into Cueva Quebrada proper. Based on what I had seen the previous day and what I remembered from a year earlier, I wasn't sure I could fit.

David and I quickly set up our equipment and got into the water. Jen and David's girlfriend were on shore. They were going to hang out and relax in the sun while we went back to the Horse Trails. We had told them about our discovery the day before and excitement permeated our moods that morning. We were all very optimistic about the dive. I also felt a sense of sadness about it. We had worked so hard for so long looking for this connection. This was our third trip to Cozumel knowing about the possibility of the two caves being connected. We spent more than thirty hours with our focus on finding that elusive tunnel that would allow us to bring the two together as one large cave system. The adventure of the exploration might be coming to an end. In a way I didn't want it to. I wanted to keep chasing that dream. I wanted to keep exploring. I didn't want the feeling I was experiencing to end. It was bittersweet. Would I be able to replicate that feeling ever again? Would I be able to have as much fun exploring caves? Or would I compare every single dive afterwards to this moment?

With mixed emotions, we walked into the water, secured our tanks onto our harnesses, and looked at each other.

"This is it. This is going to be the dive." I told David.

He smiled back and replied, "Yes, it is. Let's do this!"

I think he was feeling the same way I was. We both wanted this to be the dive in which we connected the two caves, but we didn't want the chase to end.

We waved at the girls and dropped down below the surface to begin our swim to the opening. I entered the cave, setting the line from the entrance back to the permanent guideline, this time using one of my one-hundred-and-fifty-foot jump spools. We made our way to the Horse Trails. The swim went by quickly, and at the same time it took forever. It was about a fifty minute swim to get to the Horse Trails. We made it in record time, but it was still a long time when you have one thing in mind. It was a long time to think about and reflect on all of the dives that we had done in Dos Coronas over the past thirty-three months. This was my seventh visit to Cozumel during that period of time. It was my fortieth cave dive beneath the jungle of Cozumel. We had spent almost one hundred hours in the caves of Cozumel. It wasn't a lot in the grand scheme of things. And then again, it was.

When I arrived at the tunnel that joined the main tunnel to the Stadium, I stopped and quickly set a jump line from the guideline we had been following to the guideline I had hidden around the corner. We moved into the Stadium. The ceiling still had a tannic lake hiding it from view, but it seemed smaller. The tannins didn't extend into the tunnel leading to the Horse Trails. They stopped just at the edge of the offshoot. I popped my head up into the tannic layer and saw that it was only three feet below the ceiling this time. I turned my attention back to the chupacabra tunnel. This was the first time I was able to see that tunnel clearly. David's mask lights would not be glowing red on this dive. The tunnel was about twenty feet wide and had a light colored, rough craggy floor. The ceiling was six to seven feet above the floor. From where we entered the Stadium to the opposite wall was about seventy feet. At the wall we had to go to the left. Ten feet later we were forced to turn right to enter the rear legs of the Horse Trails.

I swam along the first trail until I came to a line intersection, the line to the right forming the belly of the horse. I placed a marker on the line, and we took the belly line. We followed the trail to the next intersection. If we went left, we would be going toward the horse's head. To the right, we were traveling down the front legs of the horse. We went right. A moment later we were in a small round room. I vividly remembered finding this room the year before. It had a few small cracks around the perimeter that were much too small to fit inside. It also had a larger opening near where I had tied my line off. I remembered thinking I would have to return to that with more air in my tanks to check it out. Unfortunately, that happened during the last dive of that trip. It was after that trip that the file mix up occurred.

I went to the end of my line. It was tied onto a protrusion on the wall to the right of the larger opening. I had left a loop on the end of it as I always did when I intended to come back to explore an area further. I looked to the left of the tie-off where the small restriction I had looked at when I first went into this room was located. For some reason, the restriction didn't look as small as it had.

I mentioned that perspective changes as experience grows. That had happened. A year earlier, the restriction looked small. It looked too small for me to attempt going through, at least with the amount of air I had left in my tanks. This time that wasn't the case. We had brought multiple stage tanks into the cave and the last one had been placed at the jump to the Stadium Room. It had taken us less than ten minutes to get from there to our location at the end of the line. My sidemount tanks were almost full. I had plenty of air, meaning I had plenty of time to work through any issues that might arise. I swam toward the restriction, arrived at the end of the line, and moved beyond it. I looked into the restriction. That's when I saw it. A thin, white line dropped down from the ceiling about ten feet away. There was a white line arrow on the line pointing up toward the hole it passed through. I couldn't see the hole it was coming through, but I knew it was there. I was looking at the end of the line I had placed down the Drain from Cueva Quebrada the day before!

I turned to David and screamed through my regulator, pointing inside the restriction. David looked into the hole and saw what I was so excited about. He started screaming as well. We pumped our arms up and down, wiggled our hips back and forth, and hugged each other. That's right, two grown men, scuba diving more than two thousand feet inside of a dark underwater cave hugged each other fiercely. This was no easy feat considering we were positioned horizontally in the cave facing each other. We brought our arms around each other's shoulders and squeezed tight. Our hard work and determination had finally paid off. We connected the two caves. Dos Coronas cave had just become the Dos Coronas section of Cueva Quebrada. It was no longer its own cave. Cueva Quebrada was no longer twenty-nine thousand feet long. It was more than thirty-eight thousand feet long including the tunnels we had lined on that side during our exploration efforts. We had done it! We finally achieved our objective of connecting the crowns!

After our celebration, it was time to get back to work. While it was nice to finally know that the caves did indeed connect and to know where that connection was, that wasn't enough for me. I had to try to make the traverse from one cave to the other. I had to physically make the connection and tie the two line ends together. I was determined to do it. I grabbed my last jump spool and secured it to the loop on the end of the line. It was a short distance. I wouldn't need my explorer reel for this push. I looked at David one final time. Then I turned back toward the restriction. I had learned the day before that I would not be able to pass through the Drain with both tanks clipped at my sides. The restriction wasn't wide enough. I unclipped my left sidemount tank from the waist strap and pushed it in front of me, making my profile narrower. I started into the restriction.

As I stated before, it was tight. Very tight. This was probably the smallest, tightest restriction I had ever been in. I struggled just to get to my other line ten feet away. The sharp-edged cave fingers were doing their damndest to prevent me from reaching it. I kept waiting for them to start to spin around and spit me out. I kept going anyway. I wiggled and maneuvered. I placed my spool on the floor and pulled with my right arm. I pushed with my heels. I slowly made progress. Some might criticize me for making contact with the cave. I can assure you no damage was done. Those fingers didn't break. That rock was solid. There weren't even any marks left on them. There was no layer of dust to diminish the visibility.

I finally reached the line. I touched it. It was the most difficult ten feet I had ever traveled. It was also the most rewarding. I let out some extra line from my spool and cut it. I then looped the line around the other line and tied them together. The caves were officially connected. I retrieved two markers I had made especially for this occasion. One had Cueva Quebrada written on it and the other had Dos Coronas written on it. Each marker also included both of mine and David's names. I placed the arrows on the lines pointing in their respective directions. The connection was now complete.

That wasn't enough for me. I looked up into the Drain. I had already been down it with my upper body. I was this far. I had to try. I pushed the tank I was holding in front of me up the Drain into Cueva Quebrada. Then I pushed myself up toward the hole. It was a struggle. I had to twist my body and wiggle past the fingers. Progress was slow. I wondered what David was thinking back in the room watching me through the restriction. I knew he wouldn't be following. He had already passed up on the Little Grinder and this was much worse. I reached up and grabbed the rim of the Drain and pulled. I pulled my head up so my eyes were just above the level of the floor of Cueva Quebrada. I looked around the room and recognized it immediately. Not that I had doubted my location. This was all just so surreal. I kept expecting to wake up from a dream. I kept expecting that none of this was really happening. I carefully set my sidemount tank down on its side atop the smooth floor of the upper level. I needed both hands for the next part.

I placed my arms on either side of the Drain hole rim and pulled up with all of my might. I felt the walls of the Drain tugging at me, trying to keep me from getting through. I pushed with my feet and pulled with my arms. I still wasn't worried about damaging the cave. It was too strong and tough to damage. Nothing was breaking. No formations were giving way. I moved up inch by inch. I could only imagine what it looked like to David from his viewpoint behind me. First, he watched me try to get down the Drain the day before, and then he had to watch me climbing out of it. He was probably worried I wouldn't get back through. The thought crossed my mind. I knew where I was, though. I knew I was only eleven hundred feet from Cenote S1. There wasn't continuous guideline between me and Cenote S1, but I knew the route and I could use my safety spools to connect the lines so I wouldn't be swimming completely off of one line to get to another. I had a plan and if I couldn't get back through the Drain, I would signal to David to go out the way we had come, and I would meet him on the surface. I wasn't ready to implement that plan quite yet. I wanted us to exit together.

I managed to get through the Drain and pop out into Cueva Quebrada. I had done it! I had not only found the connection, but I had traversed from Dos Coronas to Cueva Quebrada. I took a moment to let the feeling sink in. I had been coming to Cozumel for almost three years and visited the island seven times and done twenty-four dives in Dos Coronas and nine dives in Cueva Quebrada. We had discovered the possibility of a connection about halfway through our adventures. We had done a combined total of thirty-three dives in both and managed to connect the two in only seventeen dives. It was quite an accomplishment. I was overwhelmed.

I was also sad. This journey had come to an end. What we had been so focused on for three trips was over. Sure, there was still lots of exploration to be done on Cozumel. I wanted to survey Cueva Quebrada and create a new map that included the Dos Coronas section. I might find more virgin cave passages during that process. We had already added more than fifteen hundred feet of newly lined tunnels to Cueva Quebrada aside from what we had done in Dos Coronas. That was over the course of seven dives. There was potential for a lot more.

My moment of reflection came to an end. Before I turned my attention to getting back through the Drain, I did a complete three-sixty rotation to take in my surroundings. I had made it to Cueva Quebrada from the Dos Coronas opening. I stopped my rotation once I was facing the Drain. It was time to get back to it. I knew I could continue out to Cenote S1, but I didn't want to do that. I wanted to exit the Dos Coronas entrance with David. I wanted to surface and celebrate with Jen and David and his girlfriend. I wanted to look at

Dos Coronas knowing it was now a part of a much bigger thing.

I grabbed my sidemount tank and pushed it down into the Drain. My head followed. I looked to my left in the direction I had come from. I could see David's light at the end of the restriction as he waited for me. I imagined he must have had a bit of a worried look on his face. He might even have had a mild case of whiplash from shaking his head back and forth in disbelief. I knew he wouldn't follow me. He could fit through some small restrictions. He had fit through the Grinder several times. But I barely fit through the Drain.

I turned the scuba tank toward him and pulled myself down into the hole. It was easier to get my upper body into the Drain with one tank held out in front of me. That didn't last long. Once my feet got into the Drain I was stuck. I couldn't move forward. I carefully set the tank down on the floor below me and pulled with both hands. I moved inch by inch. I finally felt my legs, followed by my finned feet, drop down so they were even with my body. I moved my tank forward and kept pulling while also pushing against the back wall with my feet. Then I got stuck again. I pulled and pushed and wiggled and maneuvered. I wasn't making any forward progress. I wasn't moving at all. I had just plugged the Drain, and the connection. Something had grabbed me and wasn't letting go.

I reached back with my right hand and felt around my harness and buoyancy wing. The fingers coming from the wall or ceiling must have grabbed one of those. I just needed to find where my equipment was snagged and get it loose. I didn't feel anything. I tried to push and pull some more. Still nothing. Maybe whatever was grabbing me was doing it from below. I reached down between my legs and felt around. That's when I felt it. The pouch containing my backup lights, safety spools, and line markers that I kept clipped onto my center rear D-ring had gotten wedged in between a couple of larger protrusions coming from the wall to my left. The protrusions weren't letting go of the pouch, and I wasn't moving forward as long as it was attached to me. I pushed myself back slightly to put some slack on it and reached behind me. I searched for the D-ring that it was clipped onto, but it wasn't where it was supposed to be. I felt around until I found it positioned much lower along my body than it should have been. I found the bolt snap holding the pouch in place and unclipped it.

With that done, I tried to move forward again. This time I moved with a little more ease. It wasn't free movement. The fingers were still grabbing other parts of me and trying to keep me from escaping this tomb. I was moving forward though. I pulled and pushed myself out of the horizontal shaft and eventually popped out into the round room where David was waiting for me. I must have looked like an overdue newborn coming through the birth canal.

I signaled David to wait, and I turned around to retrieve my pouch. I looked into the restriction and saw my pouch laying on the floor about six feet away. I secured my sidemount tank back onto my harness. I could get through that first part of the restriction with it in place. Then I reached in to grab the pouch. On second thought, I should have left the tank unclipped. It was a tight squeeze. I stretched my arm as far as I could, but still couldn't reach the pouch. I grabbed my reel and used it to extend my reach. I managed to swipe the pouch with the edge of the reel and pulled it closer. I finally got it close enough to grab. When I attempted to clip the pouch back onto its D-ring, I once again noticed that the D-ring was not where it was supposed to be. It had slid down the crotch strap and instead of being positioned over my upper buttocks, it was in between my legs. It was at the lowest point of the strap. I tried to pull the D-ring back up the strap, but I didn't have the leverage to do it while wearing the harness. I wasn't about to remove my harness more than two thousand feet inside of the cave, so I clipped the pouch to a D-ring on my waist strap instead.

In retrospect, I should have removed the harness. Not only had the rear center D-ring been moved from its position, but other hardware had been repositioned. My shoulder straps were pulled off center and the lumbar plate that connected the waist and back straps was also off center. Apparently, I had pulled and pushed so hard when the pouch was trapped that it had shifted everything on my harness. I felt completely off center during that entire swim out. My body kept tilting to the left. I struggled to rotate it back to the right and remain balanced.

It was the best exit from a cave while also being quite uncomfortable. I was thrilled with what we had accomplished, but I was miserable in my harness. Twenty-four hundred feet through several restrictions was a long way to swim with an unbalanced rig. I wasn't going to let an unbalanced rig ruin my mood, though. We made it out of the cave and surfaced about fifty feet from the shoreline. David and I looked at Jen and his girlfriend with the biggest smiles on our faces. We pumped our arms in the air and turned to hug each other again. I could hear the girls screaming from the shore to my left. They knew we had done it.

Epilogue

We finally connected the crowns, but the exploration was far from over. One project was complete, but there were many more in our future. The next day, as we set out our wetsuits and gear to dry, I sat down in front of my laptop and typed out an announcement on Facebook.

> Yesterday, during a 2-hour dive in Sistema Dos Coronas located in Cozumel, Quintana Roo, Mexico, David and I made the connection to Cueva Quebrada increasing the total length of Cueva Quebrada by more than 8000' (greater than 37000' confirmed now, likely 40000' once all data is compiled). This places Cueva Quebrada as the longest system on Cozumel and the fifteenth longest system (possibly fourteenth) in Mexico. The connection is through a very tight restriction that requires removing tanks and some contortion followed by an area we have named the Grinder but it is passable and now has line in it. If we didn't have stage tanks back in Dos Coronas we would have exited on the Cueva Quebrada side, which actually would have been easier... That will be for the next trip.

We received lots of praise from other cave divers. Some of them had known about our project and what we were trying to accomplish. Most had no clue until that day. One of the divers from Ygor's team made a comment that I should have invited the original team members on the trip to take part in the connection. I guess he thought I was clairvoyant and knew it was going to happen during this trip. He apparently had also forgotten that I had extended invitations during several previous trips and the invitations were all declined. There will always be one in the crowd.

We spent the rest of the day exploring the topside of the island, eating good food, and just relaxing. We were happy to have made the connection, but sad to have that project completed. We were also looking forward to doing more exploration beneath the jungle of Cozumel. We even talked about what we would do during the next trip. It was decided that we would change our focus to surveying the existing lines in Cueva Quebrada from the Cenote S1 and Cenote 1km entrances. Now that I had more than ten thousand feet of passage surveyed in Cueva Quebrada, more than one fourth of it, I wanted to continue to survey it and produce a new map. There was still a lot of work to be done.

I continued to travel to dive the caves located beneath the jungle of Cozumel. It would be almost three years before I returned to Dos Coronas again. The purpose of that dive was to photograph the cave. My good friend, Laurent Miroult, who was also a former cave diving student of mine, had developed into a fantastic cave diving photographer. I wanted to get some photographic documentation of Dos Coronas. We went back to Winter Wonderland and got some fantastic photographs of the cave. A year later, I returned to the cave, once again to get more photographs with Laurent. I also began getting video footage of the cave.

We had already found most, if not all, of the unexplored tunnels in Dos Coronas during our previous dives. There could be short runs of tunnels here and there, but they would be few in numbers. David and I had scoured that place looking for the connection to Cueva Quebrada. There wasn't much, if anything, that we missed. I returned to Dos Coronas with a couple of my former students a few years later. I had invited them to join me on a trip to Cozumel and wanted to show them the cave. David and I had maintained our focus on the left side of the passage when we were doing our exploration. This time I focused on the right side. That was when we found two more tunnels. I let one of the guys take the lead on the first tunnel we found. I had the pleasure of getting it on video. You can find it on my YouTube channel in the Cozumel playlist. It is titled *Cody pops his cherry – Dos Coronas section of Cueva Quebrada.* It was only a few hundred feet, but every bit counts. It was also a beautiful tunnel. I had a blast watching Cody run line through his first Cozumel virgin cave passage.

A few minutes after finding that passage, I found another one. This one was a bit smaller. I took the lead and about a hundred and fifty feet later I emerged into another tunnel that already had line in it. I had finally found my connection between the Swamp Land and the Lava Tube. Unfortunately, it didn't join the Lava Tube very far into the tunnel. It was still a nice discovery. Since then, I've visited Dos Coronas at least once a year. I haven't found any additional unexplored passages, but as I've been writing this book, it's brought back some memories of areas that I want to give another look. I'll be revisiting them with the intent of simply extending the lines rather than connecting them to another cave.

* * *

The Cueva Quebrada exploration has taken more of my attention since 2014 when David and I made the connection between it and Dos Coronas. Ten years later and it's still a project in progress. Over the past ten years, so much has happened in Cueva Quebrada. It is now among the top ten longest caves in Mexico. Its original twenty-nine thousand feet of explored tunnels has almost tripled. The total length of the cave is currently sitting at more than eighty-five thousand feet. Steve and Judy Ormeroid get credit for about five thousand feet of that. They found a couple of very beautiful tunnels that head farther south. I even managed to extend the end of one of their lines. By the time you read this the total length of Cueva Quebrada might be greater than one hundred thousand feet in length, or at least close to it.

My next installment of *Beneath the Jungle of Cozumel* is about my exploration efforts in Cueva Quebrada. That book will focus on my discovery of the Escondido section, or the Hidden Passages. This is a section I found at the end of another line through a low sidemount restriction. This section alone has more passages in it than all of Cueva Quebrada as outlined on the original map. That's more than twenty-nine thousand feet of lined passages.

I'm sure there will be more books about Cueva Quebrada that follow. There's so much to that cave, and the exploration is far from done. You can also expect a book about my exploration in Paraiso de Aerolito. I mentioned in the book that Aerolito originally had twenty thousand feet of lined cave passages. I have expanded that to more than twenty-six thousand feet, including discovering a lower section that passes below the main cenote. I'm still exploring Aerolito as well. Until then, I'll see you from beneath the jungle of Cozumel.

Map of the Dos Coronas section of Cueva Quebrada

Thanks for reading *Beneath the Jungle of Cozumel: Connecting the Crowns*!

Please take a moment to leave a review on Amazon. Reviews help provide more exposure for books. The more reviews a book has, the more likely Amazon will be to show it in search results. A simple statement is all that's needed to help boost exposure. But if you're so inclined, a more thorough review is always appreciated. Rob reads the reviews and uses suggestions to help improve his writing. You can find a link to the Amazon listing on the List of Works page at www.RobNeto.com/list-of-works

If you liked this book and want to see more by Rob Neto, please visit www.RobNeto.com for a list of his other books. Rob has written a thriller series which incorporates diving, specifically cave diving, into the stories. At the time of this publication, three were available. He was also working on the second book in this series, as well as the fourth book in the Beyond series, and a standalone political thriller novel. Rob has plans for an adventure series similar to this one that is based on his explorations in the underwater caves of Florida.

Once you're on the website, make sure to subscribe to the monthly newsletter. Email addresses are not sold or distributed, and you will only receive one email per month to update you about Rob's books and alert you to any price specials. You'll be the first to hear about new series, new books, and to see cover reveals.

See you in the next book!

ABOUT THE AUTHOR

Rob Neto is a cave diver who lives in the Florida panhandle just minutes away from some of his favorite caves. He is a cave explorer and retired cave and technical diving instructor. He spent more than ten years teaching scuba diving in Arizona and Florida. He is also the author of the book Sidemount Diving The *Almost* Comprehensive Guide, the first comprehensive book about sidemount diving. With almost three hundred pages of information and photos, Sidemount Diving is on its 2nd edition and has been translated into Dutch, German and Spanish, and is currently being translated into more languages. Rob published his first novel, *Beyond the Grate,* in July 2023. *Beyond the Grate* was awarded a Silver Award in Suspense Thrillers by the Global Book Awards in September 2023 and has received numerous reviews on Amazon, GoodReads, and Facebook. Rob is already working on the fourth book in the Joey Simmons series, *Beyond the End of the Line.* He is also working on *Beneath the Jungle of Cozumel: The Hidden Passages Book 2,* as well as a couple of other books. Visit his website at www.RobNeto.com to subscribe to his newsletter and keep up with his new releases.

Rob is married to his wonderful, supportive wife of almost twenty-two years and has a household of furry family members. At the time of this publication his family consisted of four dogs, one inside cat, and several outside cats.

Coming Soon!

Beneath the Jungle of Cozumel:
The Hidden Passages
Book 2

Join me as I continue my adventures in exploring the caves of Cozumel. In my next book, I tell the tales of my exploration of Cueva Quebrada and finding the Hidden Passages. I appropriately named this section Escondido, the Spanish word for hidden. Not only did I discover a new section, but a buddy of mine and I also discovered two new cenotes! This brought the total number of cenotes in Cueva Quebrada to twelve. The exploration done in that section made the Dos Coronas exploration seem like child's play. You'll also get a sneak peek at a section of my map that has never before been seen outside of my exploration group!

Don't miss the next book about my exploration *Beneath the Jungle of Cozumel!*